P9-CKA-442

RACE RELATIONS

305.8
St34r

RACE RELATIONS

A Critique

Stephen Steinberg

WITHDRAWN

LIBRARY ST. MARY'S COLLEGE
Stanford Social Sciences
An Imprint of Stanford University Press
Stanford, California

3-13-09

15.17

YBP

Stanford University Press
Stanford, California

©2007 by the Board of Trustees of the Leland Stanford Junior University.
All rights reserved.

No part of this book may be reproduced or transmitted in any form or by any means, electronic or mechanical, including photocopying and recording, or in any information storage or retrieval system without the prior written permission of Stanford University Press.

Printed in the United States of America on acid-free, archival-quality paper

Library of Congress Cataloging-in-Publication Data
Steinberg, Stephen.
  Race relations : a critique / Stephen Steinberg.
    p. cm.
  Includes bibliographical references and index.
  ISBN 978-0-8047-5326-5 (cloth : alk. paper) -- ISBN 978-0-8047-5327-2 (pbk. : alk. paper)
  1. Race relations. 2. Racism. 3. Prejudices. I. Title.

HT1521.S65 2007
305.8--dc22

                              2007007300

Designed by Bruce Lundquist

Typeset at Stanford University Press in 10.5/15 Adobe Garamond

Dedicated to
Julius and Phyllis Jacobson,
Herbert Hill, and Stanford Lyman
Disturbers of the intellectual peace
in the struggle against racial and economic injustice.

.

CONTENTS

PROLOGUE   A PERSONAL ENCOUNTER WITH THE CANON   I

PART I   THE ORIGINS AND IDEOLOGICAL
           UNDERPINNINGS OF THE
           RACE RELATIONS PARADIGM   5

PART 2   RACE: THE EPISTEMOLOGY OF IGNORANCE   4I

PART 3   ETHNICITY: THE EPISTEMOLOGY OF
           WISHFUL THINKING   III

           Acknowledgments   I49
           Notes   I53
           Index   I8I

RACE RELATIONS

A PERSONAL ENCOUNTER
WITH THE CANON

> He has understood the system so well because he felt it first
> as his own contradiction.
>
> *Jean-Paul Sartre, Introduction to*
> *Albert Memmi's* The Colonizer and the Colonized[1]

IN 1974 I CROSSED PATHS WITH GUNNAR
Myrdal, the illustrious author of *An American Dilemma*,
published in 1944. This landmark study, lavishly funded by the Carnegie
Corporation from its offices on Fifth Avenue in New York City, was prompted by a rise of racial tensions in Northern cities where Southern blacks had
migrated in search of opportunity. Its ambitious agenda was to provide a
comprehensive account of race in America. It was the largest and most costly
social research project to date, and upon publication *An American Dilemma*
became an instant classic. Now, thirty years later, at the age of seventy-five,
Myrdal had come to New York, to work on *An American Dilemma Revisited*
in collaboration with Kenneth Clark, the eminent black psychologist whose
research, like Myrdal's, was cited in the 1954 Supreme Court decision that
racial segregation in public schools was unconstitutional.[2]

Benjamin Ringer, the chair of Sociology at the CUNY Graduate Center, organized a weekly seminar of faculty and students on the subject of race in America. Each week a different professor was assigned responsibility for kicking off the seminar by presenting the results of his or her work. When it was my turn at the lectern, I decided to undertake a retrospective examination of the criticism of *An American Dilemma* by contemporaneous critics on the Left who challenged Myrdal's celebrated study.

My purpose was not to engage in personal or political mischief. On the contrary, I thought, naively as it turned out, that Myrdal would welcome this challenge from a neophyte, and might find it productive to revisit old debates and to engage his critics as he launched his new study of race in America. I had been particularly persuaded by Oliver Cox's brilliant critique of *An American Dilemma*. Cox praised Myrdal for turning up a vast body of useful facts about race in America, but he assailed his theoretical framework, especially his failure to explore the structural basis and material sources of prejudice. As Cox wrote: "Myrdal does not bring to light the social determinants of this well-known dilemma: he merely recognizes it and rails against its existence."[3] Myrdal's error, according to Cox, was his uncritical focus on racial beliefs. "If beliefs, per se, could subjugate a people," Cox wrote sardonically, "the beliefs which Negroes hold about whites should be as effective as those which whites hold against Negroes."[4] Another critic, Herbert Aptheker, the Communist intellectual, pummeled Myrdal with sarcasm over the very title of his book: "It is perhaps understandable how an adviser to and an official of the government of Sweden, which treated the late war against fascism as a dilemma and preferred neutrality . . . might decide to christen the fact of the exploitation and oppression of the American Negro people a dilemma—'a situation involving choice . . . between equally unsatisfactory alternatives.'"[5] I found all of this enormously persuasive, even revelatory, and I was deeply curious to find out how Myrdal would answer his critics.

Only later did I learn that Myrdal had a visceral antipathy to Marxism, and that, like many other exalted figures, he did not take well to criticism, especially of the work that made him famous. I was spared his umbrage, however. As fate would have it, on the day Steinberg was slated to go one on one with Myrdal, the seat that Myrdal occupied at the head of the table was empty. Myrdal had left for Stockholm to receive the Nobel Prize!

It was perhaps for the better that I was left to shoot hoops by myself. I was oblivious to the fact that such a confrontation was fraught with peril for me as a junior faculty member. Had Myrdal been there, he never would have written the letter of recommendation that presumably clinched my award of a prestigious National Endowment of the Humanities fellowship for the next academic year. Perhaps it is just as well that I did not raise the hackles of our illustrious guest by confronting him with heretical ideas that exposed his vulnerabilities. All the same, the entire episode left me with a nagging question: How is it that Myrdal became an exalted figure both inside and outside academia, while Oliver Cox, his brilliant critic, fell into obscurity, relegated to teach at black colleges? This question has far-reaching implications for the sociology of knowledge. What does Myrdal's elevation and Cox's marginalization tell us about the formation of sociology's canon? About the racialization of knowledge? About the occlusion of ideas that smack of Marxism?

This quandary provided the starting point for my book *Turning Back: The Retreat from Racial Justice in American Thought and Policy*, published in 1995. I devoted the first chapter to a critique of *An American Dilemma* and the liberal orthodoxy that it did so much to engender. There was poetic justice when my book received the Oliver C. Cox Award for Distinguished Antiracist Scholarship, presented by the Section on Racial and Ethnic Minorities of the American Sociological Association. Clearly, the very fact that such an award exists proves that today there is political space for opposition to hegemonic discourse that did not exist when Cox's prolific writings were studiously ignored by mainstream sociologists.

Although I followed Cox's lead by challenging Myrdal's theoretical structure, I had great admiration for Myrdal the man. In *What Is History?* Edward Carr writes, "Study the historian before you begin to study the facts."[6] Indeed, it is always revealing to know the person behind the text, and to make connections between the author's personality and sensibilities, on the one hand, and the ideas inscribed indelibly on the printed page, on the other. I admired Myrdal's boundless energy and the exuberance he brought to his intellectual endeavors. Yet at times this exuberance was an intellectual liability: Myrdal's critics accused him of being too reverential of the United States and too optimistic about the future of American democracy, and therefore prone to underestimate the extent that racism was embedded in institutions and therefore immune to change. On a personal level, however, Myrdal's exuberance was of course endearing, all the more so in an elderly man who seemed totally invested in his work.

At another of our weekly seminars, a psychologist presented the results of his empirical research on philo-Semitism. I'm not entirely sure, and neither apparently was Myrdal, what admiration of Jews had to do with loathing of blacks. In any event, when the formal presentation was over, Myrdal turned to me and said scornfully: "That's what's wrong with you American sociologists. Rome is burning, and you're doing this."

Though just a passing comment, it reveals tons about Myrdal's intellectual style and worldview. Myrdal had a capacious mind and he was always riveted on the big picture. As project director of the Carnegie study, he commissioned scores of empirical studies on a wide range of issues, but it was his talent and his achievement to take this vast body of empirical material and piece it together, like a giant jigsaw puzzle, to reveal the big picture about race in America. Whatever objections one might have to *An American Dilemma*—and I am on record with mine—it was a work of breathtaking scope. Myrdal's harsh verdict about American sociology remained with me: Was American sociology preoccupied with the minutiae and the superficies of race? What role did sociology play in the Civil Rights Revolution? What did sociology do while Rome burned?

This, indeed, is the starting point of the present study.

[Dear Reader: As we go forward in what I regard as a shared intellectual journey, I will periodically address these asides to you. I do so because as I tell the story of sociology's record on race and ethnicity, I feel a need to get off my academic horse, as it were, and to shift rhetorical frames so that I might engage you, the reader, in the direct and unembellished parlance of personal dialogue. It is rather like characters in a theatrical drama stepping out of their roles, and in a stage whisper, addressing the audience about the drama unfolding before their eyes. The rhetorical effect is to allow us mutually, as author and reader, to see the action on another level, to apply a different, more familiar lens that cuts through the pretense of hallowed scholarship.]

PART ONE

THE ORIGINS AND IDEOLOGICAL UNDERPINNINGS OF THE RACE RELATIONS PARADIGM

> To trace the black man in American sociology is tantamount to tracing the history of American sociology itself.
>
> *Stanford Lyman,* The Black American in Sociological Thought[1]

N INETEEN SIXTY-THREE WAS THE YEAR the Civil Rights Revolution reached its explosive climax. Pressures had been building up for nearly a decade, as grassroots insurgency evolved into a full-fledged political movement, replete with organizations, leaders, goals, and strategies, all aimed at the complete dismantling of the Jim Crow system that was the stepchild of slavery itself. Protest leaders tapped the smoldering resentments of African Americans over the indignities and abuses of racial segregation and second class citizenship, and mobilized these resentments into a political movement that threw the entire society into crisis. In hindsight, the Civil Rights Revolution has the appearance of a linear and inexorable progression, beginning with Rosa Parks's courageous act of defiance, and culminating a decade later with the passage of landmark civil rights legislation in 1964 and 1965. Actually, the movement was one of fits and starts. Confronted as it was with powerful and intransigent institutions, the movement at times stalled and even tottered on the brink of defeat.

Indeed, 1962 was a year notable for its setbacks. To wit:

• The Supreme Court declined to review a ruling that overturned a Washington State law barring racial discrimination in the sale or rental of publicly aided housing.

• The Kennedy administration failed to put forward civil rights legislation.

• In Albany, Georgia, Martin Luther King led demonstrations protesting segregation of the city's public facilities, but city officials cunningly refused to resort to violence that invariably backfired by generating headlines and sympathy for the movement. Without the glare of publicity, the demonstrations petered out.

• In New Orleans, segregationists sponsored reverse freedom rides by giving 1,000 blacks free one-way rides to any Northern city of their choice.

• President Kennedy's bill to create a Department for Urban Affairs was killed by the House Rules Committee.[2]

Inexplicably, 1963 was the year that the pendulum shifted the other way, as the movement recovered from setbacks and extended protest to the North, vitiating the assumption that racism was just a "Southern problem."

• Martin Luther King was arrested in Birmingham, Alabama, on Good Friday, April 12. The next day the Birmingham campaign was launched, producing the images of fire hoses and police dogs that are forever etched on the national memory.

• On June 23, Martin Luther King led 125,000 people on a Freedom Walk in Detroit, signifying the extension of protest to Northern cities.

• In July and August there were mass demonstrations at construction sites in New York City, leading to the arrest of some 800 demonstrators.

• On October 22, 1963, designated "Freedom Day," virtually every black student in the Chicago school system stayed home in protest against segregation, and thousands marched on City Hall.

• On August 28 Martin Luther King and Bayard Rustin led the famous March on Washington, the largest civil rights demonstration in history, in which a coalition of civil rights groups, labor unions, and white liberals marched "For Jobs and Freedom." Note that "jobs" was given priority over "freedom," though the march also sought to mobilize support for President Kennedy's civil rights bill that was tied up by Dixecrats in Congress.

- The Birmingham protest persisted, involving the arrest of more than 3,000 people.

It is difficult to capture through this litany of events the electrifying sense of crisis that gripped the nation. Basically, it was a constitutional crisis over whether the federal government or the states had jurisdiction over civil rights. The nation was again torn apart along the very fault lines that had produced the Civil War: the division between the slavocracy and the rest of the nation, this time over whether Jim Crow was protected under the doctrine of states rights, which the founding fathers had inserted in the Constitution to appease the slaveholding South. In essence, the Civil War was being fought again, initially in the courts but now in the streets of the old Confederacy. Instead of the Union Army, there were legions of civil rights protesters, mobilized by disciplined organizers. Southern authorities—ranging from U.S. senators, to state governors, to local sheriffs, to lynch mobs—played out their scripted role as defenders of the old order, which yielded a steady stream of disturbing television images beamed into homes across the nation, and indeed the world.

The asymmetry of ordinary citizens—descendants of slaves demonstrating for elementary civil rights—juxtaposed against fire hoses, police dogs, and other instruments of state power, had all the earmarks of a morality play dramatizing the perpetual struggle between good and evil, except that it was being enacted on the stage of history with a disfranchised people crying out for justice. A number of recent historians have stressed the role that foreign policy considerations played in shaping national policy. Against the background of the Cold War, how could the United States compete for "the hearts and minds" of people in the Third World when its own Third World minority was subjected to glaring humiliation and abuse? Even so, it is doubtful that the 1964 Civil Rights Act would have passed but for the assassination of President Kennedy on November 22, 1963. In the context of this national tragedy, liberals in Congress were able to invoke cloture on a civil rights filibuster for the first time, assuring passage of the 1964 Civil Rights Act and the 1965 Voting Rights Act. With this legislation, the civil rights movement had achieved its principal objective: the end of second class citizenship. Of course, there is bitter irony in the fact that this legislation only restored rights that were supposedly secured by Reconstruction Amendments a whole century earlier, and that these rights were restored only after a protracted and bloody struggle that pitted defenseless protestors against powerful institutions of a racist state.

Despite the depth of the racial crisis, it was a long time before the reverberations penetrated the American university, where even the architecture and landscaping suggest a refuge from the seamy and chaotic world outside. This warrants a moment's reflection. The monastic ambience of the university has its origins in a time when college functioned as a breeding ground for gentlemen, and the curriculum emphasized Greek, Latin, theology, and the classics. How is a monastic conception of the university possible in a field like sociology, whose very subject matter includes the seamy and chaotic business of race? Could sociologists remain stubbornly detached in the face of such glaring injustice? Was it not a professional obligation, if not a moral imperative, for sociologists to dirty their hands, to become engaged? Let us return to the question: What did sociology do while Rome burned?

WHILE ROME BURNED

It should come as no surprise that sociology remained on the sidelines during the critical early phases of the Civil Rights Revolution. Sociology was not alone. In the case of political science, only six articles containing the word "Negro" in their titles, and four with the word "race," were published in the *American Political Science Review* between 1906 and 1963.[3] Nor did the black liberation movement receive much support even from the nation's public intellectuals, as Carol Polsgrove shows in *Divided Minds: Intellectuals and the Civil Rights Movement*. According to Polsgrove, "when white intellectuals were faced with the challenge of racial equality, they hesitated—fearful, cautious, distracted, or simply indifferent."[4] Among the luminaries whom Polsgrove singles out for criticism are such literary figures as Robert Penn Warren, William Faulkner, and Norman Mailer; public intellectuals such as Reinhold Neibuhr and Hanna Arendt; and leading scholars such as C. Vann Woodward and David Reisman. According to Polsgrove, some of these intellectuals were swayed by romantic attachments to the Old South. Others succumbed to the pressures of McCarthyism and the Cold War. Still others feared a reactionary backlash that would

engulf liberalism and bring down the Democratic Party. This is why they hesitated and counseled moderation and gradualism. To be sure, there were some
intellectuals and scholars who provided ardent support for the movement, and
who opposed the "neo-Confederates," as they were derisively called. But as
Polsgrove shows, most remained silent. Writing in *The New Republic* in 1956,
Lawrence Dunbar Reddick, a black historian, fired this salvo:

Countless editors, scholars and men of letters, in and out of the South, who personally might shrink from killing an insect, give their sanction to the intransigence of
the racists. Is it too much to say that there is a connection between the essays, edi-
torials and novels of the literary neo-Confederates and the howling mob that blocks
the path of little Negro children on the way to school integration?[5]

In the case of sociology, culpability goes even further. Here we have a designated field, ambiguously called "race relations," that purports to practice
objective social science but whose knowledge claims inescapably have moral
consequences, either in subverting racism, or alternatively, providing scientific
legitimation for the prevailing racial order. Without doubt, most sociologists
proudly see themselves and their discipline as engaged in an antiracist project,
and cite the role that social science played historically in discrediting the Social
Darwinism that once buttressed notions of racial superiority and inferiority.
My contention, however, is that sociology has too long bathed in self-congratu-
lation over the achievement of some of its founders in discrediting biological
racism and establishing the irreducibly social character of "race." The singular
achievement of American social science was to bracket "race" with quotation
marks, signifying that it is a social construction and not a biological fact. But
W. I. Thomas famously wrote: "If men define a situation as real, it is real in its
consequences." This raises the paramount question: What role did sociology
play in relation to the *consequences* of this biological fiction? To return to the
question I posed earlier, what role did sociology play "while Rome burned,"
when the grievances of blacks erupted into a movement demanding elementary
rights of citizenship, and the entire nation was thrown into crisis?

In a 1993 paper entitled "Race Relations as Social Process: Sociology's
Resistance to a Civil Rights Orientation," Stanford Lyman showed that
generations of social theorists evaded or downplayed civil rights as a matter
of social urgency. Instead, they advanced theoretical models that projected

racial amelioration as part of an evolutionary process of societal change. "Since the time for teleological redemption is ever long," Lyman writes sardonically, "blacks might consign their civic equalitarian future to faith in the ultimate fulfillment of the inclusion cycle's promise." Lyman issued the following verdict, "Sociology . . . has been part of the problem and not part of the solution."[6]

Sociology's reckoning with its failure to champion civil rights took an unusually public form. It occurred at the 1963 meetings of the American Sociological Association when Everett Hughes delivered his presidential address under the title, "Race Relations and the Sociological Imagination." "Why," Hughes asked, "did social scientists—and sociologists in particular—not foresee the explosion of collective action of Negro Americans toward immediate full integration into American society?"[7]

This was an extraordinary moment in the annals of social science. Here was Everett Hughes, the eminent president of the American Sociological Association, issuing a public confession of intellectual failure in the most public of venues: the annual meetings when sociologists gather with ceremonial expectation to hear the presidential address. By uncanny coincidence Hughes's address occurred on the very day of the historic March on Washington, the largest civil rights demonstration in the nation's history. Whatever else needs to be said, Hughes deserves credit for his intellectual candor and for raising provocative questions about sociology's failure to anticipate the Civil Rights Revolution.

Hughes was willing to go only so far in challenging the received wisdom, however. This was evident even in the way he framed the question. If our eminent president had critical distance from his profession and the role that he played in it, he might have asked, why did *the sociological establishment* fail to anticipate the Civil Rights Revolution? Framed in this way, the question is almost self-explaining. Like the other movements of the 1960s, the civil rights movement was a movement "from below." These were grassroots movements by subaltern groups challenging their subordination by powerful institutions. Notwithstanding its claims to the contrary, the sociological enterprise is an elite formation. It routinely selects its practitioners from the privileged strata of the population, its research programs depend heavily on funding from government and foundations, it is centered in elite institutions of higher learning, and this ivory tower offers a remote and rarefied vantage point for observing the world below. True, we send emissaries "into the field," as we say, like voyagers to a foreign land who come back with narratives to enlighten the rest of us about "how the other half lives." The problem, though, is that these emissaries typically see the world through an ideological lens that reflects their position of racial and class privilege, not to speak of the dominant paradigm in the field and the prevailing ideologies in the society at large.

The net result, in matters of race, has been an "epistemology of ignorance," to use the trenchant phrase that political philosopher Charles Mills coined in *The Racial Contract*. "One has to learn to see the world wrongly," Mills writes, "producing the ironic outcome that whites will in general be unable to understand the world they themselves have made."[8] With these liabilities, how could establishment sociology have anticipated the Civil Rights Revolution? Indeed, the thrust of Mills's devastating critique is that like other fields of knowledge, sociology has functioned to provide epistemic authority and scientific legitimation to systems of racial hierarchy, from slavery down to the present. To echo Lawrence Dunbar Reddick's comment above, to the extent that these systems of knowledge condone or fail to repudiate racism, they are implicated in epistemic violence.

Not only did Hughes pose the question in the wrong way, but his answer was also sadly deficient. All that Hughes was willing to concede was that "our conception of social science is so empirical, so limited to little bundles of fact applied to little hypotheses, that we are incapable of entertaining a broad range of possibilities, of following out the madly unlikely combinations of social circumstances."[9] No doubt, narrow empiricism obscured "the big picture," but narrow empiricism is not innocent of politics. For a discipline that did not *want* to see the big picture, narrow empiricism provided an ingenious smoke screen. It is a method perfectly tailored to an epistemology of ignorance. As the adage goes, one can "look" but never "see."

Hughes came closer to the truth when he wrote: "Why should we have thought, apart from the comfort of it, that the relations of the future could be predicted in terms of moderate trends, rather than by the model of the slow burn reaching the heat of massive explosion?"[10] But what was behind the presumption that the vector of change would be "moderate," and why was this regarded with "comfort," or rather by whom? Could this reflect the fact that all but a few professional sociologists were white and middle-class in origin, and that *they* could afford to be patient? Or that they were less exercised over the routine violence embedded in the Jim Crow system than by the disorder engendered by the black protest movement? Was it not also the case that the prevailing models in sociology, notwithstanding their disclaimers of neutrality, were wedded to the existing racial order, or at best, a kinder and gentler version of the existing racial order? Since the sociological establishment rarely heard, much less heeded, the voices emanating from the bottom of black society, how *could* it have anticipated black insurgency?

In point of fact, there were people who were not averse to "the slow burn reaching the heat of massive explosion," though they were not part of the sociological establishment. These were mavericks on the Left who *did* focus on the denial of civil rights, who *did* conceptualize racism as a structural problem, who *did* call for an overhaul of major institutions, who *did* advocate a politics that would transform the nation's racial order. But for these very reasons they were dismissed as ideologues who did not share a commitment to objective social science. Three names come instantly to mind: W.E.B. Du Bois, Oliver Cox, and C.L.R. James. All three were African Americans with pronounced Marxist leanings. In contrast to the prevailing race relations paradigm, their Marxism provided them with a paradigm that allowed them to both anticipate and champion the cause of civil rights, as can be gleaned from the following quotes:

- Du Bois in 1906, at the meeting of the Niagara Movement in Harpers Ferry that spawned the NAACP: "We will not be satisfied to take one jot or tittle less than our full manhood rights. We claim for ourselves every single right that belongs to a freeborn American, political, civil and social; and until we get these rights we will never cease to protest and assail the ears of America."[11] It bears repeating: this was 1906, a half-century before the Birmingham boycott that galvanized the civil rights movement.

- Cox in 1944, in his masterpiece, *Caste, Class, & Race*: "We cannot defeat race prejudice by proving that it is wrong. The reason for this is that race prejudice is only a symptom of a materialistic social fact. . . . The articulate white man's ideas about his racial superiority are rooted deeply in the social system, and it can be corrected only by changing the system itself."[12]

- C.L.R. James in 1947, in a piece entitled "The Revolutionary Answer to the Negro Problem in the U.S.A.": "Let us not forget that in the Negro people, there sleep and are now awakening passions of a violence exceeding, perhaps, as far as these things can be compared, anything among the tremendous forces that capitalism has created. Anyone who knows them, who knows their history, is able to talk to them intimately, watches them at their own theaters, watches them at their dances, watches them in their churches, reads their press with a discerning eye, must recognize that although their social force may not be able to compare with the social force of a corresponding number of organized workers, the hatred of bourgeois society and the readiness to destroy it when the opportunity should present itself, rests among them to a greater degree than in any other section of the population of the United States."[13]

Far from failing to anticipate black insurgency, these prescient scholar/activists erred in thinking that insurgency would occur much sooner than it did! So did a next generation of black scholars who for the most part remained "behind the veil," a term made popular by W.E.B. Du Bois. Whether black scholars remained behind or in front of the veil, there emerged a black radical tradition—sometimes muffled, at other times assertive—that has challenged the main currents of thought on race and racism among mainstream sociologists.[14] If Everett Hughes had been plugged into this black radical tradition, he would not have been in such a quandary about why sociology "did not foresee the explosion of collective action of Negro Americans toward immediate full integration into American society." *[Dear Reader: Put yourself in the shoes, or rather the skin, of Du Bois, Cox, or James—men who had been agitating for civil rights for decades—and imagine them sitting in the audience, hearing the president of the American Sociological Association puzzling over sociology's failure to "foresee" the civil rights upheaval.*

It is not difficult to imagine what Cox was thinking. No doubt he would recall, with bitter irony, that in 1948 Hughes reviewed Caste, Class, & Race *in* Phylon, *a journal founded by W.E.B. Du Bois. Hughes failed utterly to engage any of the major themes or arguments in the book. He devoted the entire review to defending sociology's pet concept of "caste," which Cox maintained was irrelevant to the American situation. In the next issue Cox wrote a polite rejoinder, accusing Hughes of only reading chapter 22 on* The Modern Caste School of Race Relations, *"with scarcely a condescending glance at the other twenty-four chapters."[15]*

It is doubtful as well that Hughes bothered to read the testimonial that Herbert Aptheker wrote for W.E.B. Du Bois in the very same issue that published his review of Cox's opus. Aptheker quoted Du Bois, fifty years earlier, speaking at the first annual meeting of the Equal Rights Association: "We must agitate, complain, protest and keep protesting against the invasion of our manhood rights; we must besiege the legislature, carry our cases to the court and above all organize these million brothers of ours into one great fist which shall never cease to pound at the gates of opportunity until they fly open."[16] Small surprise that sixteen years after his flimsy review of Cox's book, Everett Hughes was dumbfounded at sociology's failure to foresee the Civil Rights Revolution!]

Indeed, one has to look no further than the program for the 1963 meetings itself. There were only two sessions on "Race and Ethnic Relations," both organized by Seymour Leventman. Five of the ten papers dealt with such esoteric subjects as "Status Conflicts within a Hindu Caste"; "Ethnic Self-Identity of Two Eskimo Villages"; "Racialism, Miscegenation and Acculturation in Africa and the Americas." Several others delved in theoretical abstraction. For example: "Toward a General Theory of Minority Groups"; "Minority Responses to Intergroup Situations." To echo Myrdal, this is what sociology did while Rome burned.

Only one paper came close to dealing with the burning issue of the moment: C. Wilson Record's paper "The Politics of Desegregation." Who was this person who shattered the image of rarefied erudition? Wilson Record was a leftist who received his Ph.D. from U.C. Berkeley and taught at Sacramento State College. A year later he published *Race and Radicalism*, a history of the relationship between the NAACP and the Communist Party, the two groups that *did* champion the black cause, and indeed planted seeds of protest that came to fruition after 1955.

One wonders whether Everett Hughes, as he peered out at his audience, was cognizant of the fact that it consisted of a sea of white faces. In 1967 there were only 121 Negro doctorates in sociology in the entire nation, representing about one percent of all sociologists. Almost all of these (83 percent) came from just ten institutions, with the University of Chicago at the top of the list (twenty black doctorates). The institutions that had four or fewer black doctorates included Yale, the University of Wisconsin, the University of Michigan, Northwestern, Boston University, and Harvard. Furthermore, most black sociologists were denied access to teaching positions in "white" universities, and taught in black colleges.[17]

Consider the epistemological implications of having a field devoted to the study of "race relations" in which blacks had only token representation and, to make matters worse, those who deviated from the dominant discourse were cast to the margins. In his 1971 essay "In Defense of Black Studies," James Moss wrote:

> The sociology that I learned, and the concepts I internalized, were all cast within the framework of white perceptions and white interpretations. Indeed, while many will dispute this, the sociology I brought away with me from Columbia was the sociology of the white experience, with its Anglo-Saxon and Teutonic roots. It certainly did not nor does it now touch, except peripherally, upon the sociology of the black experience either in this country, or in Africa or the Caribbean.[18]

Indeed, we need to ask whether sociologists were unknowingly reflecting "their Anglo Saxon and Teutonic roots." Were they, against their intentions, practicing a "white sociology" that reflects white interests and viewpoints? Put yet another way, is the "epistemology of ignorance" a failure of the white imagination?

Let us reflect on the title that Hughes chose for his peroration: "Race Relations and the Sociological Imagination." The term "sociological imagination," of course, derives from C. Wright Mills, who famously wrote: "Perhaps the most fruitful distinction with which the sociological imagination works is between 'the personal troubles of milieu' and 'the public issues of social structure.'"[19] Had Hughes taken Mills's conception seriously, he might have challenged the logic of reducing racism to troubled "race relations," and instead probed the structural foundations of racism that engendered and gave warrant to social protest. This might have led him to explore the long history of African American grievance and resistance that culminated, on the very day that he spoke, in the historic March on Washington demanding "Jobs and Freedom." And it might have also led him to critically examine the process of knowledge production within sociology that accounts for its failure to anticipate or grasp the meaning of the civil rights upheaval. Unfortunately, Mill's seminal construct—"the sociological imagination"—has been so diluted that it now refers to virtually any cerebral activity on the part of sociologists.

Let us also scrutinize Hughes's other term of discourse: "race relations."

Of course, any sociologist will recognize this as the conventional nomenclature, derived from Robert Ezra Park, who was Hughes's mentor at the University of Chicago. Indeed, Hughes launched his peroration with an exegesis of Park's foundational scholarship. In doing so, however, he went fishing in the wrong theoretical waters. Instead of using the racial upheavals of the moment to reflect critically on Park's race relations model, Hughes searched in vain in Park's writing to find some shred of knowledge or insight that would shed light on the escalating racial crisis.

Think of the logical asymmetry here between the empirical events and the conceptual umbrella under which they are subsumed. On the one hand, we have a subjugated people rising up through a grassroots movement to challenge a system of state-sponsored racism that amounted to what Howard Winant has aptly called "a racial dictatorship," enforced by legislatures, courts, police, and in the final resort, by the lynch mob.[20] On the other hand, a theoretical paradigm blandly called "race relations."

While the term "race relations" is meant to convey value neutrality, on closer examination it is riddled with value. Indeed, its rhetorical function is to obfuscate the true nature of "race relations," which is a system of racial domination and exploitation based on violence, resulting in the suppression and dehumanization of an entire people over centuries of American history. Marxists did not shy away from calling "race relations" by its right name: "racial oppression." This was the title that Bob Blauner chose for his 1972 book, *Racial Oppression in America*, an icon-shattering work that challenged the race relations paradigm, and in doing so, made conceptual sense of the nation's racial crisis.[21] Nor did Martin Luther King shy away from calling race relations by its right name. As early as 1957 he wrote in *Phylon*:

There comes a time when people get tired of being trampled over by *the iron feet of oppression*. There comes a time when people get tired of being plunged across the abyss of exploitation where they experience the bleakness of nagging despair. . . . As they look back they see the old order of colonialism and imperialism passing away and the new order of freedom and justice coming into being.[22]

Alas, here we come to a jolting realization: that "race relations" is the language of the oppressor, whereas "oppression" is the construct—the rhetorical weapon—of the oppressed.

Consider the difference between the two terms. "Race relations" obscures the nature of the relationship between the constituent groups in a cloud of ambiguity. In contrast, "racial oppression" conveys a clear sense of the nature, magnitude, and sources of the problem. Whereas the race relations model assumes that racial prejudice arises out of a natural antipathy between groups on the basis of difference, "racial oppression" locates the source of the problem within the structure of society. Whereas "race relations" elides the issue of power, reducing racism down to the level of attitudes, "racial oppression" makes clear from the outset that we are dealing here with a system of domination, one that implicates major political and economic institutions, including the state itself. Whereas "race relations" implies mutuality, "racial oppression" clearly distinguishes between the oppressor and the oppressed. Whereas "race relations" rivets attention on superficial aspects of the racial dyad, "racial oppression" explores the underlying factors that engender racial division and discord. Whereas the sociologist of "race relations" is reduced to the social equivalent of a marriage counselor, exploring ways to repair these fractured relationships, the sociologist of "racial oppression" is potentially an agent of social transformation, forging a praxis for remedying racial inequities. Yet we have a profession that rejects "racial oppression" as tendentious, and pretends that "race relations" is innocent of ideology, merely because it is allied with the racial status quo.[23]

More is involved here than semantics. Everett Hughes's presidential speech had all of the earmarks of a paradigm crisis. According to Thomas Kuhn in *The Structure of Scientific Revolutions*, a paradigm crisis occurs when scientists lose faith in the system of ideas and practices that they previously accepted as constituting valid science.[24] The problem, as we have seen, is that Hughes was not willing to go much beyond his quizzical admission that sociology failed to anticipate the revolutionary events that were swirling around him even as he spoke. "The decision to reject one paradigm," Kuhn writes, "is always simultaneously the decision to accept another."[25] But our befuddled president of the American Sociological Association had made no such decision to reject the old paradigm, and thus he missed the opportunity to venture onto new intellectual terrain and to contemplate the possibility of a new paradigm.

Even so, Hughes's address was an act of courage at a crucial historical moment, and could have been construed as a clarion call to rethink old assumptions. I have interviewed several scholars of race who attended Hughes's address. According to these eyewitnesses, the speech had very little impact, certainly nothing approaching the drama of "a paradigm crisis." According to Seymour Leventman, "Most people didn't get it. The small group who got it blamed structural functionalism. In those days there was still a lingering of the functionalist mentality, best represented by Talcott Parsons, that was too oriented to the status quo."[26] Other eyewitnesses convey the impression that Hughes's address was a humdrum event, and there was no sense that something momentous had transpired.

Hughes's address received little or no press attention, even though it could have been seen as a newsworthy event against the background of the March on Washington. Like all presidential addresses, it was published in the *American Sociological Review*, but according to the *Citations Index*, it was rarely cited, and as far as I know, never anthologized except for inclusion in a posthumous volume of Hughes's own papers.[27] In *Sociology and the Race Problem*, James McKee notes that only a few sociologists took up the provocative question that Hughes raised about sociology's failure to anticipate or to apply its collective wisdom to explaining the Civil Rights Revolution.[28]

In short, this was a "paradigm crisis" that wasn't. Despite the seismic events in society at large, mainstream sociologists, including Hughes himself, hunkered down and clung to Park's antiquated race relations model. As Kuhn observed, scientists easily rationalize away discrepant facts by cramming them into preconceived conceptual boxes, and they cling to the received wisdom until events or scientific advances make it absolutely impossible to do so. Thus it passed that sociologists fiddled while Rome burned.

The sorry end result is that a paradigm that was invented *four decades before* the Civil Rights Revolution continues as the reigning paradigm *four decades after* the Civil Rights Revolution. Even today most sociology courses on race are listed in college catalogs under the rubric "Race Relations" or "Race and Ethnic Relations." At the least, this is a sign of intellectual stasis, and as I show in the pages that follow, the main currents of thought in sociology still reflect the fundamental assumptions and conceptions of race and racism that were embedded in the race relations model, as first propounded by Robert Park at the University of Chicago in the 1910s. Thus, not only did sociology fail to anticipate the Civil Rights Revolution, not only did it give scant attention to the historic events that were occurring in Washington as sociologists convened for their annual meeting, but even in the aftermath of the civil rights upheaval, sociology stayed the course. It is difficult to escape the conclusion that, insofar as mainstream sociology is concerned, the Civil Rights Revolution failed to produce a corresponding revolution in the realm of ideas.

This is problematic, to say the least, for a sub-field that is dedicated to the study of race, one that purports to welcome new ideas, but that stubbornly lags behind the curve of history, unwilling to jettison obsolete models or to search for new truths. Of course, there have been exceptions: as we have already seen, there were prescient voices all along that did anticipate the civil rights upheaval. Furthermore, in the aftermath of the Civil Rights Revolution, beginning with Blauner's *Racial Oppression in America*, there emerged a canon of anti-hegemonic discourse. For the most part, however, the old guard rationalized away the failures of Park's race relations paradigm, or made token changes that served only to extend its life. On the whole, the sociological establishment persevered, unfazed by its own conspicuous failures.

Precisely for this reason, it becomes intellectually imperative to reach a clear understanding of the origins and ideological underpinnings of Robert Park's race relations model. By treading down this path of inquiry, we are in effect tracing the life history of an "epistemology of ignorance."

THE STRANGE CAREER OF ROBERT EZRA PARK

Robert Park once greeted Richard Wright with the question, "How in hell did you happen?"[29] Let us turn the table, and ask the same question of Robert Park. How in hell did this lad from Red Wing, Minnesota, who oscillated between different career trajectories, finally end up, at the ripe age of fifty, as a professor at the University of Chicago where he emerged as the "father" of the famed Chicago school of race relations?[30] Even though he was new to the field, Park was catapulted to prominence, oddly enough, by collaborating with Ernest W. Burgess in writing a textbook, *Introduction to the Science of Sociology*, which was dubbed "the Green Bible" because it was the standard textbook in the field for nearly two decades and known for its green cover.[31]

As in other aspects of Park's life, this fateful development owed much to serendipity. The story is an interesting one. Burgess had received his Ph.D. in sociology at the University of Chicago in 1913, and in 1916 was invited back as an instructor. Everett Hughes has described what happened next:

Burgess was expected to teach an introductory course. He asked a Professor Bedford, who was teaching such a course for his outline. Bedford refused to give it, saying that he would have to get up his own course. Thereupon the older Park and the young Burgess worked out a set of readings and outlines which, after use in classes, became the famous Park & Burgess, *Introduction to the Science of Sociology.*[32] *[A star is born!]*

The volume was first published in 1921, with a second edition in 1924. Strangely, an abridged "student edition" was published in 1969, with an introduction by Morris Janowitz. *[What clearer sign of intellectual stasis! Indeed, the editor tells readers that the volume was not being republished merely for its historical value, but rather because so much of the original volume is "remarkably up to date." Can you imagine republishing or reading a 48-year-old textbook in biology, or English, or for that matter, history? Why suppose that the verities four decades before the Civil Rights Revolution, when white supremacy was official state policy, would have anything but retrograde bearing on contemporary events?]*

Despite the success of the textbook, Park's personal reputation as a leading scholar was mostly a posthumous phenomenon. According to Herbert Blumer, one of Park's illustrious students, "Dr. Park's impact on American sociology was much greater through his training and guidance of graduate students than through a reading of his sociological writings."[33] His reputation as a preeminent scholar of race waited until 1950, seven years after his death, when another of his students—none other than Everett Hughes—collaborated in the publication of a three-volume series of Park's articles. The first paperback edition of *Race and Culture* was issued in 1964, just as the civil rights crisis engendered intense interest in the study of race. *Race and Culture* rapidly emerged as a canonical text in the emerging field of "race relations," a term that entered the sociological lexicon through Park's "race relations cycle."

In the pages that follow, I attempt to fill the gap between Park's upbringing in Minnesota and his emergence as a luminary at the University of Chicago. My goal is to identify the combination of biography and history that accounts for both the genesis of Park's ideas and their embrace by the sociological establishment.

Some insight into Park's psychology can be gleaned from an autobiographical note that he dictated to his secretary and was found after his death in 1944. Park began as follows:

I can trace my interest in sociology to the reading of Goethe's *Faust*. You remember that Faust was tired of books and wanted to see the world—the world of men. At any rate, after leaving college I gave up a position as teacher in a high school at Red Wing, Minnesota, and went to Minneapolis on the chance of getting a job as a reporter.[34]

This fragment of self-analysis contains the key to understanding the twists and turns in Park's life course. Here was a restless and conflicted man who tired of the pristine and cerebral life of the university, and sought action and adventure in "the world of men." But after each foray into that world outside, Park's internal radar brought him back to the university.

Thus, after graduating Phi Beta Kappa from the University of Michigan, Park embarked on an eight-year career as a reporter that began in Minneapolis and ended up in New York, which Park described as "the Mecca of every ambitious newspaperman." He then spent a year at Harvard, before venturing off to Germany, which was the major center of intellectual ferment where social philosophy was evolving into sociology. For four years Park studied with Georg Simmel in Berlin and Wilhelm Windelband in Heidelberg, and returned to Harvard in 1903 to complete his doctoral dissertation entitled "Masse und Publikum" (Crowd and Public). By his own account, he was a person adrift: "I spent most of the time putting my thesis in shape. It was a thin little book and not very easy to read. I had expected to produce something shining and was terribly disappointed and discouraged."[35]

"By this time," Park tells us in his autobiographical note, "I was sick and tired of the academic world and I wanted to get back to the world of men." Quite by chance, in 1904 Park met an official of the Congo Reform Association (CRA), a group based in England that was waging an international crusade against the ravages in the Congo by King Leopold of Belgium.[36] In a stunning example of how European powers carved up the Third World among themselves, an international conference in 1887 granted Leopold imperial possession of the Congo. Its name—the Congo Free State—itself embodies the myth of imperialism: that it was a philanthropic undertaking that would bring the fruits of civilization to Africa. Of course, behind this rhetorical smokescreen were raw economic interests. Leopold amassed immense wealth,

first from the import of ivory and later through the import of rubber to sat-
isfy the rubber boom that followed the invention of the inflatable bicycle tire
and the automobile. Leopold's colonial administrators imposed a system of
forced labor that held women as hostages and required men to meet quotas
for rubber extraction. The brutalities associated with forced labor came to
light through the efforts of the Congo Reform Association, whose most illustrious adherent, Joseph Conrad, depicted the ravages of colonialism in
*Heart of Darkness. [Dear Reader: Without going mad, juxtapose two images in
your mind: one of a plundered land and a people subjected to ruthless exploitation and grotesque violence; the other of well-groomed couples with aristocratic
airs riding their bicycles through a Brussels park on a Sunday afternoon. Such
are the contradictions of imperialism!]*

Park took a position with the CRA, first as publicist and then as secretary,
though hardly out of idealistic fervor. One of his biographers quotes him as
saying: "Any ambition that I had ever had to be a reformer had quite vanished
by that time. But I had nothing to do. I was quite discouraged about the prospects in America of Collective Psychology as I had conceived of it. I was ready
to take up newspaper or literary work again. The Congo Reform Association
offered an opportunity."[37] Park never set foot in Africa, but used secondary
sources and interviews with eyewitnesses to write a series of three muckraking
articles for *Everybody's Magazine* between November 1906 and January 1907 that
provided graphic accounts of Leopold's atrocities, replete with photographs of
children with severed hands. Whatever his professed misgivings about social
reformers, Park threw himself into the mission of the Congo Reform Association with energy and conviction. This is noteworthy because, as I show later,
the passion and fire found in Park's Congo papers provide a puzzling contrast
to the prolixity and torpor that mark his academic writing.

Park's first article, sarcastically entitled "A King in Business," began with
rhetorical flourish: "A new figure looms large on the horizon of Europe! A figure
strange, fantastic, and ominous—the king who is capitalist, *le roi d'affaires*;
the man who unites in himself the political and social prestige of a reigning
monarch with the vast material power of a multimillionaire." This vibrant
language is a far cry from the doctoral student who berated himself for "a
thin little book that was not easy to read"! Park went on to lampoon the daily
press, "which writes history by flash-light," presenting a flattering portrayal

of Leopold, and masking his "rape of the Congo." And he derisively stripped away the façade of Leopold's "Society for Studies in the Upper Congo." "The name had a harmless and academic sound," Park wrote. "It was, however, but a mask for the real enterprise, which was commercial and political."[38]

In his second article, "The Terrible Story of the Congo," Park launched another verbal barrage:

Who is the owner of the vastest private estate in the world—900,000 square miles of it? Who is the promoter of the most stupendous scheme of loot and robbery that modern times can show? Who single-handed, has laid waste a country, drenched a land in blood, offered up tens of thousands of human lives on the altars of his greed and his lust for gold, and hoodwinked the powers of the earth into believing that he did it in the interest of philanthropy and civilization? Who but Leopold, King of the Belgians? . . . who played a game of chess with the nations, with 20 million black men as his helpless pawns.[39]

[Please, DR, insert a mental bookmark here, that we might compare the style and substance of "The Terrible Story of the Congo" to The Story of the Negro, *which Park ghostwrote for Booker T. Washington.]*

Park's final article, "The Blood-Money of the Congo," was relentless in its ridicule of "the Philanthropist of the Congo and of Belgium":

You have learned the methods whereby he has coined into gold the sweat and blood of a dying people; you have watched mutilated men and women staggering under baskets of rubber beneath the lash of his armed and brutal sentries; you have seen fourscore severed hands, the mummied hands of living victims, impaled on stakes before a smoking fire as evidence from his agents of duty well performed. And now, inevitably you ask:

"What does it all mean? What becomes of this vast wealth, wrung from a nation's agony? Who benefits by its outpouring? It comes to him, millions of dollars of it, every year; where does it go, and what does its owner do with it?"

Where does it go, this blood-stained Congo gold? Into the fairy palaces, the wonderful gardens of enchantment in which this grim old, gray old king delights.[40]

Potent stuff! Yet for all of Park's fierce denunciation of Leopold's Congo, it would be a mistake to conclude that he was an archenemy of imperialism and colonial domination. This is worth underscoring because it provides clues to

Park's mindset as he shifted his focus from Africa to race in the United States. Again, it is best to let Park speak for himself:

I discovered what I might have known in advance—that conditions in the Congo were about what one might expect, what they have since become, though not by any means so bad, in Kenya. They were, in short, what they were certain to be whenever a sophisticated people invades the territories of a more primitive people in order to exploit their lands and, incidentally, to uplift and civilize them. I knew enough about civilization even at that time to know that progress, as James once remarked, is a terrible thing. It is so destructive and wasteful.[41]

"To uplift and civilize." This was the logic of imperialism, or at least its public face. "Progress . . . is a terrible thing." Translated: imperialism is violent and "stuff happens," to use Donald Rumsfeld's infamous phrase in relation to another imperialist venture—the American war in Iraq. As terrible as this "stuff" is, it is the price of progress. Alas, we arrive at the naked truth. The problem with Leopold was that he was giving colonialism a bad name! His atrocities had exposed the lie of colonialism: the pretense that it was motivated by the philanthropic intention of bringing the fruits of civilization to these backward peoples. This was the façade that Park was attempting to restore, even as he railed against Leopold's excesses.

Given his worldview, it should come as no surprise that Park soon found himself in league with the man who penned the following words: "notwithstanding the cruelty and moral wrong of slavery, the ten million Negroes inhabiting this country, who themselves or whose ancestors went through the school of American slavery, are in a stronger and more hopeful condition, materially, intellectually, morally, and religiously, than is true of an equal number of black people in any other portion of the globe."[42] The author of these words was Booker T. Washington, in his 1901 autobiography, *Up from Slavery*. One can detect the same stream of ideas that we found in Park's Congo papers. Slavery was "a terrible thing," but it nevertheless rescued these benighted people from savagery. This was precisely the moral justification for slavery—invented, refined, and adapted to changing circumstances, for over two centuries. One might wince at the excesses of slavery, and as with Leopold, one might repudiate slave owners who used gratuitous or extreme violence. But can it be denied that slavery, for all of its ills, was an instrument of progress? Were not American Negroes better off than blacks anywhere in Africa? Were they not better off than even serfs in Europe? Indeed, this was the theme of an entire book, ghostwritten by Park himself, after he and Washington traveled to Europe in 1910, ostensibly to determine the answer to this strange and specious question.

As a twist on our previous question, we might now ask how in hell did this unlikely partnership between Robert Ezra Park and Booker T. Washington happen? And what did this suggest about the intellectual baggage that Park carried with him when he eventually left "the world of men" and returned to the ivory tower, this time as a professor at the University of Chicago and "the father of the study of race relations."

One of Park's responsibilities at the CRA was to ghostwrite articles signed by notables. Washington was nominally a vice president of the CRA, and in 1904 Park wrote an article under Washington's name entitled "Cruelty in the Congo Country."[43] In private conversation, Park discussed the need to establish a system of education in the Congo along the lines of Tuskegee, which resulted in an invitation to visit Tuskegee.[44] Thus began a nine-year collaboration. Park was employed as Washington's publicist and ghostwriter, a position that had been initially offered to W.E.B. Du Bois, who taught at Tuskegee. Du Bois declined, and rightly so, since he was about to publish *The Souls of Black Folk*, in which he excoriates Washington for representing "the old attitude of adjustment and submission."[45] Park would prove to be a more reliable ideological bedfellow.

Why did Park forsake his career in journalism and agree to assume an essentially subordinate role as publicist and ghostwriter for Washington? One answer is that Park did not have notable success as a journalist: he had few bylines to boast about and relied on his inheritance to support his wife and four children, who remained in Wollaston, Massachusetts. In contrast, Washington was an internationally renowned figure, at the height of his fame and influence.[46] As he had done when he reached other crossroads in his life, Park was drawn to "the world of men." He once wrote: "I was disgusted with what I had done in the University and had come to the conclusion that I couldn't do anything first rate on my own account. I decided the best thing to do was to attach myself to someone who was doing something first rate. Washington was not a brilliant man or an intellectual, but he seemed to me to be doing something real. So I went."[47]

As Fred Matthews contends in *Quest for an American Sociology: Robert E. Park and the Chicago School,* Park's role as publicist was vital to Washington's success.[48] Publicity was the lifeblood of Tuskegee. Publicity was necessary to elicit contributions from wealthy philanthropists, to curry political favor with white politicians, to build ties between blacks and whites in the South, to promote the ideals embodied in the Tuskegee experiment, and to trumpet the success of moral education so as to counter prevailing stereotypes of blacks. The ideological function of publicity was that it sustained the myth of "uplift"—the notion that blacks could transcend oppression and misery—even at a time when the scaffolding of the Jim Crow system was being erected.[49]

Perhaps Park's greatest contribution was in bolstering the image and reputation of the Wizard of Tuskegee, as Washington was called. Thus it fell upon Park to craft the public image that made Washington into a spokesman for the race. Park put his talents as a journalist to work, not only as press agent for Washington, but, as has been noted, also as ghostwriter. Washington's autobiography, *Up from Slavery,* was published before his encounter with Park, though this too was largely ghostwritten by another white journalist who relied on notes and drafts written by Washington.[50] Park had a hand in the sequel, *My Larger Education* (1911), and in *The Story of the Negro* (1909), an account of blacks at the turn of the century.[51] Then Park and Washington collaborated in writing *The Man Farthest Down* (1912), based on the trip the two men took across Europe in 1910, with the singular purpose of finding out if blacks in the United States were better off than the peasants in Europe. This time Park bridled at his role as ghostwriter, and proposed that he be listed as joint author. Washington refused, but acknowledged Park as a "collaborator" and in the introduction provided a self-serving account of the respective contributions of each of them.[52]

In terms of the history of ideas, two vexing issues present themselves. First, what import are we to give to the fact that this white man played such a crucial role in crafting Washington's public image, and even in telling *The Story of the Negro?* In this book readers are told that hardship and injustice are the fate of "every race that has struggled up from a lower to a higher civilization."[53] To have Park writing these words amounts to a subtle form of "blackface," as Park, in his role of ghostwriter, got into the skin of this illustrious black leader. Indeed, Park once wrote, "I became, for all intents and purposes, a Negro myself."[54]

Yet, perhaps Park had it backwards: it was not that he "became" a Negro, but rather that, like the minstrel player, he crafted the Negro to his own image. Perhaps Park was unwittingly a purveyor of "whiteness" as he became Booker Taliaferro Washington's voice to the world.

Conversely, we have to inquire into what influence Washington had on Park. What about the intellectual baggage that Robert Park carried with him when he became a professor at the renowned University of Chicago, just as sociology was in its formative stage? Indeed, John Stanfield has gone so far as to declare, "Booker T. Washington, through his sponsorship of Robert E. Park, was a founder of the Chicago school of race relations."[55] Though this may be an overstatement, it behooves us to ask a series of questions. Did the theories that Park propounded from his cloistered office at the University of Chicago embody ideology and perspectives he acquired during his nine-year stint as publicist and ghostwriter for Booker T. Washington? Did Park give scholarly exposition to Washington's accommodationist logic, whose central feature was the avoidance of conflict and acceptance of the racial status quo? Is this why sociology failed to confront, much less oppose, racial oppression? Does this bring us closer to understanding why sociology failed to anticipate the Civil Rights Revolution?

Before addressing these questions, let us unravel the mystery of how Robert Ezra Park morphed from ghostwriter to professor when, at the age of fifty, he was hired in 1914 as a part-time assistant lecturer at the University of Chicago and subsequently emerged as "the father of the race relations school."

As happens in life, luck and circumstance played a fateful role. According to Park's biographers, it all turned on a chance encounter in 1912 with W. I. Thomas, a professor in the fledgling Department of Sociology at the University of Chicago, at a conference on "The Education of Primitive Man." *[Dear Reader: Don't race on to the next sentence, as I did initially. Stop and ponder the bevy of assumptions that allowed erudite scholars to convene a conference on "The Education of Primitive Man." Think about the implications of tagging blacks as "primitive" in need of "education." Indeed, as we will see, this construction provides the ideological linkage between Booker T. Washington, Robert Ezra Park, William Thomas, and the Chicago school of race relations.]*

The conference, held at Tuskegee, was Park's brainchild, though it was sponsored and funded by Washington. Some 3,700 persons were invited, and

the Department of State distributed a notice to all governments that had
"Negro possessions." Park sounded the keynote for the conference by posing
the question: "How far is it possible by means of education to abridge the ap-
prenticeship of the younger to the older races, or at least to make it less cruel
and inhuman than it now frequently is?"[56] Here we encounter the linchpin
of Washington's ideological system: that there is a hierarchy of "older" and
"younger" races in terms of their level of civilization, and that education is the
mechanism for lifting "the primitive" to the level of "civilized" man.

Indeed, this is precisely the argument advanced by Dinesh D'Souza in his
1995 book, *The End of Racism.* D'Souza rejects the idea that racism is a problem, insisting that whites are only reacting to the "uncivilized" behavior they
observe among blacks. The remedy, then, is to close "the civilization gap" between the races. Indeed, in advancing this thesis D'Souza invokes the name of
Booker T. Washington: "The supreme challenge faced by African Americans is
the one that Booker T. Washington outlined almost a century ago: the mission
of building the civilizational resources of a people whose culture is frequently
unsuited to the requirements of the modern world."[57]

For Park, as for D'Souza eight decades later, the key to racial progress is
closing the civilization gap, and the way to do this is by educating blacks. Only
then will the condition of blacks become "less cruel and inhumane." Note that
there is no provision in this schema for curbing the cruelty and inhumanity
of the Jim Crow system that was being enacted into law at the very time that
Washington and Park preached the gospel of education. Rather, it is blacks
themselves who are to be transformed—through the medium of education.
Thus instead of lowering racist barriers, the convenient and wildly inaccurate
assumption is that those barriers are not insurmountable, so long as blacks
have the requisite education.[58]

As Washington's intellectual defenders are quick to point out, his position
offered a hopeful alternative to the reigning paradigm that defined blacks as
genetically inferior and thus beyond redemption. This, as we will see, is precisely the claim to fame of the Chicago school of race relations: its renunciation
of scientific racism. We have to ask, however, whether this merely marked a
shift from genes to culture, thus diverting attention away from the structure
of oppression and placing responsibility for racial uplift on blacks themselves.
Booker T. Washington's famous autobiography *Up from Slavery* might just as

well have been entitled *Up from Savagery*, since the project of racial uplift was conceived as one that entailed the socialization of blacks, through education, from a "savage mentality" into the mindset of "civilized man." Was this the core belief that served as the basis of the unusual collaboration between Booker T. Washington and Robert Ezra Park, and that provided Park with entrée into the lofty world of the academy?

In *Robert E. Park: Biography of a Sociologist*, Winifred Raushenbush, Park's personal assistant, devotes an entire chapter to "The Convergence of William I. Thomas and Robert Park," rich in detail about this fateful encounter.[59] Thomas's presentation was entitled "Education and Cultural Traits." According to the Tuskegee student newspaper, "Professor Thomas revived the old question of the fitness of the Negro as a race to acquire the culture of the white man and participate in the white man's civilization, but he did it in a novel and surprisingly witty manner."[60] Whether because of the confluence of their ideas or a deeper personal connection, or both, Park and Thomas struck up a friendship that can only be described as passionate, as evident from an exchange of letters between the two men. Four days after the conference, Thomas sent a letter to Park that began: "My dear brother in Christ: I am amazed to find how ignorant I was before I met you and how wise I seem to be now," and was signed: "Good Hunting, W. I. Thomas."[61] And a month later: "My dear Park: Your two letters reached me together. It has been the greatest thing that ever happened to me to meet you, and if we can pull this thing off, as we are going to, and eventually get together and teach alongside it will make life interesting."[62] Park later wrote, in more temperate language, "I found in Thomas, almost for the first time, a man who seemed to speak the same language as myself. When, therefore, he invited me to come to Chicago and give a course on the Negro, I was delighted to do so."[63] Securing an appointment for Park was no easy matter, however. Thomas enlisted the help of Albion Small, chair of the Sociology Department, who had met Park a decade earlier at the summer home of his father-in-law, a prominent Supreme Court judge in Michigan.[64] The strands of fate seemed to come together, though at first Small was only able to offer Park a part-time position as an assistant lecturer in the Divinity School. According to Morris Janowitz, a future chair of the department, it was only "after many years of agitation" that Park, through Albion Small, was able to secure a regular appointment in the Department of Sociology.[65]

Thus it passed that in the winter quarter of 1914 Park taught his first course in the Department of Sociology and Anthropology on "The Negro in America." Here is the description in the college catalog:

Directed especially to the effects, in slavery and freedom, of the contacts of the white and black race, an attempt will be made to characterize the nature of the present tensions and tendencies and to estimate the character of the changes which race relations are likely to bring about in the American system.[66]

According to Raushenbush, "This course was certainly one of the first dealing exclusively with black Americans to be given in any predominantly white university in the United States and may, indeed, have been the first such course."[67] Indeed, even black colleges, dependent as they were on white philanthropy, shied away from putting "race" on their curricula. In 1915 the board of trustees at Howard University *[Howard University!!]* turned down a request for a course on "interracial relations," along with a faculty proposal for a course on "Negro problems."[68] *[In 1995 a professor at the University of Connecticut proposed a course on "White Racism," and was embroiled in controversy and ensnarled in bureaucratic red tape until the course was finally approved a year later.[69] As the French expression goes: Plus ça change, plus c'est la même chose.]* Park of course deserves credit for breaking through the wall of silence and making race a subject for scholarly inquiry. On the other hand, he did so in a way that was politically safe, beginning with his conception of "race relations." Thus began Park's illustrious career as "father" of the Chicago school of race relations.

This development calls forth a number of tantalizing questions. How did Park morph from the deferential assistant to Booker T. Washington into a professor at the renowned University of Chicago? How did he make the transition from the firebrand who used his journalistic talents to denounce King Leopold's ravages in the Congo into the detached scholar in a profession that explicitly proscribed political advocacy? And, to return to the question I posed earlier, what elements of his Tuskegee experience, and Washington's weltanschauung on race, did Park bring with him as he traversed the figurative midway and entered the awe-inspiring campus of the University of Chicago, with its gothic spires, gargoyles, and magnificent cathedral, the benefaction of John D. Rockefeller? Was Park a reincarnation of Booker T. Washington in academic garb, preaching the gospel of education at a time when the final nails were being driven in the coffin of Reconstruction? In *Quest for an American Sociology*, Fred Matthews provides a cogent answer to this important question: "The attitudes which Washington tried to inculcate as a shield against total despair in the Alabama of 1910 were absorbed by Park, and transmitted through him a generation later to an audience of white (and even Negro) social scientists who then preached to a very different audience the 'good news' that political action to protect civil liberties against community mores was futile."[70]

According to St. Clair Drake, in the hiatus between Park's decision to leave Tuskegee in the spring of 1912 and his appointment to the University of Chicago in the fall of 1914, Park "spent three years retooling for an academic career in the department of sociology. . . . He did so by intensive reading and constant discussion with W. I. Thomas," who had received one of the first Ph.D.s in sociology from the University of Chicago in 1896.[71] During this period Park drafted a paper, "Racial Assimilation in Secondary Groups, With Particular Reference to the Negro," strategically published in the prestigious *Publication of the American Sociological Society*, the precursor to the *American Sociological Review*.[72] This also served as the basis of a lecture Park delivered at the University of Chicago in the spring of 1913. Essentially this was his "job talk," his chance to prove his mettle as a scholar.

What is immediately striking about Park's paper on "racial assimilation" is his abrupt change of rhetorical frames. Gone are the passion and fire, the polemics, and the moral outrage that jumped off the page of his Congo papers. Instead, his paper opens with the detached voice and insipid prose of the social scientist: "The race problem has sometimes been described as a problem in assimilation. It is not always clear, however, what assimilation means." *[Let the hairsplitting and obfuscation begin!]*

Park's core argument was that assimilation was a dominant feature of modern societies. "The modern Italian, Frenchman, and German is a composite of the broken fragments of several different racial groups. Interbreeding has broken up the ancient stocks, and interaction and imitation have created new national types which exhibit definite uniformities in language, manners, and formal behavior."[73] But then the conundrum: the racial exception. The United States has been able "to swallow and digest every sort of normal human difference, except the purely external ones, like the color of the skin."[74]

If I could make a quantum leap into the past and attend Park's job talk, I would throw three questions at the candidate:

1. You say that this country has been able "to swallow and digest every sort of normal human difference, except the purely external ones, like the color of the skin." But you haven't made clear why the happenstance of skin color should have such profound consequences. In other words, why doesn't your race relations model, which fits the experience of European immigrants so well, apply to people of color?

2. You note that unlike European immigrants, who try to escape assimilation, "the Negro has had his separateness and consequent race consciousness thrust upon him, because of his exclusion and forcible isolation from white society." Yet you seem to accept these deplorable conditions with equanimity, as an inexorable fact of life! What happened to the idealism and fire in your Congo papers? How is it that you denounced racial violence in the Congo with such fervor, and here in the United States, where blacks are forcibly segregated, denied basic civil rights, and subjected to mob violence, you speak only of "kindly relations between individual members of the two races" and "mutual sympathy and understanding" between the races?

3. You cite your erstwhile employer, Booker T. Washington, as arguing that blacks are emerging as "a nation within a nation." As you may know, W.E.B. Du Bois has recently published a book, under the evocative title *The Souls of Black Folk*. Let me quote a passage from this book:

   "Mr. Washington distinctly asks that people give up, at least for the present, three things—

   First, political power,

   Second, insistence on civil rights,

   Third, higher education of Negro Youth,—and concentrate all their energies on industrial education, and the accumulation of wealth, and the conciliation of the South."[75]

   Do you agree with Washington that "at least for the present" blacks should give up their demands for political power and civil rights? And while we're talking about Du Bois, what do you think about his study of *The Philadelphia Negro*, in which he documents the many racist barriers in jobs and housing that prevent the "assimilation" of blacks? Why do you think *The Philadelphia Negro* was never reviewed in the *American Journal of Sociology*, which is published by the very men sitting in this room? And why, in your disquisition on "Racial Assimilation in Secondary Groups," do you say next to nothing about the massive denial of rights to Negroes? How can they "assimilate" when they are segregated by law in the South and surrounded by a sea of bigotry in the North?

Alas, here we bump up against the difference between fantasy and reality. Had I accosted Park with such prickly questions, what can we imagine would have been the outcome? No doubt I would have been disdained as "a Washington basher" and shunned into silence. As for Park, well, had he so much as hinted that he favored civil rights for blacks, he would have been accused of violating the principle of value-free social science and committing the sin of "advocacy." For sure, he would have been rejected for the position that he coveted at the University of Chicago, and we would not now be assessing the influence of Robert Ezra Park on the study of race in America!

It is not my contention that, minus Park, the historiography of race would have been fundamentally different. After all, Park was hired precisely because he was in sync with the prevailing intellectual and ideological currents, and without Park, some other person would have emerged to serve as the exemplar of the race relations school. A likely prospect was W. I. Thomas, who had staked out a position similar to Park's in his paper on "Education and Cultural Traits" at the conference on the Education of Primitive Man. Thomas was the dominant influence in the Chicago school until his career ended in ignominy in 1918 when scandal-mongering newspapers reported that he was registered under a false name with a married woman in a Chicago hotel.[76] Instead, the wheel of fortune operated in reverse: after Thomas's expulsion, Park emerged as the key figure in the Chicago school. *[Don't miss the irony here: that Thomas's private breach of puritanical codes of sexuality elicited severe condemnation, whereas racism, which entailed the debasement of an entire people, was accepted with equanimity, or at best, gratuitous hand wringing.]*

Another prospective candidate for Park's pedestal was Sarah Simons, the niece of Lester Ward, the celebrated "father" of American sociology. Simons's disquisition on "Social Assimilation" was published in five parts in the *American Journal of Sociology* in 1901 and 1902. However, like most of academia at that time, Chicago's sociology department was a male bastion.[77] Surely, some other white male would have been found to fill the role of exemplar of the race relations paradigm. Yet it was Park's destiny to fulfill this role, and he had a unique credential: his personal connection with the illustrious Booker T. Washington, and through him, the black world. What better person to serve as the proverbial "friend of the Negro" and the chief architect of the Chicago school of race relations?

At the risk of stretching fantasy into the absurd, let us imagine Robert Park making a quantum leap forward, landing in Chicago's Department of Sociology in 1978, the year that an obscure professor, William Julius Wilson, was catapulted into national prominence with the publication of a book with a magical title, *The Declining Significance of Race*. Coming as it did at the end of the Second Reconstruction, Wilson's ascent was a rerun of Booker T. Washington's meteoric rise after his 1895 speech at the Atlanta Exposition. Although Wilson once declared himself a social democrat and favors governmental programs for "the truly disadvantaged," the public controversy around his work centered on the fact that, like Washington in his time, Wilson shifted attention away from "political agitation" and a demand for "rights," to racial uplift through education and the acquisition of skills. With overtones reminiscent of Washington, Wilson held that "talented and educated blacks, like talented and educated whites, will continue to enjoy the advantages and privileges of their class status."[78] Finally, both men backed away from political action (or what Washington called "artificial forcing"), and emphasized the development of the education and job skills that delivered the black middle class from degrading poverty. Thus, Robert Park would have felt very much at home in Chicago's Department of Sociology that housed William Julius Wilson. Yet another sign of intellectual stasis, of how little sociological thinking on race had changed from Park to Wilson![79] *[Again, Plus ça change, plus c'est la même chose.]*

EXCURSUS: A NOTE ON THE POLITICS OF "OBJECTIVITY"

Every student of sociology is schooled in the dogma of value-free social science, whose central dictum is that social scientists must strive for objectivity. This idea is usually traced to Max Weber who, in his famous essay on "Science as a Vocation," admonished social scientists to eschew politics. *[Dear Reader: If you've never eschewed anything before, you can begin now: with politics. This will require something of an intellectual lobotomy, but that is another matter.]* Weber issued this uncompromising edict: "The prophet and the demagogue do not belong on the academic platform."[80] In plain language, the business of sociology concerns what *is*, not what *should be*.

However, in the formative years before professional sociology emerged as a discipline—before it bowed to the false god of objectivity—it was not only interested in what *should be*, but it used this as a prism for assessing what *is*. I am alluding to the Progressive Era at the turn of the century when early sociologists were unabashed social reformers. The reform impulse came from two unlikely sources: evangelical Protestants and social workers, both of whom were committed to the betterment of society. These early sociologists—or more accurately, pre-sociologists—did not eschew advocacy: they did not flinch at taking positions on such contentious issues as child labor, the right to strike, compulsory arbitration, progressive taxation, and municipal ownership of utilities. Indeed, in a paper on "Scholarship and Social Agitation," published in the *American Journal of Sociology* in 1896, Albion Small, the founder of Chicago's Department of Sociology, reviewed the litany of problems of the industrial age, declaring: "Scholars are shirkers unless they grapple with these problems."[81] For these early sociologists, it was an article of faith that the methods of science could be applied to the study of society, and that this knowledge could be used for the betterment of humankind. Some scholars went a perilous step further: they took positions on the contentious issues of the day. They openly defended labor unions, opposed monopolies, advocated public ownership of public utilities, opposed child labor, and so on. This was the political soil that gave rise to the discipline of sociology.

However, the years in which the Progressive Movement flourished were also the years that the scaffolding of Jim Crow was being erected in the South and the Fourteenth Amendment effectively nullified as a guarantor of rights for blacks. For all their fervor in championing the cause of child labor and the poor, for all their belief in "progress," most progressives fell silent when it came to the retrogression of black rights as Reconstruction unraveled. As one historian put it: "While the Progressive reform movement of the early twentieth century was seeking to enlarge democratic perspectives for white society, the Negro was being pushed to the nadir of his experience since emancipation."[82]

Before sociology could become established in universities as a legitimate field of study, it had to pass muster with the trustees. Invariably, these trustees were prominent businessmen or philanthropists whose power and beneficence led to their appointment. As Walter Metzger writes in *Academic Freedom in the Age of the University*, "In the final decades of the last century, the leaders of American business began to support our universities on a completely unprecedented scale."[83] Earlier I alluded to the cloistered atmosphere of the university, but this was a carefully crafted illusion. In reality, the university was a political minefield where permissible dissent was held within a narrow range of accepted belief and practice. In her book, aptly titled *Advocacy & Objectivity*, Mary Furner presents us with this lead-in to her chapter on "Permissible Dissent":

A cartoon on the cover of *Life* showed the dignified figure of a university president and former economist leaving the college gate with his suitcase, while a plump trustee nailed a want ad to the ivy-covered pillar. The message read: "WANTED: By the Corporation of Brown University, a young man of submissive disposition as president. A reasonable amount of scholarship will not be a disqualification, but the chief requisite will be an obsequious and ingratiating behavior toward millionaires and an ability to RAKE IN THE DOLLARS. Opinions and first-class board furnished by the Corporation. No gentlemen encumbered with a back-bone need apply."[84]

The cartoon in *Life*, almost unimaginable today in a national magazine, was prompted by a series of highly publicized academic freedom cases in the 1890s. The most serious involved Richard Ely, a prominent economist at Johns Hopkins University who was one of a number of young economists who hailed from evangelical Protestant families, but had become disillusioned with the idea that the church could be an instrument of social change. Instead, they turned to social science, which they regarded as a secular instrument for reaching God's kingdom on earth.[85] Ely wrote articles in both the popular and religious press supporting labor during the upheavals of 1886, and he waged a battle in professional journals against laissez faire economics. He soon found himself embattled, vilified as a socialist, and pressured by the university to temper his language.[86] Eventually Ely left Johns Hopkins for the University of Wisconsin, only to find himself under political attack that culminated with a public trial by the university regents. In the end Ely was exonerated, but only after he issued a public statement affirming that if the charges against him had been true, he would have no right to teach in the university.[87]

Another economist, Henry Carter Adams, whose father had been a leader in the Iowa band of antislavery Congregational ministers, had been fired from his position at Cornell because, according to historian of science Dorothy Ross, "he roused the ire of Cornell benefactor, Russell Sage." *[Dear Reader: Stay tuned, because the name of Russell Sage, monumentalized in the Russell Sage Foundation, comes up again later in this narrative.]* Eventually Adams secured a position at the University of Michigan, but only after he issued a public statement in which he retreated from his earlier radicalism, and essentially foreswore any allegiance to socialism.[88]

The assault on academic freedom reached into the University of Chicago's Sociology Department with the Bemis case, described in detail in Mary Furner's book, *Advocacy & Objectivity.* In a chapter on "The Perils of Radicalism," Furner writes: "Sympathy with the labor movement was tantamount to subversion; support of public ownership of gasworks or streetcar lines attacked the interests of the private capitalists who owned them and the politicians who dispensed the franchises."[89] Edward Bemis was a student of Ely who expounded the dangerous belief that utilities were so powerful and important, and prone to monopoly pricing and graft, that they should either be owned by municipalities or closely regulated by government.

Educated at Amherst and Johns Hopkins University, Bemis was brought to the University of Chicago as a young professor in 1892. However, he quickly fell out of the graces of the conservative chairman of the Economics Department, who banished him to teach extension courses. After Bemis joined the fight for municipal control of the city's gas supply, *[Dig this!]* the Chicago gas trust retaliated by denying the university cut-rate prices so long as Bemis remained on the faculty! In January 1894 Bemis, who was a tenured professor, received a letter from President Harper notifying him that "in the long run you can do in another institution because of the peculiar circumstances here, a better and more satisfactory work to yourself than you can do here." *[In plain English: you're fired!]* On another occasion Harper complained, "It is hardly safe for me to venture into any of the Chicago clubs," and ordered Bemis not to make any more public statements on controversial issues. Bemis refused to resign, and his battle to retain his position became a cause célèbre. Critics blamed Rockefeller, the Standard Oil Company, the Chicago and Northwestern Railway, and the Chicago Gas Trust for pressuring the university trustees to fire Bemis. President Harper's rejoinder *[Get ready for this one.]* was that Bemis was fired because his teaching was inadequate.

One of the people to whom Bemis turned for help was Albion Small, the chair of the Sociology Department, who would hire Robert Park a decade later. Small, too, had been an Ely student, and two years later would publish the article in the *American Journal of Sociology* admonishing sociologists not to be "shirkers" when it came to social reform. Although Small agreed with Bemis on municipal ownership, he was clearly under pressure from President Harper, and equivocated, telling Bemis that "in these days a man is not considered scientific, who claims to speak on more than one small corner of a subject."[90] *[Remember Everett Hughes's lament that sociology missed the Civil Rights Revolution because "our conception of social science is so empirical, so limited to little bundles of fact applied to little hypotheses" that we fail to take in the big picture?]* Then Small disclosed his personal formula for survival: "There is so much misapprehension of Sociology as a science of reform that, although I hope to take up reform movements years hence, I am now going off in my lectures into transcendental philosophy so as to be as far as possible from these reform movements and thus establish the scientific character of my department."[91]

Here was a startling admission that validated the thesis of Furner's book: that advocacy was sacrificed on the altar of objectivity, and that this was a precondition for the admission of sociology into the academy as a legitimate field of inquiry. The clear message was that any professors who engaged in advocacy did so at their own peril.

I have devoted considerable space to the Bemis case for two reasons. First, it goes a long way toward explaining the intellectual metamorphosis of Robert Ezra Park. Clearly, Park knew that he had to *[ahem]* eschew both passion and advocacy in order to make it across the political minefield leading to the ivory towers flanking John Rockefeller's cathedral. Second, the Bemis case brings to light an astounding paradox: that the doctrine of objectivity was itself politically motivated! What a remarkable a feat of self-contradiction: while pretending to uphold standards of objectivity, its underlying purpose was to drive social reformers out of the university, and above all, to prevent Marxism from making inroads into the emerging social sciences. In effect, the doctrine of "objectivity" normalized the status quo, and tagged any attempts to challenge established institutions or prevailing systems of belief as motivated by "politics." Thus, "objective" meant acceding to prevailing opinion, and as C. Wright Mills once commented, "biased" was applied to points of view that were not politically acceptable.

Thus, "race relations" rather than "racial oppression" would provide the conceptual umbrella for the study of race in America. And scholarship would proceed without the benefit of a Marxist theory of conflict, with its grounding in historical materialism and its focus on political economy. Even those zealous social workers (mostly female) fired up with the idealism and pragmatism of the Progressive Era would be banished from the academy, all in the name of "objectivity."[92] What a perfect ground rule for an epistemology of ignorance!

PART TWO

RACE: THE EPISTEMOLOGY
OF IGNORANCE

One could say then, as a general rule, that *white
misunderstanding, misrepresentation, evasion, and self-
deception on matters related to race* are among the most
pervasive mental phenomena of the past few hundred
years, a cognitive and moral economy psychically
required for conquest, colonization, and enslavement.

Charles W. Mills, The Racial Contract[1]

ROBERT EZRA PARK ENTERED THE RANKS
of academe during the "nadir" of racism, when the last
nails were being driven into the coffin of Reconstruction. As one historian put
it, citing President Wilson's imposition of Jim Crow policies in the federal civil
service in 1913: "Thus, as the Progressive movement reached its peak, and the
nation prepared to embark on a war to save the world for democracy, the black
man found himself more threatened, more despised, and more discriminated
against in his own land than at any time since emancipation."[2] This was a period that witnessed the resurgence of the Klan and mob violence (more than
1,100 blacks were lynched between 1900 and 1914).

This was also the period of "the Great Migration" of Southern blacks to
Northern cities, triggered by labor shortages that resulted from the cutoff of
European immigration by the First World War. In Chicago, a burgeoning
population of blacks settled on the South Side, where the cloistered University
of Chicago was located, surrounded by a few upscale neighborhoods that relied

on the Hyde Park Improvement Protective Club to keep the black "invasion" at bay.[3] How did social scientists, even in their headstrong determination to prove their scientific prowess, avert their eyes from the racism that was visible to the naked eye, and that finally erupted in the 1919 Chicago riot? How does one go about studying race without crossing the forbidden line into "advocacy"? How does one remain "neutral" in the face of transparent evil? In addressing these questions, we learn something about the rules of sociological method as they apply to an epistemology of ignorance:

Rule 1: Detachment. Robert Park once wrote: "Detachment is the secret of the academic attitude."[4] Park's collaborator, Ernest Burgess, reports that Park actively discouraged students from becoming "activists or propagandists." According to Burgess, "Park told them flatly that the world is full of crusaders. Their role instead was to be that of the calm detached scientist who investigates race relations with the same objectivity and detachment with which the zoologist dissects the potato bug."[5] *[Hmm, the potato bug.]* Another of Park's collaborators gives us this pithy description of Park's rejection of sociology as a moral enterprise: "The aim was not to find out who is right or wrong, but to learn what IS and how it CAME TO BE."[6] But as Stow Persons, author of *Ethnic Studies at Chicago, 1905–45*, points out, "Park's emphasis on detachment involved a repudiation of the influence of John Dewey, which had been very strong at Chicago."[7] Dewey emphasized the unity of thought and action, and held that to understand the world is to transform it. Conversely, an epistemology of ignorance is not innocent of politics, but on the contrary, provides epistemic authority for the status quo.

Rule 2: Evasion. An epistemology of ignorance speaks through silence. The failure to speak out or even take notice implies or functions as acquiescence to the status quo. Writing in 1914, a year that witnessed a spate of lynchings, W.E.B. Du Bois expressed his fury by switching fonts, as he wrote: "Woodrow Wilson and millions of others have given no encouragement to lynching except by silence! *Except by silence!* EXCEPT BY SILENCE!"[8]

The Chicago race riot of 1919, in which the killing of a black teenager on a beach triggered a week of violence that left thirty-eight dead, tested the limits of scholarly detachment. One might think that such an event, barely two miles from the University of Chicago campus, would have captured the attention of the University of Chicago's leading race scholar, especially given his professed appetite for "action." As director of Chicago's Urban League, Park was called upon to head up the official investigation of the causes of the riot. Strangely, Park did not involve himself directly, but instead delegated this to his prize black student, Charles Sturgeon Johnson. Park's baffled biographer writes: "In view of his interest in conflict, it is curious that he did not do any personal study of the riot or even discuss it in his essays on race relations."[9] Ah, yes, "race relations." That was about pacification, not conflict. There was no place in the race relations paradigm, which envisioned a process of steady accommodation and ultimate assimilation, for marauding white gangs killing blacks on the streets of Chicago, a half century after the abolition of slavery. Park was silent because his entire teleological model predicting steady progress was utterly vitiated by events on the ground.

Rule 3: Transcendentalism. As we have seen, Albion Small's personal formula for squelching his own reformist impulses was to drift off "into transcendental philosophy so as to be as far as possible from these reform movements and thus establish the scientific character of my department."[10] Adopting evolutionary theory was tantamount to donning spectacles that brought the long view into focus, but simultaneously eclipsed the reality perceptible to the naked eye. As Stow Persons writes, "the long view tended to impose its complacence on short-range problems."[11] Thus, from an evolutionary standpoint the 1919 Chicago riot was but an unfortunate blip, perhaps worth the attention of the news reporter or the social reformer, but not the practitioner of "the science of society." Of course, this elision itself had political implications. As an observer of what *is* and how it *came to be,* the sociologist was consigned to being a helpless bystander of history. Through its silences and opacities, social science became an instrument of the racial status quo, barred from even imagining a more humane and democratic alternative.

Rule 4: Sophism. When events make it impossible to avert one's eyes, then blatant and inconvenient facts can be disguised under a cloak of euphemism. In popular discourse, segregation was called "the Southern way of life." A segregated balcony in a theatre was called "nigger heaven." A lynching was called "coon cooking." Needless to say, erudite scholars eschew such vulgarities, but they invent neologisms appropriate to their rank. They speak of "a caste system." Of "racial etiquette." And of—the mother of all euphemisms—"race relations." The impact of this nomenclature is to normalize and naturalize racial oppression, to pretend that it is consensual, and to conceal its violent underpinnings and periodic atrocities. The overriding purpose of this wordplay is to obscure what is morally repugnant and indefensible about racism. A popular adage holds, "Don't piss on me and call it rain." Applied to the sociologist, it might read: "Don't deny me my rights, my livelihood, and my dignity and call it 'race relations.'"

These are four rules of sociological method that Robert Park mastered, presumably with coaching from W. I. Thomas, before his "job talk," which allowed him to pass muster with Albion Small and his minion.[12] Still other "rules" will come to light as we follow Robert Park further along his quixotic career path.

In 1913, the same year that Park published his first paper and applied for a teaching position at the University of Chicago, he published a second paper, on "Negro Home Life and Standards of Living." The venue was the prestigious *Annals of the American Academy of Political and Social Science*, in a special issue on "The Negro's Progress in Fifty Years."[13] The title speaks volumes. It encapsulates the trope of "progress" that was the hallmark of Booker T. Washington's Tuskegee project, and that is embedded in the evolutionary logic of the race relations paradigm. Yet once again, note the mind-boggling asymmetry between lofty erudition and the facts on the ground. At a historical juncture when blacks were a downtrodden people, when doctrines of white supremacy and racial segregation were being enacted into law, and when the Klan and mob violence were on the rise, here was a major social science publication crowing about a half century of "progress." And here was our "father of the study of race relations," with an article on "Negro Home Life and Standards of Living" that reads like an antebellum glorification of slavery.[14]

"Negro Home Life and Standards of Living" shows that Booker T. Washington and Robert Ezra Park were made of the same ideological cloth. It is also important because of its striking parallels with the argument that William Julius Wilson would advance a half century later, when the Second Reconstruction was unraveling. Both Park and Wilson trumpeted the "progress" of the black middle class and construed this as indicative of waning racism.

As with Wilson, the starting point for Park is class differentiation among blacks, reflecting the emergence of a class of privileged blacks:

Before the Civil War there were, generally speaking, two classes of Negroes in the United States, namely free Negroes and slaves. After the Civil War and the abolition of slavery, the plantation Negroes remained, for the most part, upon the soil and formed a class of peasant farmers. . . . In recent years the number of occupations in which Negroes are engaged has multiplied. . . . The descendants of the free Negroes and of those slaves who started with superior advantages directly after the war have gone very largely into the professions. . . . There has grown up in recent years a vigorous and pushing middle class, composed of small contractors, business men of various sorts, bankers, real estate and insurance men. . . . At the same time, from among the peasant farmers, there has grown a small class of plantation owners. . . . The growth of a Negro middle class, composed of merchants, plantation owners and small capitalists, has served to fill the distance which formerly existed between the masses of the race at the bottom and the small class of educated Negroes at the top.[15]

Park's emphasis, however, is on home living standards. This is his account of farmers in the region around Christianburg, Virginia:

The homes of the Negro farmers in this region would be regarded as comfortable for a small farmer in any part of the country. They are frequently two-story frame buildings, surrounded by a garden and numerous out-buildings. The interior of these homes is neat and well kept. They contain a few books, some pictures and the usual assortment of women's handiwork. *A general air of comfort and contentment pervades the homes and the community. Nearby there is a little six months country school.*[16]

In his description of Negro home life, Park deploys the word "little" no fewer than ten times in five paragraphs: "little farms," "little cottages," "little rude huts with two or three rooms and a few out-buildings," "a little stretch of sandy soil which the spring flood never reached," "little communities," "little societies," "little churches," "a little garden in the rear of the house and a general air of thrift and comfort about the place." Yet what is Park's overall conclusion? That "the Negro has made *great progress* in many directions during the past half century."[17] How, one might ask, does "little," even repeated tenfold, add up to "great progress"? Here we encounter two more rules of race's epistemology of ignorance:

Rule 5: The Inverted Metric. Progress should always be measured by the standard of the past. This is even implied in the artful title of Booker T. Washington's autobiography, *Up from Slavery.* With slavery as the baseline of measurement, it is easy to demonstrate "progress." The thinking goes as follows: Granted, the vast majority of blacks are impoverished, but at least they are free. True, blacks are denied elementary rights of citizenship, but at least they are not slaves. On this logic, the true nadir of the black experience was Middle Passage, and life has been getting better for black folks ever since! Indeed, this perverse logic has been carried even a step further. In a 1901 article in the *American Journal of Sociology*, Sarah Simons wrote: "Although the process began with the enslavement of subject peoples, this was certainly an improvement over extermination."[18] There we have it: These subhumans should be grateful for not being annihilated! Predicated as it is on the dehumanization of the racial "other," the inverted metric makes it possible to observe glaring differences in the life condition of blacks and whites, and yet to celebrate them as indicating "progress," reaching the facile conclusion that race is of "declining significance."

Rule 6: The Moral Calculus of Race. In *Stigma*, Erving Goffman conceived of race as embodying a stigma that rendered the bearer as "not quite human."[19] Indeed, as a social system, racism diminishes the humanity of black people, and relegates them to positions of inferiority that diminish their life chances. If it is assumed that blacks are "not quite human," then it is well and good that these diminished people have "little farms" with "little huts." If, on the other hand, we follow W.E.B. Du Bois's example, and "tell the story as though Negroes were ordinary human beings,"[20] then progress must be measured by the standards that prevail for whites. These "little farms" and "little huts" and "little churches" will be seen as a measure of the extent to which blacks have been cheated of their birthright and even their humanity. In other words, "what *is*" is gauged not by "what *was*" but rather by "what *should be*."

It is not that Park presents a totally rosy picture. Elsewhere in his article he notes that black farmers in the South are worse off than blacks in the North; that Southern cotton mills exclude blacks; that in the North immigrants have "crowded out" blacks, even in occupations like barbers and waiters where they previously had a foothold; that labor unions exclude blacks from the skilled trades. But applying the inverted metric, these problems are dismissed as challenges for the future, allowing Park to end on an upbeat note that celebrates the "great progress in many directions during the past half century." Park's final comment is an invocation of Washington's faith in education as a panacea. Park exults: "nowhere do the fruits of education show to better advantage than in the home of the educated Negro."[21] It was tempting to say that this is a page that might have come directly out of Booker T. Washington's *The Story of the Negro*, except that this book was ghostwritten by Park himself!

Without doubt, when Park morphed from ghostwriter to professor, he brought with him unusual background and experience on matters of race— for a white man, that is. However, most of this experience was based on his years at Tuskegee and his travels throughout the South. Ironically, his move to Chicago in 1914 coincided with the beginning of the Great Migration, which also marked the beginning of a transformation of America's black population from country to city, and from South to North. As Fred Matthews shrewdly observes, "History had begun to make Park's moral preferences anachronistic even as he brought them to the classroom."[22]

Perhaps this also helps to explain why Park avoided direct involvement in the study of the 1919 Chicago riot. As commented earlier, when the Illinois Commission on Race Relations was looking for somebody to head up a study of the riot, Park delegated this to his first black student, Charles S. Johnson, whom Park had already appointed as his research director at the Chicago Urban League. Although only twenty-six years of age and officially the Associate Executive Secretary of the Riot Commission, Johnson was the principal author of the report, ultimately published as *The Negro in Chicago*.[23] In some respects the report reflected Park's teaching, especially with its early chapter on "The Migration of Negroes from the South," its 95-page chapter on "Racial Contacts," and its 158-page chapter on "Public Opinion in Race Relations." Park's influence is also evident in its omissions, particularly its tendency to *[here we go again]* eschew power, as concept or social reality.[24]

In other ways, however, Johnson went far beyond his mentor. Gone were the ahistorical philosophical abstractions that rendered the events on the ground as unfortunate but inevitable blips on the template of evolution. On the contrary, *The Negro in Chicago* provides a graphic account of the gritty reality of race. Gone too was the posture of Olympian detachment. Despite its impassive tone, *The Negro in Chicago* was animated by a deep concern for the plight of blacks, together with a blanket condemnation of racism. The chapter on "The Negro Housing Problem" documents the pervasive racism that relegated blacks to "the Black Belt" on Chicago's South Side, where the physical condition of most houses was poor and neglected by owners. Furthermore, blacks who moved into white neighborhoods were confronted with "objection" manifested "in studied aloofness, in taunts, warnings, slurs, threats, or even the bombing of their homes."[25] Followed by white flight.

The chapter on "The Negro in Industry" provides a more hopeful account of rapid incorporation of blacks into the workforce of major industries. Most employers interviewed by the commission's investigators commented favorably on the quality of their black employees and their tense but successful relations with whites on the job. The unions were another matter, however. Some unions, especially those affiliated with the AFL, relegated their black workers to segregated locals. The craft unions that Marx called "the aristocracy of labor" were the worst offenders. The Electricians Union, for example, had only one Negro in a membership of 11,000. Much the same pattern existed among unions of machinists, sheet metal workers, plumbers, and steamfitters. Even so, the commission concluded on an upbeat note: "The policy, wherever it exists, of excluding Negroes from unions, whether by direct or indirect means, is considered wrong and shortsighted by the great majority of labor leaders."[26]

As can be seen from this overview, *The Negro in Chicago* went far beyond its mandate to account for the riot, and used this event to provide a comprehensive account of the condition of blacks in Chicago. What is noteworthy for our purposes is the extent to which it broke the "rules" of the epistemology of ignorance. Instead of ahistorical abstraction, Johnson gave us a historical account in minute and graphic detail. Instead of evasion and denial, we have a blunt confrontation with systemic racism in housing, industry, and public life. Instead of the inverted metric by which the injustices visited on Chicago's blacks could be pasted over with a narrative of "progress," emphasizing how much better off they were than in the South, the report implicitly compared living conditions of blacks to the norm for whites. Instead of the moral calculus that treated blacks as though they were less than fully human, the commission's report treated blacks as deserving of all rights of citizenship. Instead of studying blacks as objects of inquiry, it also treated them as subjects whose voices are heard, through interviews that probe and record their experiences and attitudes. Instead of adopting a posture of helplessness in influencing the course of history, the report ends with eleven pages of recommendations, though these were politically safe and clearly calibrated to avoid offending the political establishment.

Thus, as Chicago reeled from a calamitous race riot only blocks away, Robert Park remained sequestered in his ivory tower, and left it to his enterprising black student to plunge into "the world of men." Charles Johnson conducted the most exhaustive study of race in America to date. In the reformist spirit of the founders of sociology that had been smothered under professionalism, Johnson applied the methods of social science to uncover facts that would be useful to social reformers. Though no one, least of all Johnson, saw his work as representing a nascent "black sociology," there was clearly a distinctively black imprint reflected in a resolve to address the wrongs visited upon blacks, rather than to rationalize them away in theoretical abstraction. Johnson had come out from behind the veil, however cautiously and however measured his rhetoric, and presented at least the rudiments of a black alternative to the prevailing discourse.

Not that Charles Johnson was a "radical." Indeed, some contemporaneous black critics assailed him for being "a white man's negro," by not going nearly far enough to advance the black cause. Undeniably, *The Negro in Chicago* was stronger on analysis than it was on action. For all of its condemnation of racism, it stopped short of demanding sweeping changes to the racial status quo. Yet this internecine wrangling between Johnson and his critics is itself indicative of the extent to which there was a black sensibility and voice that challenged the epistemology of ignorance. This again raises the key question: Was the race relations paradigm that Robert Park propounded essentially a "white" perspective on race, reflecting "white" interests and a "white" point of view?

THE RACE RELATIONS CYCLE DECONSTRUCTED

A contemporary student who peruses "the Green Bible"—Park and Burgess's *Introduction to the Science of Society*—will be surprised to discover that their famed "race relations cycle" was more than a theory of race. Their race relations cycle provided the theoretical scaffolding for their entire volume. In effect, Park and Burgess advanced a racial theory of human evolution.

Thus, the Green Bible begins with a Rousseau-like reflection of human nature and the social condition of peoples who live in relative isolation. This is the stasis that is disrupted through migration or conquest, the two mechanisms that "bring different races together." Racial intermingling, in turn, is the catalyst that puts the race relations cycle into motion. Whole chapters are then devoted to each of the four sequential stages of the race relations cycle: contact, conflict, accommodation, and assimilation. Here, alas, was the grand evolutionary schema for the study of society, the dynamic process whereby history is forged and new races and cultures come into existence.

Inasmuch as the *Introduction to the Science of Sociology* was the leading textbook for the first two decades of sociology's establishment as a discipline, it might be said that sociology as a discipline evolved out of a racial ontology. As Stanford Lyman has observed, "the famous Chicago School of sociology was animated by its interest in the adjustments of immigrants, races, and ethnic groups to American society."[27] We can say with only slight exaggeration that American sociology had its roots in an effort to provide erudite justification for racial hierarchy.

This statement, of course, goes against the prevailing view in sociology of the Chicago school of race relations. Most commentators heap praise on Park and his colleagues for their repudiation of theories associated with Spencer and the Social Darwinists, which held that blacks were biologically inferior and destined by nature to occupy the lower stratum in society. Indeed, this was the argument advanced by the very first two treatises on sociology in America—George Fitzhugh's *Sociology for the South* and Henry Hughes's *A Treatise on Sociology*, both of which were pro-slavery tracts. For Park, racial hierarchy was not rooted in the germ plasma of races, but in culture (thus the title of his posthumous collection, *Race and Culture*). Unlike Social Darwinism, which consigned the inferior races to permanent subjugation, Park's schema carried forth the optimistic possibility that the lower races could be brought to the level of the higher races through a gradual process of assimilation. The chief mechanism for accomplishing this evolutionary goal was signified by the title of the conference that brought Park together with Thomas: "The Education of Primitive Man." Just as missionaries brought Christianity to the heathen, the educator was now envisioned as the emissary who would provide secular deliverance by bringing civilization to the benighted races. There was a deeply conservative flip side to this proposition, however. Aside from education, there was not much that society could do to speed up the wheels of evolution. As Ralph Turner has pointed out, "For all of his concern with race relations, it is striking that the achievement of social and economic equality never emerges as a dominant goal in Park's thought."[28]

In a series of subsequent essays Park applied the racial evolutionism of the Park-Burgess textbook specifically to racial and nationality groups in the United States. "In the relations of races," Park wrote, "there is a cycle of events which tends everywhere to repeat itself."[29] Here is one synopsis of Park's race relations cycle:

Park maintained that when large populations of diverse races come into contact, conflict and competition invariably resulted. Stabilization occurred when one race became dominant and the other accommodated itself to an inferior position. As part of the mechanism of accommodation there developed an "etiquette of race relations" which maintained "social distance" between the races, enabling them to coexist, although not on an egalitarian level. While competition and conflict produced prejudice and accommodation in the short run, the process of assimilation would inevitably occur. Park, studying the race situations of his own time in the United States, dealt chiefly with the mechanism of competition and accommodation, and never tried to explain how assimilation would ultimately be achieved.[30]

In a nutshell, this is the famed race relations cycle with its four stages—contact, competition, accommodation, and assimilation—that has been recited like a catechism by generations of sociologists on doctoral exams, oblivious to its ideological underpinnings. If we don a different pair of conceptual lenses, suddenly a bevy of hidden meanings and assumptions come into focus. Consider the following:

Contact. What an extraordinary euphemism for colonialism! We are talking here of the systematic plunder of an entire continent over centuries by Western powers. This began with a global slave trade that transported an estimated 112 million Africans to the New World, to provide slave labor for the plantation economies. *["Contact." Does this word encapsulate Europe's rapacious encounter with Africa, or is it a verbal smoke screen that conceals it? Would this word be deployed to describe what happened when two aircraft plummeted into the World Trade Center?]*

Competition. Another euphemism for conquest and slavery! The rhetorical function of this word is to gloss over the subjugation of an entire people through brute force. *[Oh, now I get it: "competition" is what the genocidal wars against Native Americans were all about. We won, they lost.]*

Accommodation. [This word should send bells ringing in the ears of anyone familiar with Booker T. Washington, the apostle of accommodation.] Stripped of its veneer, "accommodation" refers to the process whereby racial subjugation reaches grim finality, so that the vanquished group is rendered incapable of more than token resistance, and relations between the oppressor and oppressed are normalized through law and custom. "Etiquette," according to the dictionary, refers to socially prescribed codes of manners or behavior. Just think of the hidden implications of deploying such a word to describe the system of dehumanizing practices that were designed to remind blacks at every turn of their inferiority to whites. When a black person must step off the sidewalk to clear the way for a white passerby, or is forbidden to pass a car occupied by whites on the highway, or must enter the home of a white person through the back door, or occupy the back of a bus or the balcony of a movie house, this is not "etiquette" but suffocating and dehumanizing oppression, all the more humiliating because it is grafted on the smallest and most personal aspects of life. Instead of confronting the brute reality of racial oppression, Park's race relations model incorporated the accommodationist logic associated with Booker T. Washington, projecting accommodation as a necessary stage in a long-term assimilation process that would civilize the primitive.

Assimilation. This is the final stage, where the subordinate group eventually merges culturally and biologically with the dominant group, thus eliminating the basis of conflict. As Park wrote at the end of one of his essays: "Races and cultures die—it has always been so—but civilization lives on."[31] *[Ho, hum, races come and go.]* Thus, even though the "clash of civilizations" might be messy and chaotic, this was the price of progress. Hence, progress—the advance of civilization—was the pot of gold that lay at the end of the sociological rainbow, to borrow a phrase from Albion Small. *[Wonderful that this epic story of human slaughter and oppression has a happy ending!]*

Let us return to the passage from Charles Mills's *The Racial Contract* that I used as the epigraph for this essay: "One could say then, as a general rule, that *white misunderstanding, misrepresentation, evasion, and self-deception on matters related to race* are among the most pervasive mental phenomena of the past few hundred years, a cognitive and moral economy psychically required for conquest, colonization, and enslavement." We see now that Park's race relations paradigm provided just that: a cognitive and moral economy for conquest, colonization, and enslavement, all in the name of "progress" and the advance of "civilization." As the author of a 1908 article in the *American Journal of Sociology* put it: "The African race, with the advantage of contact with our more advanced stage of evolution, has made more progress in a few generations than any other race has done in the same time."[32] Thus with a rhetorical sleight of hand, the race relations model provided a cognitive basis for misrepresentation, evasion, and self-deception, allowing sociologists, following Park, to imagine themselves as "friends of the Negro," even as they provided epistemic authority for racial oppression.

Here we arrive at a crucial insight: *the logic of imperialism was imbricated onto the race relations cycle.* Indeed, the very language of "race relations," with its cycle of "contact," "competition," "accommodation," and "assimilation," provided an indispensable ideological smoke screen for imperialism itself. Nor can it be said that this represented an early stage on the learning curve of a new discipline. There was, all along, an alternative to the race relations paradigm, one that did not cast a blind eye on oppression, but rather, on the contrary, made oppression central to its system of ideas. However, Marxism was banished from respectable scholarly discourse, and the race relations model was invented as its politically acceptable alternative.

Therefore, it should come as no surprise that, when it came to foregrounding imperialism, only a few lone Marxists have been willing to tread down this ideologically forbidden path. In *The Sociologists of the Chair: A Radical Analysis of the Formative Years of North American Sociology, 1883–1922*, Herman Schwendinger and Julia Schwendinger show how the acclaimed "father" of American sociology, Lester Ward, was a Social Darwinist who adapted Spencer's theory of social evolution into a theory that posited higher and lower races who were thrown into a deadly conflict that conferred civilization onto the lower races.[33]

[In 2005 the American Sociological Association (ASA) proudly celebrated its centennial, and prominently featured Lester Ward, the first president of the ASA, in its program. There is a lesson here in how a field mindlessly elevates certain figures into icons, and in doing so, fails to come to terms with its past. Consider this: in 1907 Lester Ward speculated that black men raped white women because of a "biological imperative" to improve the quality of their genetic pool, and that

black women submitted to the sexual advances of white men for the same reason. That's not all: according to this revered pioneer of sociology, whites who lynched black rapists were defending their genetic stock, driven by a "biological law of self-preservation."[34] Alas, like the nation's founding fathers who were slaveholders, sociology's first president was capable of racist drivel. Instead of sentimental twaddle (to borrow a phrase from W.E.B. Du Bois), how much better it would have been had sociology celebrated its centennial by acknowledging and repudiating the complicity of its founders in "a cognitive and moral economy psychically required for conquest, colonization, and enslavement."

The larger question, central to this book, is whether sociology can ever turn over a new leaf without first confronting and disowning its own sullied past. Far from doing so, the American Sociological Association sold ASA Centennial posters, ASA Centennial postage stamps, and merchandise consisting of such items as Centennial mugs, tote bags, mouse pads, and bibs. Not to mention Centennial T-shirts for both sociologists and dogs. There is also a documentary, premiered at the meetings, entitled Lester F. Ward: A Life's Journey, *which portrays Ward "as a staunch advocate for women's rights, a vigorous critic of the racism of eugenics,"[35] but fails to deal with Ward's crackpot ideas about race.[36] No less than the nation, sociology displays a banal tendency to celebrate its past and venerate even presidents who were slaveholders. Instead of all this hoopla, how much better it would have been had sociology confronted its complicity in racism's sordid history.]*

Following Ward, other theorists argued that racial conflict was an essential feature of the state, that war was an instrument of progress, and that colonialism spread the fruits of civilization to the culturally backward regions of the world. As Schwendinger and Schwendinger write, "the race-conflict theories, taken as a whole, were little more than an apology for imperialism."[37]

Imperialism. This is the "i" word that rarely appears in the canon of sociological writing on race. To be sure, sociologists today, with near unanimity, repudiate the scientific racism that prevailed early in the twentieth century. However, with the exception of a few irksome "radicals" who are not taken seriously, mainstream sociologists fail to recognize the connection between these retrograde ideologies and the imperialistic projects of that period, or the insidious ways the logic of imperialism is embedded in the race relations paradigm. As Schwendinger and Schwendinger argue, "The founders of American sociology adopted social Darwinian ideas in order to buttress their own racist and imperialist doctrines."[38] Most of the founders and pioneers of sociology to whom we pay homage were men who subscribed to the idea, derived from Spencer, that there was a racial hierarchy consisting of higher and lower races, with the liberal addendum that it was the white man's burden to elevate the primitive.

Thus, the notable contribution of the Chicago school of race relations was to define the lower races in terms of culture rather than genes. Against the background of scientific racism, this was a major and significant theoretical turn, but its insidious function was to provide an updated and more credible ideological rationale for racial hierarchy and for imperialism itself.

R. W. Connell makes precisely this argument in an incisive paper, "Why Is Classical Theory Classical?" Connell begins with the observation that the formative period of sociology was very much bound up with imperialist expansion. Contrary to what is generally assumed, the pioneers of sociology had a global perspective. Indeed, they were obsessed with the "difference between the civilization of the metropole and an Other whose main feature was its primitiveness."[39] This difference was paired with "the idea of 'progress' from the primitive to the advanced," which, according to Connell, was "both the key assumption of sociological research and the major object of sociological theory."[40] Alas, now we can grasp the historical and ideological context behind the conference on "The Education of Primitive Man," where Thomas and Park had their fateful encounter, as well as the racist subtext of the famed Green Bible. At bottom, stripped of its rhetorical veneer, "race relations" was really about "the social relations of imperialism."

Park's flight into abstraction, his embrace of the evolutionary theory so fashionable at the time, camouflaged the brute realities of colonialism, so copiously and graphically documented in his Congo papers. Now we can better understand Park's metamorphosis from journalist to sociologist. Even discussion of the morality or ethics of imperialism, or the brutality and inhumanity associated with imperialism, was considered a breach of "science." No one has stated it more clearly than Connell: "The idea of the evolutionary superiority of the settlers and their institutions replaced missionary religion as the main justification of empire."[41]

Connell is astute to situate knowledge production within the context of the United States' venture into empire. Yet it is astounding how rarely the word "imperialism" appears in the immense canon of race relations, even though imperialism was the political context for that euphemistic "contact" that put the race relations cycle into motion. Of course, as a nation we well understand that the American colonies were subjected to intolerable oppression under the yoke of British colonialism, leading to a triumphant War for Independence. However, no sooner had the new nation won its independence than it cast an imperial eye to the territories that lay beyond the beachhead on the East Coast. What else was "manifest destiny," if not a blueprint and ideological justification for imperial expansion from the Atlantic to the Pacific, including the annexation of a third of Mexico's national territory? The end of the nineteenth century, when sociology was taking root as a discipline, was also a period of several overseas adventures, including the Spanish-American War, which led to the occupation of Cuba and the Philippines, followed by the annexation of Hawaii, Samoa, Guam, and Puerto Rico.

Enter the scholar, whose distinctive role, as John Hope Franklin has written, is to provide "ideological justifications and rationalizations . . . for actions that had already been taken."[42] To quote Connell again: "Sociology was formed within the culture of imperialism and embodied a cultural response to the colonized world."[43] Indeed, without bringing the "i" word to center stage, one can hardly comprehend the emerging gestalt of the Chicago school of race relations.

Thus, Social Darwinism, with its hierarchy of higher and lower races, provided perfect justification, first for slavery, and then for the conquest and dispossession of Indians and Mexicans who stood in the way of "the westward march." Never mind the multitude of Indians and Mexicans stomped under imperial feet. To quote Park again, "Races and cultures die—it has always been so—but civilization lives on."[44] At the turn of the twentieth century, Social Darwinism was also deployed to provide the logic and justification for several of the nation's imperialist ventures. As E. Berkeley Tompkins shows in *Anti-Imperialism in the United States: The Great Debate, 1890–1920*, both the defenders and critics of imperialist policies laced their arguments with racism. Defenders proclaimed "the more civilized and enlightened nations had a mission to perform by taking over the backward peoples of the earth."[45] On the other hand, critics replied that "the United States already had a plethora of unresolved racial problems, which would only be increased by colonialism."[46] Indeed, the racialized debate between imperialists and anti-imperialists raged at precisely the time that sociology was struggling to become established at Chicago and other leading universities. Thus it came to pass that the language and the logic of imperialism were inflected on sociology during its formative years.

From the foregoing discussion, we can identify two more "rules of sociological method" that buttress an epistemology of ignorance:

Rule 7: Ahistoricism. Racism is plucked out of the societal context that engendered and sustained it, treated as a phenomenon sui generis—one that exists unto itself, disembodied from the matrix of institutions of which it is a part. Racism has no history, but rather springs forth as a natural antipathy to difference, mitigated as groups pass through the inexorable race relations cycle.

Rule 8: Reductionism. Racism is reduced to the level of individual predispositions and attitudes. Theoretical reductionism combined with methodological reductionism to produce a multitude of studies to measure the extent and sources of prejudice in individuals, all with the ultimate aim of disabusing bigots of their benighted beliefs. Here, alas, was an incredible inversion of "white social science." The major paradigm involved a praxis that ministered to the oppressor rather than to the oppressed! The thrust of social research and social policy was directed, not at improving conditions for blacks, but at reforming attitudes among whites. Liberation for blacks would have to wait for whites to undergo a therapeutic transformation.[47]

BLACK SOCIOLOGISTS: WALKING THE FINE LINE

No doubt some readers will react with skepticism or umbrage to my claim that the founders of the sociology of race were, however unwittingly, practicing a white sociology that reflected the perspectives and interests of the dominant white majority. They will see this argument as "overgeneralized" and "overheated," or in common parlance, "over the top." One lame defense, readily available, is that the entire society was racist, and that, whatever its limitations, Chicago sociology was a vast improvement over the scientific racism that it replaced in that it rejected the idea that the darker races were inherently inferior. True enough, but as Thomas Kuhn writes, the death of one paradigm necessarily involves the birth of another, and my contention here is that the race relations paradigm was saturated with assumptions that were racist and reactionary. This is why it is imperative to bring to light the subtle ways that sociology, from its very inception, has provided intellectual legitimacy for a racist order, even as it imagined itself as that proverbial "friend of the Negro."

Upon reflection, how could sociology *not* have been "white," given that blacks were systematically excluded from the discipline, except for a token handful who were shunted off to teach in black colleges, cut off from the mainstream?[48] Prior to World War I only fourteen blacks in the United States received a Ph.D. in sociology.[49] Even as late as 1936 over 80 percent of black Ph.D.s were employed by Atlanta, Fisk, and Howard universities, and it was not until 1942 that a major university hired a full-time tenure-track African American professor.[50] Only four blacks were among the 750 contributors to the *American Journal of Sociology* between 1916 and 1940.[51] Thus, there was no significant black presence in the discipline to provide a reality check on the knowledge claims that were spewed forth by a white establishment. Before I am accused of "essentialism"—that is, of assuming that blacks and whites uniformly have different viewpoints—imagine if the tables had been turned and the "founding fathers" of the study of race had been African American men and women ensconced in elite universities and generously subsidized by foundations. Would the discourse have been centered on "race relations" rather than "racial oppression"? Let us take seriously Otto Klineberg's taunt: "What would our field be like if the books had been written by Hottentots or Eskimos rather than by Europeans and Americans?"[52] The answer, I fear, is self-evident, and casts an epistemological shadow over the entire sociological enterprise.

One thing is clear: racial exclusion was an institutional mechanism in the production of an epistemology of ignorance. A few resourceful and talented blacks did manage to cross the color line, but to do so, they had to pass muster with the gatekeepers whose function was to bring blacks into the professions, but to assure that, if they departed from the prevailing wisdom, they would do so within carefully delimited strictures. In any event, upon graduation black Ph.D.s invariably were shunted to black colleges. This was true even of Franklin Frazier, who was elected as the first black president of the American Sociological Association, but never received an offer for a tenure-track position in a predominantly white university, and spent his career in a racially segregated academy.[53]

Nor did black colleges necessarily provide the soil for the germination of an alternative epistemology reflecting black interests and a black point of view. As Anthony Platt writes in his biography of E. Franklin Frazier, "prior to World War I Afro-American colleges were not hospitable to nonconformists. They were ruled by white boards of trustees who demanded obsequious faculty and docile students."[54] As late as World War II the trustees and administrators of black colleges were invariably white, and so were most faculty.[55] Add to that the insidious role of foundations, which dispensed the grants that kept these institutions afloat and that controlled intellectual productivity. In 1961 Franklin Frazier noted with characteristic bluntness: "It seems that ever since the Negro has been free, some foundation has watched over his destiny. Right after Emancipation the Peabody Fund was giving him wrong advice. Then later on the Rosenwald Fund corrupted his leaders."[56] Thus, not only were there innumerable barriers to prevent blacks from entering the profession, but still other mechanisms were deployed to assure that those few blacks who circumvented these barriers would not challenge hegemonic discourse on race.

We can explore this process at work at the University of Chicago, which emerged as the major center for the training of black sociologists. Two factors explain this unusual development. One was the largesse of the Julius Rosenwald Fund, which was one of the nation's largest philanthropic foundations and was almost exclusively devoted to race relations and fortuitously located in Chicago. Julius Rosenwald was born in Springfield, Illinois, the son of middle-class, German Jewish immigrants. After a stint in the family clothing business in New York, he opened up a clothing store in Chicago, and eventually became the major owner and chief executive of the Sears, Roebuck & Company. Thanks to his philanthropy, Rosenwald was a trustee of both Hull House and the University of Chicago. According to his biographer, he was so moved upon reading Booker T. Washington's *Up from Slavery* that he devoted himself to promoting the education of African Americans.[57] Not only was he a major benefactor of Tuskegee, but he also helped to build some 5,000 schools throughout the South, as well as YMCAs in Chicago and other cities. The Julius Rosenwald Fund, chartered in 1917, three years after Robert Park joined the faculty of the University of Chicago, also provided grants and fellowships for black graduate students in sociology. In this capacity, Rosenwald and Park collaborated in the production of what amounted to a neocolonialism in the realm of ideas.[58]

Again, for readers who think that I have carried cynicism too far, consider this: During the years that Julius Rosenwald was building schools in the South and subsidizing black graduate students at the University of Chicago, the Sears Roebuck company had a color line that excluded blacks from its workforce. After Rosenwald's death in 1948, Edwin Embree, the president of the Rosenwald Fund, wrote a biographical essay that ruefully acknowledged that "Mr. Rosenwald was saddened by his inability to change the discriminatory practices in his own firm and the Chicago office building that he owned. . . . [F]earing that he might create antagonism against the very people he was trying to help, he did not unduly press these efforts."[59] *[Give me a break!]* This hypocrisy did not go unnoticed in the black community. In 1938 an editorial in the *Pittsburgh Courier*, a black newspaper, that was critical of "Jewish exploiters" elicited a storm of protest from Jews who cited the work of the Rosenwald Fund in helping blacks. In a subsequent editorial, the *Courier* asserted that "we are not ungrateful," but went on to cite the fact that his Sears Roebuck refused to hire black workers, and concluded with this zinger: "Thus the graduates of Rosenwald schools can go without bread so far as the Rosenwald business institution is concerned. We are grateful but we are hungry."[60] Grateful but hungry: such are the contradictions of philanthropy!

The other factor that explains why Chicago emerged as the major center for the training of black sociologists was Robert Ezra Park. To be sure, Park deserves credit for defying racism and bringing black students into the University of Chicago. Beyond that, he functioned as a mentor and provided research training, thus spawning the "first generation" of black sociologists. Park's efforts were an extension of his years at Tuskegee, reflecting his commitment to Washington's civilizing mission through education. Even after his retirement from Chicago in 1933, Park continued to teach black students at Fisk University. Clearly, the hallmark of Park's career was his unique ability to operate on both sides of the color line.

Before we heap too much praise on the "father" of the race relations school, it behooves us to consider the flip side of his patronage. Park was more than a champion of black inclusion into sociology. As Butler Jones has suggested, his extensive contacts with blacks, not to speak of the Wizard of Tuskegee, imparted Park with "credentials for assuming within the inner circles of the power elite the role of spokesman for blacks in sociology."[61] He was also its primary gatekeeper. It was Robert Park who selected which black applicants to bring to Chicago. Then, through his tutelage, he molded them intellectually in the dogma of his race relations model. And finally, he placed them on a career trajectory that secured their futures. Is it any wonder that they dedicated their books to Park and showered praise on him? The thorny question, though, is whether Park, through his patronage, was able to exercise "surrogate control" over the direction of a next generation of black sociologists, as Jones alleges.[62] The net effect was to create a black presence in sociology that did not pose a threat to the hegemony of the race relations model. And given the insidious ways the logic of imperialism was inscribed on the race relations model, it is difficult to avoid the conclusion that Park's much ballyhooed contribution in spawning a first generation of black sociologists indeed amounted to neo-colonialism in the realm of ideas.

Is this criticism fair, especially when leveled against the man who did more than anybody else to breach the color line in sociology? When, one might ask, is patronage *not* control? Quite simply: when it does not exact ideological conformity or ingratiation as its price. Did Park's black students mold themselves to Park's position and squelch criticism because of personal loyalties, professional debts, or fear of falling out of favor with their mentor? Or were they able to steer an independent course, within safe limits, without arousing the ire of their mentor? Or yet again, were they free to openly challenge his positions on "race relations"? As I show below, these three alternative paths were taken, respectively, by three of Chicago's first generation of black sociologists: Charles Johnson, Franklin Frazier, and Oliver Cox. They chose different paths, but all three are living proof of Davarian Baldwin's claim, "Black scholars brought new eyes to the study of race."[63]

Charles Sturgeon Johnson

The preceding pages gave us a glimpse of the paternalistic relationship that Robert Park had with Charles Johnson, which led to Johnson's appointment to the Chicago race riot commission, on which Julius Rosenwald also sat. What better demonstrates the nexus between politics, corporate wealth, foundations, the university, and the token black scholar who is brought in to defuse the potentially dangerous racial division in Chicago following an explosive riot? Does this mean that Johnson deserves Butler Jones's epithet, "an establishment nigger"?[64] To be sure, Johnson worked within the establishment. On the other hand, his indictment of white racism, though muted, was unmistakable. Oliver Cox's observation of the black leader applies with equal force to the black scholar: "He must be a friend of the enemy. He must be a champion of the cause of Negroes, yet not so aggressive as to incur the consummate ill will of whites."[65]

Of course, such people are always subject to accusations of opportunism, since they reap the rewards of their collusion with "the enemy." In Charles Johnson's case, as Park's protégé he was appointed as research director at the Urban League, then appointed as associate executive director to the Chicago riot commission, which led to an appointment to the Social Science Department at Fisk University, where he went on to become editor of the National Urban League's journal, *Opportunity*, and to cultivate contacts with philanthropic organizations and foundations, allowing him to function as a powerbroker. Finally, he became the first Negro president of Fisk University.

On the other hand, as I suggested earlier, Johnson did provide a distinctly black perspective on the Chicago riot, in which he brought to light the conditions associated with racial segregation in housing and jobs that engendered the hostilities that erupted in the riot. During his career, Johnson was a prodigious researcher, and produced books like *Shadow of the Plantation* and *Growing up in the Black Belt* that sympathetically documented the black plight.[66] As editor of *Opportunity*, he provided an outlet for scholarship that also brought attention to the black condition. Finally, he used his position as chairman of sociology at Fisk, along with his access to foundations, to subsidize a steady stream of research, including a book series published by Fisk University Press. Johnson was no radical, but neither does he deserve the tag of "establishment nigger." There is no denying though that Johnson's effectiveness depended upon his toeing an ideological line that allowed him to curry favor with Park and the foundations. When Park retired from Chicago in 1933, Johnson brought him to teach at Fisk. The story doesn't end there. After Park's death in 1944, a new social science building on campus was named Park Hall, and after Johnson's death, renamed Park-Johnson Hall.[67] A fitting monument to the Park-Johnson axis!

E. Franklin Frazier

If Charles Johnson reaped the benefits of remaining on the safe side of "the line," the career of E. Franklin Frazier, another of Park's early black students, demonstrates the perils of crossing the line. In 1912 Frazier arrived as an undergraduate at Howard, the same year that Park resigned his position at Tuskegee and began his transition into sociology. In terms of their politics, the two men were like meteors on a collision course, which raises the tantalizing question of how Frazier eventually emerged as Robert Park's "most complete student," according to G. Franklin Edwards.[68] As will be seen, Frazier had to undergo something of an intellectual metamorphosis, reminiscent of the one that Park underwent when he morphed from the firebrand of the Congo Reform Association into Booker T. Washington's compliant associate.

In his incisive biography *E. Franklin Frazier Reconsidered*, Anthony Platt portrays Frazier as something of a youthful radical.[69] When Frazier enrolled in 1912, Howard was different from black colleges in the South that were modeled after Booker T. Washington's vocational education. Most of the deans and faculty were black, and instead of industrial education, its curriculum emphasized the classics and liberal arts. Frazier took a challenging regimen of courses, but he studiously avoided sociology because the professor, Kelley Miller, was closely identified with Booker T. Washington. Instead, he gravitated to socialist groups on campus, and was a member of the Intercollegiate Socialist Society (ISS), which had a chapter on campus. He was also vice president of the NAACP and president of his senior class. Hence, Frazier combined the two strands of race and radicalism that came together in the black radical tradition, though he ventured forth into a world that was hospitable to neither.

Frazier's first job was teaching math at Tuskegee, which, given his radical bent, was a predictable disaster. Platt provides this account:

These experiences at Tuskegee left Frazier embittered about the politics of black education in the South but with a sharp awareness of the depths of racism as well as an increasing consciousness of his political commitments. Whatever respect he had felt for Booker T. Washington, with whose policies he profoundly disagreed, turned to disgust with the "reactionary policy" of Tuskegee under Moton's leadership [Moton was Washington's successor].[70]

A year later Frazier enrolled in an M.A. program in sociology at Clark University, where he did his thesis on Afro-American socialism as it was reflected in *The Messenger*, a magazine founded by A. Philip Randolph and Chandler Owen that railed against capitalism and racism. These early signs pointed to the making of a radical. Yet, according to Platt, Frazier acquired a knack for simultaneously taking radical positions and observing "the etiquette of disinterested neutrality" required of the social scientist. As Platt put it, "Frazier had to operate within narrow ideological and theoretical constraints if he wanted to get past the gatekeepers of professional sociology."[71]

Frazier once crossed the line and it nearly cost him his career. In 1924 he wrote an article entitled "The Pathology of Race Prejudice," which was a thinly disguised parody of white sociology. Instead of whites putting blacks under the magnifying glass, here was a delicious role reversal: a black man subjecting whites to clinical examination. According to Frazier, the average racist meets all of the defining characteristics of dementia! Most of all, he suffers from a "Negro complex" that leads him into irrationality verging on lunacy. "How else than as a somnambulism of the insane and almost insane," Frazier asks with feigned incredulity, "are we to account for the behavior of a member of a school board who jumps up and paces the floor, cursing and accusing Negroes, the instant the question of appropriating more for Negro schools is raised?"[72] Frazier goes on to assert that whites, including white women who accuse innocent blacks of sexual advances, are merely projecting their own illicit desires onto blacks, another sure sign of mental pathology. The only reason the Negro complex passes as "normal," according to our self-certified psychopathologist, is that it is so widely shared. In a final jibe, Frazier reminds the reader that "the inmates of a madhouse are not judged insane by themselves, but by those outside."[73]

Frazier was engaged in daring and dangerous intellectual frolic, turning the bigot's racial obsessions onto the bigot, in effect treating racism as a collective pathology. Frazier had the cheek as well to send his parody off to the *Atlantic Monthly* and other national publications. Rebuffed, he turned to academic journals. The rejection letter from the *Journal of Applied Sociology* claimed that the journal "has a policy of avoiding as far as possible the publication of argumentative articles."[74] As Anthony Platt points out, the charge of "argumentative" is leveled only against writers who challenge the prevailing wisdom. No such judgment was made of Robert Park's pronouncement on the temperament of the Negro: "He is primarily an artist, loving life for its own sake. His *métier* is expression rather than action. He is, so to speak, the lady among races."[75] The venue for this nugget of wisdom was none other than the Green Bible: Park and Burgess's famed *Introduction to the Science of Sociology*. Thus we see a double standard inherent in the epistemology of ignorance: No matter how outrageous, knowledge claims of whites are accorded normative status, whereas dissenting viewpoints are spurned as "argumentative" and expunged from the canon.

After three years of persistent effort, Frazier found a publisher—*Forum*, a journal that relished controversy.[76] Platt provides this account of the maelstrom that ensued:

Within a week of his article's appearing in *Forum*, Atlanta's *Constitution* carried an editorial condemning this "psychopathologician" as "more insane by reason of his anti-white complex than any southerner obsessed by his anti-Negro repulsions." Sam Small, editor of the newspaper, was particularly incensed by Frazier's "revolting" suggestion—"the vilest this writer has ever encountered in a lifetime"—that "the white woman desires the negro." Another newspaper editorialized that "it is generally accepted that he, Frazier, was suffering from some mental trouble and was as insane as those he alleged were insane. . . . The professor happens to be one of those highly educated Negroes who has disassociated himself from his people in pursuit of social equality" continued the *Atlanta Independent*. "He is over-educated."[77]

Over-educated, indeed! Frazier was spouting truths that were unacceptable even to the erudite professors at the University of Chicago who forged the sociological canon on race. Here was the seminal beginning of what much later came to be called "whiteness studies"—a reversal of the lens whereby whites instead of blacks were made the object of inquiry. Frazier was having his fun, and to add to the irony, his parodic intentions eluded most commentators who could not fathom the farcical nature of racism.[78] After the publication of his article, Frazier—who had already changed his pen name from Edward F. Frazier to E. Franklin Frazier in order to conceal his identity—received death threats and fled Atlanta, with a .45 in his belt, leaving blacks chortling about "Frazier's farewell to the South."[79]

The timing of Frazier's article could not have been worse, since it was the very month (June 1927) that he arrived in Chicago with a grant from the Rockefeller Foundation to begin his doctoral education. A few months before the publication of his article, Frazier had written Burgess and Park to enlist their help in completing his doctorate, and had proposed undertaking a study of the Negro family. Consistent with his role as gatekeeper, Park wrote back in April: "We are hoping to have you with us next year, and are looking forward to your work here as a preparation for a thoroughgoing study of the Negro family. There is no study connected with the Negro that is so important, in my opinion."[80] Thanks to Platt's assiduous research, this exchange is part of the historical record. But let us make another quantum leap back into history. What if Frazier's mischievous piece on "The Pathology of Race Prejudice" had been published three months before instead of three months after he sent off his letter of inquiry to the gatekeepers at Chicago? In all probability the gate would have come slamming down, and E. Franklin Frazier might never have entered the ranks of sociology. Or imagine that instead of indicating a desire to work on the black family, which eventually materialized into his dissertation and his ticket into the profession, what if our brash upstart had proposed to continue his research on "the pathology of race prejudice"? Or what if he had proposed a study of "racial oppression," focusing on the flagrant denial of civil and human rights? Without doubt, he would have been banished from the academy, like countless other black dissidents throughout history.

Oliver Cox once said of Frazier: "Franklin knows how to walk the fine line." Frazier's version of double consciousness brings to light yet another rule of an epistemology of ignorance:

Rule 9: The Racial Optic. Blacks, not whites, must be the "problem" under examination and thus the object of inquiry. Indeed, in the vast canon of studies on race, nearly every aspect of the black body and soul has been scoured in a misdirected search for the reasons for racial hierarchy. This began with craniometry—an entire field that flourished in leading universities, predicated on the assumption that the configuration of the skull accounted for the superiority of whites and inferiority of blacks. Similar scientific inquiries involved meticulous measurement of breasts, buttocks, genitals, and even ejaculation distance.[81] When IQ tests came on stream, scores of studies were conducted documenting the lower IQ of blacks. With the emergence of the social sciences, attention was shifted from biology to culture. Early studies focused on temperament and culture. Later, the focus was on black families, neighborhoods, and communities, all assumed to be deficient. Still more recently, the focus has been on hip hop culture and gangsta rap, which are blamed for the troubles that afflict black youth. Though not necessarily by intent, these studies yielded a picture of wholesale social disorganization and cultural pathology. On the other hand, as Frazier's spoof was intended to show, white people and white society are not subjected to scrutiny, with the single exception of superficial and redundant studies of racial prejudice.

Clearly, in proposing a study of the Negro family, and making blacks rather than whites the object of inquiry, Frazier had learned to "walk the line" that allowed him to get by the gatekeepers. Yet at other times in his career he reflected the radical proclivities of his youth and challenged intellectual and political orthodoxies. It can be said of Frazier that he became adept at walking *both* sides of the line. This is even reflected in the dedication to his opus, *The Negro in the United States*, which reads as follows:

To W. E. BURGHARDT DuBois and to the Memory of ROBERT E. PARK
Two Pioneers in the Scientific Study of the Negro[82]

Frazier's duality was also reflected in his rhetoric. As Platt shrewdly observes: "Frazier used two styles: a sociological language in his academic publications and in his other writings—essays, letters, and stories—the polemical language learned in political debates at Howard and in the pages of the *Messenger*."[83] Thus, in his first incarnation, as a sociologist, he commanded respect and was elected as the first black president of the American Sociological Association. Then again, in his second incarnation, as the man who was dubbed "Forceful Frazier," he challenged intellectual orthodoxies and roiled the political waters. Of course, these two selves were intertwined, since Frazier could use his credentials as a respectable sociologist to reach positions that allowed him, when it mattered most, to challenge the intellectual and political establishment.

Forceful Frazier's finest hour came when he was appointed by Mayor Fiorello LaGuardia to head up a blue-ribbon commission to study the 1935 Harlem "race riot." Unlike earlier riots in Chicago and East St. Louis where whites ran amok and committed violence against blacks, in this case blacks were the perpetrators of violence, though it was intended as protest and directed at property, not people. It was triggered by a false rumor that a teenager accused of pilfering a penknife in Kress's Department Store had been beaten to death by police. This unleashed a day of mayhem in which stores were trashed, looted, and set ablaze. Mayor LaGuardia called on the prominent chairman of Howard's Sociology Department to head up his commission, but he got more than he bargained for. Instead of pious denunciation of violence and disorder, the report took a more radical tack from its opening sentence: "This relatively unimportant case of juvenile pilfering was only the spark that set aflame the smoldering resentments of the people of Harlem against racial discrimination and poverty in the midst of plenty."[84] The report went on to document the massive exclusion of blacks by all of the city's major employers: the Consolidated Gas Company, the Rapid Transit Company, the hotel industry, the Metropolitan Life Insurance Company, and the unions in the construction trades, clothing and textiles, and teamsters and chauffeurs. The report concluded that employment discrimination is the principal factor "that arouses so much resentment in the Negro worker."

The first recommendation of the report was that "the city enact an ordinance to the effect that no contracts may be given to any firm or labor union that discriminates against Negro workers."[85] Essentially Frazier had provided the logic and blueprint for affirmative action policy, thirty years before the term "affirmative action" was coined. In doing so, however, he had crossed the forbidden line by locating the source of blame, not on rioters, but on racist institutions. The result is another sobering reminder of what happens when one crosses that line: LaGuardia refused to release the report to the public. It would still be collecting dust in an archive except that somebody leaked the report to the *Amsterdam News*, New York's premier black newspaper, which printed it in its entirety. *[It doesn't require much imagination to guess the likely source of this leak.]*

Oliver Cromwell Cox

If Charles Johnson operated within the establishment and Franklin Frazier wavered back and forth across "the line," Oliver Cox was the quintessential maverick who steered an independent course that not only defied and challenged the prevailing wisdom, but also blazed entirely new avenues of inquiry. His biographer, Christopher McAuley, attributes his streak of defiance to his Caribbean upbringing.[86] However that may be, Cox's critical acumen clearly derived from his grasp of Marxist theory, and for this he paid the price: he was dismissed as an ideologue who violated the principle of scientific objectivity. According to one study, three-quarters of the academic reviews of his books referred to him as "a Marxist."[87] This tag gave readers permission to don their blinders and dismiss Cox's scholarship out of hand.

What was it about Cox that warranted his excommunication from the community of scholars? As Sean Hier writes in an essay entitled "Structures of Orthodoxy and the Sociological Exclusion of Oliver C. Cox," when Cox published *Caste, Class, & Race* in 1948, "his work came into conflict with the ahistorical, functionalist-oriented orthodoxy of 'race relations' and American stratification studies, as well as a considerable proportion of the epistemological orthodoxy of the sociological elite, centered at the University of Chicago."[88] Marxism offered an alternative to ahistorical functionalism. The hallmark of Cox's writing was its steadfast focus on the political economy of racism.

Let us return to that nugget of Cox's wisdom that I quoted earlier: "We cannot defeat prejudice by proving that it is wrong." Cox challenged the tendency in social science to reify racism, which is to say, to treat it as a disembodied ideology that, like some kind of evil spirit, required exorcism. Enter the professional exorcist, the sociologist or psychologist, whose mission is to apply the tools of social science to counter and invalidate these mistaken stereotypes and behaviors. For Cox, this was an exercise in mystification, so long as it failed to connect these beliefs and practices to the system of economic exploitation in which they are anchored. Yes, slavery was wrong, but why did the pleas of abolitionists fall on deaf ears? Because slavery was, as its defenders conceded, "a necessary evil." It provided cheap labor for a plantation system that produced raw material—cotton—that went to those textile mills that were the foundation of industrialization both in Europe and the United States. Here was a formulation that *made sense* of racism. For Cox, racism was not merely a moral transgression, but the tip of an iceberg: the enslavement of an entire people, over centuries of time, to expropriate their labor in the genesis of national wealth.

Now we can begin to see why these simple truths were so transgressive, and why Cox's analysis had to be banished from respectable discourse. Because it called into question the myth of the United States as a democracy, constructed as it was on slave labor. Because it did not balk at placing blame on the doorstep of capitalism. Because it conceived of racism, not as the benighted fantasies of uneducated minds or warped personalities, but as the toxin that was woven into the fabric of the nation. Because it did not reduce racism to the beliefs and actions of misguided individuals, but rather impugned major political and economic institutions. Exorcizing the demon of racism would not suffice: the thrust of Cox's analytical system was that you had to change the system. Here is the full context of the passage I quoted earlier:

We cannot defeat race prejudice by proving that it is wrong. The reason for this is that race prejudice is only a symptom of a materialistic social fact. If, for instance, we should discover by "scientific" method that Negroes and Chinese are "superior" to tall, long-skulled blonds—and this is not farfetched, since libraries have been written to prove the opposite—then, to the powers that be, so much the worse for Negroes and Chinese. Our proof accomplishes nothing. The articulate white man's ideas about his racial superiority are rooted in the social system, and it can be corrected only by changing the system itself.[89]

Here again we encounter the breathtaking illogic of the epistemology of ignorance: a call to change the system is condemned as crossing the line from science into politics, but the obverse position—ratification of the status quo—is regarded as apolitical, faithful to the precept of "objectivity." Thus was the epistemological deck stacked in favor of the existing racial order.

Unlike mainstream scholars who cravenly expunged Marxists from the canon, Cox directly engaged the writing of his intellectual adversaries. In his 1948 magnum opus, *Caste, Class, & Race*, Cox characterized Park's race relations model as "a new orthodoxy." What was "new" was that Park "was one of the most consistent opponents of that host of pseudo scientists who take it upon themselves to explain why peoples of color are inferior to white people and how they became that way."[90] True enough, Park's memorable contribution to the sociological canon was that, like Boas in anthropology, he rejected notions of biological inferiority. Nevertheless, Cox criticized Park's conception of race relations as "weak, vacillating, and misleading."[91] Park's failing was less in what he said than in what was left unsaid. Implicitly, Park accepted the caste system as a reified fact of life, instead of tracing it to the economic processes that engendered it and sustained it down to the present. Cox's position, put simply, was that the caste system was not just "wrong," but it was useful:

"These race relations in the South have developed out of the immediate need of the white exploiting class to restore as far as possible the complete control over its labor supply, which it enjoyed during slavery."[92] The problem with Park's race relations model, according to Cox, was that "his teleological approach has diverted him from an examination of the specific causal events in the development of modern race antagonism; it has led him inevitably into a hopeless position about 'man's inhumanity to man,' a state of mind that must eventually drive the student into the open arms of the mystic."[93]

"Into the open arms of the mystic." The ultimate insult, given sociology's obsession with establishing its scientific credentials! Could it be that Marxism, with its method of historical materialism, provided a more adequate theory of race, by placing racism in historical context and bringing to light its economic functions and the role that powerful institutions played in its perpetuation? But this was a dangerous line of inquiry, precisely because it leads logically to Cox's proposition that racism is "rooted in the social system, and it can be corrected only by changing the system itself."[94] This is the forbidden insight that had to be expunged from the discourse, which was accomplished by tagging Cox as "a radical." And to make matters worse, "a black radical" whose name and prolific writing were relegated to obscurity, whereas Robert Park, the champion of the race relations model, on the basis of some sparse essays, was elevated into an icon.[95]

Cox's forthright challenge to the established orthodoxy on race brings to light what might be called "the mother of all rules" in the epistemology of ignorance:

Rule 10: Vilify the racist, not the system. It is permissible, even commendable, to rail against racism, so long as racism is conceived as an attribute of discrete individuals. Indeed, scores of surveys have been conducted over many decades that meticulously measure the prevalence and trend of negative beliefs about blacks. However, it is forbidden to cross the line and impugn major political and economic institutions for their complicity in the production and reproduction of the conditions that engender, reinforce, and reproduce these prejudiced beliefs.

Alas, this brings us back again to the ultimate reckoning with history. The epistemology of ignorance did not exist because it was the exclusive discourse during the century after slavery. All along there was a rival perspective and epistemology, but one that was studiously ignored and institutionally cast to the periphery. As Schwendinger and Schwendinger comment:

The surge in radical sociology after 1968 should not obscure the fact that for three quarters of a century since the 1890s, no important examples of a sustained *systematic* defense of Marxist scholarship by *circles* of academic scholars can be found in *any* subject-matter in *any* of the sociological journals sponsored by professional associations of sociologists in the United States.[96]

MARXISM: AN EPISTEMOLOGY OF OPPRESSION

Robert Park's achievement, as the designated "father" of the Chicago school of race relations, was to relegate theories postulating the biological inferiority of Negroes to the proverbial trash bin, and instead to cast the races in a hierarchy of evolutionary development, from "higher" to "lower" races. If, as Kuhn argues, the acceptance of a new paradigm always involves the rejection of another, it was also the case that there was all along a rival paradigm, mostly championed by African American scholars with Marxist tendencies, that explained racial hierarchy in terms of political economy, thereby riveting attention on the historical and social factors that explained racial hierarchy. Thus, one might say that adoption of a new paradigm not only entails substitution of an antecedent one, but the rejection of viable alternative paradigms as well. Indeed, the occlusion of Marxism from the canon on race and ethnicity is a remarkable and understudied phenomenon that casts a long shadow over the entire canon, and is a prime example of "the structural blindnesses and opacities" that, as Charles Mills writes, are essential to an epistemology of ignorance.[97]

For our purposes, Marxism can be described as "an epistemology of oppression."[98] On matters of race, it is the exact antithesis to "an epistemology of ignorance." Instead of denial and evasion of the grisly facts of racial oppression, Marxism not only confronted oppression head-on, but also made it central (perhaps too much so, as we will see) to its system of thought. Instead of looking at racial hierarchy from the standpoint of the oppressor, finding justification for its crimes, Marxism approached truth from the standpoint of the oppressed, who have reason to reject the mystifications and shibboleths that are contrived to justify and camouflage the wrongs visited upon them.

Changing a paradigm is like adopting a different set of conceptual lenses, where raw facts assume totally different meaning. We literally see things differently. Instead of seeing a benevolent system with a civilizing mission, we see conquest, enslavement, violent repression, merciless exploitation, and dehumanization. Instead of looking at racial hierarchy as corresponding to "higher" and "lower" ranks on an evolutionary scale, we see instead a racial oppressor and people whose racial difference becomes the basis for their oppression. Instead of seeing, as Park did in his study of rural blacks, "little farms" and "little churches," it now becomes clear that this is an imperial gaze of pacified subjects. Instead of seeing whites living in opulent splendor, we see a ruling class living off the expropriated labor of their black workers. Instead of a racial order where each group has its assigned place, we see a racial dictatorship, upheld through all of the powerful institutions of a tyrannical state. Instead of "etiquette," we see rituals of domination and submission that are utterly dehumanizing, for the oppressor as well as the oppressed. Instead of "progress," we see gains pitifully eked out through personal struggle. Instead of eventual "assimilation," we see a false promise of ultimate inclusion that serves only to pacify.

Finally, if we look at the famed race relations paradigm from the point of view of the oppressed, we see a system of thought that provides erudite justification for oppression. Indeed, while pretending to be "neutral," the race relations model concocts such an inversion of truth that the oppressed are made responsible for their own oppression. Like a Dr. Seuss story, the incredible is made plausible. Or as Charles Mills writes in *The Racial Contract*: "To a significant extent, then, white signatories will live in an invented delusional world, a racial fantasyland, a 'consensual hallucination.'"[99]

Perhaps now we are better prepared to explain the astounding failure of the Chicago school of race relations to take notice of the blatant denial of elementary civil rights. The whole purpose of an epistemology of ignorance was to camouflage oppression. Small wonder that when the Civil Rights Revolution finally exploded in their faces, the experts of "race relations," denizens of "an invented delusional world," reacted with consternation. They lacked the conceptual apparatus to grasp the reality that was unfolding before their eyes. This was rooted in an even more elementary conceptual failure. As Du Bois wrote with his unrivaled perspicacity, the fundamental problem was its inability to see the Negro "as an ordinary and average human being."[100] If we begin with this simple premise, then all of the conventional truths fall like bowling pins.

On the other hand, Marxism provided the conceptual apparatus for bringing oppression into focus. From a Marxist perspective blacks were the most
oppressed group under American capitalism—the archetypal subproletariat,
downtrodden, and therefore ripe for revolution.[101] Armed with this conceptual
weapon, the Marxists had no trouble confronting the grisly facts of racial oppression. Indeed, the "o" word—oppression—was central to their lexicon. Any
suggestion that slavery was a benevolent institution or that racial hierarchy
had a civilizing mission would strike a Marxist as imperialist poppycock. And
when black protest exploded, whether in Birmingham or Watts, far from being
inexplicable, any Marxist worth his or her salt would have seen this instantly
as the fulfillment of the Marxist prophecy of revolution.

A paradigm also provides a shorthand for those steeped in its syntax. In
1846, fifteen years before the Civil War, Marx wrote, "Without slavery there
would be no cotton, without cotton there would be no modern industry."[102]
In one epigrammatic sentence, Marx summed up the relationship of slavery
to the emerging industrial economies of both the United States and England,
dependent as they were on abundant and cheap cotton for their burgeoning
textile industries. Implicit, too, was a theory of race and racism, which turned
the prevailing conception of slavery on its head. In the Marxist schema, slavery
did not exist because of some preexisting racial animus. Rather, racism was
invented to provide justification for slavery. This was the seminal theoretical
point that led Oliver Cox to write, a century later: "Race prejudice, then, constitutes an attitudinal justification necessary for an easy exploitation of some
race."[103] Implicit, too, is a critique of the cottage industry that has existed in
the social sciences for decades, preoccupied with measuring and charting the
prevalence of prejudice and racial stereotyping. Why, the Marxist asks, focus
on symptoms rather than causes? Why this obsession with attitudes rather than
conditions? Why do we keep flogging the bigot instead of attacking a system
of oppression that spawns and nurtures bigots? En masse!

The hallmark of the Marxist paradigm was that it explained racial hierarchy in terms of political economy, and the societal interests that were served
by the suppression of rights and the exploitation of black labor. Again, it
turned the prevailing wisdom on its head. Instead of looking for the reasons
for racial hierarchy among blacks themselves—whether in their genes or their
culture—the Marxist paradigm riveted attention on those *external* political

and economic structures that were complicit in the genesis, legitimation, and enforcement of racial hierarchy. But this was the elemental truth that was taboo in the academy, which was itself enmeshed in the very system of power that was under scrutiny. What chance did Marxism have in an academy that was beholden to wealthy philanthropists and controlled by trustees who included captains of industry? Or in a political culture that was staunchly antagonistic to anything that smacked of Marxism?

Furthermore, Marxism was the convenient scapegoat for any outbreak of racial violence. The summer of the 1919 Chicago riot was dubbed "the Red Summer" because racial unrest occurred at a time of anti-Communist hysteria, and blacks who sought equality were branded as "radicals."[104] This was the context in which Charles Johnson, as proxy for Robert Park, was commissioned to conduct a study of the riot. Imagine what would have happened if Johnson had drafted a report that placed the blame for the riot on the doorstep of a capitalist system that pitted European immigrants and blacks against each other in deadly competition for jobs and wages. Charles Johnson's career would have come to a screeching halt, and Robert Ezra Park most likely would have suffered the fate of Richard Ely, Edward Bemis, and Edward Ross, all of whom were banished to remote colleges where their maverick views could be safely contained.

Now, consider the dilemma of those rare and remarkable black students who, in an era of Jim Crow, overcame multiple obstacles to enroll in colleges where they encountered a system of learning that was saturated with racism. Take Carter G. Woodson, for example. Woodson was the son of a poor family in Virginia, who had worked in coal mines, and whose thirst for knowledge led him to the University of Chicago, where he earned a B.A. in 1907 and an M.A. in 1908. Four years later he received a Ph.D. from Harvard, and was a cofounder of the Association for the Study of African Life and History. Woodson's judgment about the treatment of blacks in American institutions of higher learning is encapsulated in the title of his 1933 book, *The Miseducation of the Negro*. Woodson excoriated schools for ignoring and distorting black history, and in effect teaching blacks that they were inferior. He dismissed the learning in universities as "propaganda and cant that involved a waste of time and misdirected the Negroes thus trained." *["Propaganda and cant," hmm. Have we only become more sophisticated at masking propaganda and cant?]* In his critique of historiography, Du Bois was equally scathing: "In propaganda against the Negro since emancipation in this land, we face one of the most stupendous efforts the world ever saw to discredit human beings, an effort involving universities, history, science, social life and religion."[105]

These black scholars had to find a place for themselves in a system of knowledge that did not represent the world of race as they knew it. On a very personal level, they experienced the dissonances of these opposing episte-mologies. It is easy to see why many of them resisted the prevailing wisdom and gravitated to Marxism, if only because it did not function as apology or justification for the racial status quo. Yet these aspiring scholars had to tread carefully, beholden as they were to white philanthropists, not to speak of their professors at Chicago, who were identified with the very positions they were challenging. As we have seen, anything that smacked of Marxism was tagged as "political," and in the name of "objectivity" banished from the canon. Du Bois's fate was typical and a warning to others: as Cedric Robinson has observed, Du Bois was subjected to "vilification and neglect."[106] *[Of course, if one had to choose between death by neglect and death by vilification, the latter is clearly preferable. Vilification at least puts one's ideas into the discourse, and allows one to die fighting! Neglect leaves one with a sense of utter futility. Early in his career, when his pioneering Atlanta studies were ignored, W.E.B. Du Bois actually left sociology and assumed the editorship of the NAACP's journal,* The Crisis, *where he thought he might be more effective as an agent of change. Eventually, he came back to the academy, where he was (and still remains) the unheralded pioneer of community studies. Even his pathbreaking study of* The Philadelphia Negro *was never reviewed in the* American Journal of Sociology.*]*

THE SPARRING MATCH BETWEEN
"RACE MEN" AND "CLASS MEN"[107]

One expects vilification and neglect from one's ideological enemies. The more vexing problem was that even black intellectuals who were drawn to Marx-ism in their youth eventually took issue with key Marxist tenets. The appeal of Marxism was that it offered a compelling system of ideas that made sense of the black condition, and Marxists did not flinch at condemning racism at a time when the prevailing attitude was one of utter complacency. However, problems arose with the Marxist tendency to subsume race to class. Marxism turned a blind eye toward the factors that made the problems of blacks different from those of other downtrodden and exploited workers. Instead, doctrinaire Marxists held fast to the principle of the unity of labor, which lumped blacks together with other disparaged and exploited groups who were cast in a mutual struggle with capital. No one denied that blacks were more severely exploited and oppressed than other workers, but this was seen as a matter of degree, not of kind. Besides, whatever differences existed in the situation of black and white workers were secondary to their mutual interest in class struggle, or so it was argued, and certainly did not require a different theory or praxis. However, in this failure to recognize what was unique about racial oppression, these Marxists were out of sync with the real-life experiences of black people. Indeed, we have to ask whether Marxism is subject to the same judgment that I rendered earlier against mainstream sociology: of being "white," despite its best intentions.

Du Bois is a case in point. In 1904 he voted for Debs because, as he later wrote, the Socialists "rung truest on the race question in their theoretical statements." But theory was one thing, and politics another. Debs took the position that "there is no 'Negro problem' apart from the general labor problem." More was involved than ideological purity: Debs could not afford to antagonize working-class whites, his principal constituency, and the racism that permeated the working class made a sham of the promise of "the unity of labor." In the 1912 election Du Bois abandoned Debs with this parting salvo: "The Negro problem, then, is the great test of the American Socialist."[108]

Indeed, all through the twentieth century—from Franklin Roosevelt through Bill Clinton—the Negro problem would test the limits of the liberal/Left's commitment to blacks and its willingness to confront racism.[109] Ironically, the same paradigm that refused to mince words when it came to "oppression," had trouble distinguishing between racial and class oppression, insisting that the "real" causes of racial oppression were economic. Thus, in the Marxist framework the political enemy was not the racist, but rather the capitalist. As Du Bois found with Debs, despite verbal condemnation of racism, Marxists had trouble dealing with issues of race within the strictures of their class paradigm. Did this foregrounding of class and elision of race reflect the European origins of Marxism? Or that its white adherents were unable to grasp what was viscerally understood by most blacks: that racial and class oppression were two different animals? Were Marxists guilty of turning a blind eye to the racism that was rife among the working classes? Did this mean that blacks were rendered invisible not only by the color-blind Right, but by a color-blind Left as well?

The ambiguities of race and class were the subject of intense and often acrimonious debate within the councils of the American Communist Party (CP). The debate intensified after the Great Migration during World War I, when conflict erupted between black and white workers. There were two competing positions on "the Negro question." One held that racism was "a device of national oppression, a smoke screen thrown up by the class enemy, to hide the underlying economic and social conditions involved in black oppression and to maintain the division of the working class."[110] Adherents of this position insisted that there was nothing to do other than uniting blacks with other class-conscious workers.

A second position contended that the Negro question was more than a class or racial problem, but "the sum total of the economic, social, and political relations existing between the Negroes and the white population make this question one of an oppressed national (or racial) minority."[111] After a decade of debate, in 1928 the Sixth World Congress of the Communist International passed a resolution declaring that blacks concentrated in the Black Belt counties of the Deep South constituted an oppressed nation.[112] The corollary was that blacks had a right of self-determination to secede from the United States. Alas, the official position of the CP had swung from one of rejecting the notion that blacks were different from other exploited workers, to one of claiming that the political and social cleavages were so fundamental that blacks constituted a nation within a nation, entitled to self-determination.

This did not sit well with many left-leaning black intellectuals. Some of the black participants in the debate rejected not only the conclusion—the argument for self-determination—but also the premise of unbridgeable differences. In *The Cry Was Unity*, Mark Solomon provides this account of the objections voiced by Ron Mahoney, a black student who had been recruited to study at the KUTV, the University of the Toilers of the East, in Moscow:

The Party failed to influence blacks, he [Mahoney] said, because it approached the subject from the outside with no understanding of what goes on among the mass of blacks in the United States. And that, he said, was the problem with this question of a nation. Negroes were not 'a pure race'; in the deepest recesses of the Black Belt, the effects of assimilation could be seen in the varied hues of the people. The white rulers, Mahoney claimed, understood the forces of assimilation and pressed their antimiscegenation laws to curb them. Blacks, in fact, were losing their 'common territory' through migration to the North and to the cities of the South. Self-determination would find no response among the black public, Mahoney said.[113]

Without doubt, our sharp student from the University of the Toilers of the East was accurate in his assessment that the idea of self-determination had little traction among rank and file blacks, however much it resonated with nationalist impulses that flourished during the Garvey movement.

The dialectics of race and class were also debated among black intellectuals and activists. The issue came to a head at a 1916 conference in Amenia, New York, that spawned the NAACP. The "race men," led by W.E.B. Du Bois, argued for a frontal assault against Jim Crow segregation, denial of civil rights, and labor market discrimination. The "class men," on the other hand, countered that this position was "too narrow," insisting that the problems of the race had to be seen in the larger context of class inequality. It followed that, instead of pleading their own cause, blacks should join labor in a larger movement for social change.

Roy Wilkins, a quintessential "race man," accused the "class men" of engaging in political abstractions far removed from the realities on the ground or the political understandings of rank and file blacks. Wilkins advanced his position with conviction and eloquence:

I am convinced that the masses of Negroes in this country are concerned primarily with the injustices that beset them on every hand because of their color. They are concerned with lynching, discrimination, segregation, insult, denial of opportunities in schools, businesses, and taxation without representation. Only a small minority is at all concerned with the question of integrating the race into the economic and political pattern of the day. This may not be as it should be, but I am convinced that that is what it is. I am afraid that if we go too off too heavily on theoretic social and political and economic program, we will find out that we shall have cut ourselves loose from the support of the bulk of our followers.[114]

In turn, the "class men" parried these arguments with equal conviction and eloquence. Abram Harris, Jr., the chair of the Department of Economics at

Howard University, headed up a committee that called on the NAACP to "lay the intellectual basis for united action between white and black workers in local, state, and national politics for securing passage of adequate legislation on immediate problems, such as a) old age pensions, b) unemployment and sickness insurance, c) widows' and orphans' pensions, d) child and female labor, e) lynching, f) public discrimination and Jim Crowism."[115]

This contention at the 1916 Amenia Conference presaged the race/class debate that would reverberate down to the present: between those who argue the centrality of race and those who see this as a blind alley, insisting that blacks need to unite with other exploited workers in a collective assault against structures of inequality. Unlike the visionaries who assembled in Amenia in 1916, we have the advantage of looking backward instead of forward. What is the judgment of history with regard to the issues debated at Amenia?

It is difficult to escape the conclusion that "class men," like Ralph Bunche, were wrong in pooh-poohing the civil rights approach of the NAACP.[116] After all, if blacks were waiting for the revolution of the Marxist imagination, they would still be sitting in the back of the bus! The civil rights movement was built on the solidarities of black people, and it succeeded in dismantling the official scaffolding of Jim Crow that denied them elementary rights of citizenship enjoyed by the most exploited white workers. Granted, the "class men" were right in tagging the civil rights movement as "reformist," in the sense that it never sought a fundamental redistribution of power and wealth, but only equal black participation in that system. Nevertheless, this so-called reform was not only crucially important for blacks, but it was also a major catalyst of broader political transformation. As Aldon Morris writes: "The civil rights movement served as a training ground for many of the activists who later organized movements within their own communities. Indeed, the modern women's movement, student movement, farm workers' movement, and others of the period were triggered by the unprecedented scale of nontraditional politics in the civil rights movement."[117]

Yet the judgment of history vindicates the "class men" as well. No sooner did the movement achieve its legislative agenda than civil rights leaders struck a new refrain: "What good does it do a man," King asked rhetorically in 1967, "to have integrated lunch counters if he can't buy a hamburger?"[118] For all of its successes, the civil rights movement did not even begin to address the vast inequalities in power, wealth, and status that separated the black and white citizens of this nation. Was Ralph Bunche right after all? Were civil rights leaders naïve in believing that once the walls of segregation came tumbling down, blacks would achieve their rightful place in American society?

Fortunately, we need not choose between these rival positions: both are vindicated by history. The "race men" were clearly right in their contention that the dismantling of Jim Crow was a necessary first step in the liberation struggle. However, the "class men" were also right, as protest leaders were quick to realize, that winning formal rights left unanswered the vast economic inequalities that were the legacy of slavery. People on both sides of the race/class debate agree in principle that "race" and "class" are intertwined, and both must be confronted tactically. Yet in the practical world of politics, we are often confronted with hard choices between the one and the other. As we will see, the race/class debate emerged with renewed force in the post–civil rights period.

A REIGNING PARADIGM

A reigning paradigm, much like a reigning monarch, has pomp and circumstance working in its favor. The celebrated texts and erudite scholars associated with them are accorded honorific status, and all the rights and immunities thereof. However innocuous this may seem, it is certainly problematic from the point of view of the sociology of knowledge. Not only do established truths go unquestioned, but the people associated with them also wield power and influence in knowledge production. Aside from being ensconced at elite universities, they function as powerbrokers who influence decisions regarding what books and articles are published by leading book publishers and journals. Even more important, they influence the dispensation of funds from governmental agencies and foundations. On the other hand, as we have seen from the marginalization of black scholars, dissident viewpoints and the people associated with them are at best tolerated, and at worst vilified. The guardians of the reigning paradigm ensure that it reigns supreme.

As James McKee writes in *Sociology and the Race Problem,* "from the 1920s until the onset of a new generation and a new situation after World War II, Park's conception of a race relations cycle provided an influential model for studying the assimilation of racial minorities into modern society."[119] McKee adds that the influence of Park's race relations cycle owed more to the legion of Park's students than to Park himself. As noted earlier, Park's influence got a boost when Everett Hughes joined with several of Park's colleagues and students to publish a collection of his essays in 1950, and the paperback edition followed in 1964. The timing could not have been better. Park emerged as the "exemplar scholar" of race just at the point that race was emerging as a burning public issue.[120]

Nor was Park's race relations model restricted to the realm of ideas. It provided the intellectual framework for what came to be known as "the race relations industry."[121] On the assumption that the problem of race was one of prejudice that had to be extirpated, a vast network of organizations and whole professions were engaged in this societal project. The burden for change fell on teachers and social workers whose self-declared mission was to spread enlightenment and root out prejudice. As McKee shows, a whole nomenclature evolved, "variously labeled 'human relations,' 'community relations' and eventually, by professional choice, 'intergroup relations.'"[122] Psychologists got in on the act, and devised strategies for reducing intergroup tensions.

All of this might seem innocuous, but consider the historical context. At a time when racial segregation was encoded in law and blacks were denied elementary rights of citizenship, the practitioners of intergroup relations preoccupied themselves, not with issues of civil rights and racial justice, but rather with reducing intergroup tensions. This amounted to little more than a pacification program that sought to promote interracial understanding and cooperation, but left the racist system intact. In effect, the race relations industry was a domestic version of the Congo Reform Association, which did not attack colonialism per se but only sought to curb the atrocities that were giving colonialism a bad name. Similarly, the race relations industry, consisting as it did of big-hearted and well-intentioned men and women striving to mitigate the scourge of bigotry, utterly failed to address the core problem: entrenched racism that pervaded all major institutions of society.

McKee states the problem in more temperate language: "Whether the emphasis was upon prejudice or discrimination, the focus in either case was on the dominant group, not the minority. As prejudiced persons or as discriminators, white people were the object of analysis. They were the target of any strategy for racial change, and it was they who had to change in attitude or behavior

or both if any improvement in race relations was to be effected."[123] Think
about it: here we have a racial dictatorship *[pardon the intemperate language]*,
and there we have a race relations industry ministering to the oppressor, not
the oppressed. Instead of doing something to improve *conditions* for blacks,
all the effort is devoted to changing *attitudes* among whites, on the dubious
assumption that this will eventually translate into better treatment of blacks.[124]
It is difficult to avoid the conclusion that the entire school of "intergroup relations" was enshrouded in sanctimony and self-deception. Despite intentions
to the contrary, it served the racial status quo by fostering the illusion that
"something" was being done to alleviate the plight of African Americans. For
their part, scholars of "race relations" betrayed their own classical traditions,
which would have focused on the institutional basis for racial hierarchy and
conflict. As I suggested earlier, they are like marriage counselors, exploring
ways to repair these fractured relationships while the root problems remain
unexamined or at least unresolved.

Let me be clear: McKee provides a most welcome critique of sociological
practice on race, and his book delivers on the promise of its subtitle: *The Failure of a Perspective*. For example, McKee provides this critical assessment of
Robert McIver's strategy for dealing with racism in his influential book, *The
More Perfect Union*: "moderate in demands, gradual in pace of change; attacking discrimination at its weakest points; and adapting to the mores, that
is, avoiding 'radical' demands that might provoke a backlash."[125] Indeed, this
is an apt description of the entire race relations industry. Where McKee fails,
however, is in not engaging the scholarship and activism of those who were
not moderate in their demands, who were *not* gradual in pace of change, who
attacked racism at its core rather than its weakest points, and who did not shy
away from making "radical" demands for fear of triggering a backlash.[126]

By giving short shrift to the radical tradition that has consistently challenged mainstream social science, McKee has given us half a loaf: an incisive
critique of sociology's failures, but only a meager sense of what it will take to
"get it right." Thus, he concludes his book with a lament that "sociologists
need to learn new ways to examine race relations." True enough, but then he
shoots himself in the foot with this caveat: "Sociologists lose when they take
sides in the difficult struggle to attain racial equality."[127] This is a breathtaking assertion. My reading of McKee's book is that it is *only* when sociologists

have taken the *right* side and aligned themselves with the antiracist struggle
that they have produced a sociology worthy of its name. Besides, what does
it mean to say, "Sociologists lose when they take sides"? Remaining silent
in the face of oppression amounts to acquiescence. Failing to recognize and
condemn oppression, or calling it by its right name, allows oppression to go
unchallenged. As Howard Zinn proclaimed in the title of his book, *You Can't
Be Neutral on a Moving Train*.[128]

GUNNAR MYRDAL'S DILEMMA[129]

As we have seen, the cardinal rule in the epistemology of ignorance stipulates
that it is permissible, even commendable to rail against racism, so long as
one does not cross the forbidden line into "advocacy." Nowhere is this more
evident than in the celebrated work of Gunnar Myrdal, the Swedish economist who in 1935, in the midst of the Depression, was commissioned by the
Carnegie Corporation to undertake a comprehensive study of race in America.
An American Dilemma was an instant classic upon publication in 1944, and
a fiftieth anniversary edition was published with much fanfare in 1995. One
wonders about the logic of celebrating a book three decades after the Civil
Rights Revolution that was written two decades before the passage of the
1964 Civil Rights Act. Was Myrdal *that* prescient, or is this yet another sign
of intellectual stasis, reflecting the extent to which sociology is still wedded
to antiquated and problematic conceptions of race and racism?

Why did the august Carnegie Corporation decide to underwrite a study
on race in America that was unprecedented in scope and cost? And why did
the trustees entrust this responsibility to Gunnar Myrdal, a Swede who had
never set foot in the South? To answer these questions, we need to probe the
mindset and deliberations of the men who inhabited the gilded offices of the
Carnegie Corporation on Fifth Avenue in New York City.

As John Stanfield points out in *Philanthropy and Jim Crow in American
Social Science*, previously the Carnegie Corporation had been "the most racially exclusive of the major foundations and was very supportive of white
supremacy in apartheid societies."[130] This should alert us to the possibility that
the motivation behind the study had more to do with pacification than with
racial justice. Indeed, the study was prompted by concern over mounting racial

tensions in Northern cities during the Depression, underscored by the Harlem "race riot" only a few miles from the offices of the Carnegie Corporation. The research project was the brainchild of Newton Baker, one of Carnegie's trustees. Baker, the son of a Confederate soldier, revealed his retrograde views on race in private correspondence with Frederick Keppel, the president of the Carnegie Corporation. Baker wrote of slavery:

How many white civilizations could have dared to receive so many wild savages, who were practically uncaged animals, and spread them around over their farms in contact with their own families passes human comprehension. What has been done for the Negro in a hundred years is an unparalleled achievement and nothing but a theoretical democratic impatience can make us critical of it, though, of course, much more remains to be done.[131]

What clearer statement of the imperialist logic behind slavery and Jim Crow could there be! Not in 1800 or 1860 by an apologist for slavery, not in 1900 by an architect of legal apartheid, but in 1936 by a trustee of the Carnegie Corporation as it prepared to launch a comprehensive study of the Negro in the United States. *[As the saying goes, with friends like this, who needs enemies?]*

I do not mean to imply that Myrdal shared the retrograde mindset of his patrons at the Carnegie Corporation. It is common for grantees to be at odds with the politics and intentions of their grantors, though in receiving their largess, there is an inevitable gravitational pull that keeps grantees in check. *[No pun intended, though it is noteworthy that in the middle of the Depression Myrdal was paid roughly $280,000 in today's dollars to head up the Carnegie study.[132]]* However that may be, the obvious leverage that grantors have is in selecting the grantee. What led them to select Myrdal, a renowned architect of Sweden's welfare state? What the trustees told the public was that they wanted an outsider who could approach the study with "a fresh mind." They specifically limited the search "to countries of high intellectual and scholarly standards *[read: Europe]* but with no background or traditions of imperialism which might lessen the confidence of the Negroes in the United States as to the complete impartiality of the study and the validity of its findings."[133] *[In that case, why didn't the big wheels at Carnegie assemble a blue-ribbon panel of black scholars to choose the person to head up the study? How different would it have been had Forceful Frazier been at the helm? Not to speak of Oliver Cox!]* Surely,

Myrdal's social democratic politics came under scrutiny, but then again they blended well with the politics of the New Deal. Of paramount importance is that Myrdal's liberal credentials and personal stature put a useful liberal imprimatur on the study.

At the same time, before the trustees disbursed the largest grant in the history of social research, they made sure that Myrdal would not stray too far from what they deemed to be politically acceptable. Myrdal's biographer, Walter Jackson, unearthed a letter that Myrdal wrote to the Carnegie Corporation in October 1937, which provided the assurance that the trustees needed:

During my stay in the States in 1929–30 I found myself having a purely questioning attitude to the Negro problem. My general attitude to race problems . . . is that I am on the one hand inclined to keep very critical against the popular insistence on great biological difference in intellectual and moral qualities between races but on the other hand not apt *a priori* to postulate perfect parity.[134]

Here in this private communication Myrdal laid his cards on the table. He would embrace Park's "new orthodoxy" that renounces notions of biological inferiority, but, like the abolitionists a century earlier, stops short of advocating "perfect parity" between the races. Thus, his letter provided the trustees the assurance that they needed that he would steer clear of controversy.

With his unimpeachable liberal credentials, Myrdal was the perfect choice to rationalize the racial order that was evolving, which involved a shift away from Southern-style de jure racism to Northern-style de facto racism. Myrdal knew that he was walking through a political minefield, and deft politician that he was, knew how to appease and disarm potential critics on all sides. The best façade was strict adherence to the separation between science and politics. Indeed, in his preface to *An American Dilemma*, Frederick Keppel, president of the Carnegie Corporation, noted that the "proper function" of the foundation is "to make the facts available and let them speak for themselves," adding that it is not the role of the foundation to "instruct the public as to what to do about them."[135]

Ironically, the president of the Carnegie Corporation exposed the most grievous shortcoming of *An American Dilemma*: its failure to arrive at a set of policy recommendations to deal with the wrongs so copiously documented in the body of the study. This is doubly ironic because Myrdal had a reputation as a "social engineer" who sought to use the findings of social research to forge social policy. To be sure, the raw facts concerning black victimization cry for justice. However, Myrdal stopped short of bringing his analysis to a logical conclusion, and one can comb through the 1,300 pages of his book without finding any policy agenda from our reputed social engineer.

Given the times, Myrdal knew how far he could push a reform agenda. Had he followed through with even a proposal to restore the civil rights that blacks enjoyed in the aftermath of slavery, he would have been denounced as a "radical," and a "foreign radical" at that, and his famous book would have been consigned to the remainder bin.

There is a further irony here. Tucked away in Appendix 2 of his book, on page 1050, is the most direct and searing criticism of Robert Park that I have encountered in the social science literature. Myrdal writes:

Probably because he has no intentional conservative bias, it is difficult to find simple statements in Park's writing which exemplify the fallacy of drawing practical conclusions from factual premises alone. What we do find is a systematic tendency to ignore practically all possibilities of modifying—by conscious effort—the social effects of the natural forces.[136]

Myrdal went on to criticize Park for his "fatalism" and for "the do-nothing (*laissez-faire*) implications" of his analysis. Well stated! The problem is that this criticism applies with equal force to Myrdal himself. Obviously, Myrdal was fearful of triggering a backlash, and held his fire. How else to explain his utter failure to explore policy remedies for the injustices so copiously documented in his study?

PARADIGM CRISIS AND THE
SCHOLARSHIP OF CONFRONTATION

According to Walter Jackson, Myrdal's biographer, *An American Dilemma* "established a liberal orthodoxy on black-white relations and remained the most important study of the race issue until the middle of the 1960s."[137] Myrdal's magnum opus was particularly effective in exposing the brutalities of Jim Crow, as well as paving the way for the crucial *Brown v. Board of Education* decision in 1954. By the mid-1960s, however, as the civil rights crisis intensified,

Myrdal's famous book came under increased critical scrutiny. Proof positive that it takes a revolution to dislodge an established paradigm!

Thomas Kuhn writes: "Scientific revolutions are inaugurated by a growing sense, again often restricted to a narrow subdivision of the scientific community, that an existing paradigm has ceased to function adequately in the exploration of an aspect of nature to which that paradigm itself had previously led the way."[138] Indeed, this was the deeper significance behind Everett Hughes's 1963 presidential address to the American Sociological Association, in which he expressed bewilderment at sociology's failure to anticipate the civil rights upheaval. As racial conflict intensified and grew more violent with the explosion in Watts in 1965 and the spate of "riots" in the years that followed, it became abundantly clear that the race experts, exponents of the received wisdom, could not shed light on these momentous events. There was a growing realization that the old paradigm was useless in explaining the racial crisis that gripped the nation.

Furthermore, the reassessment of Myrdal's "classic" did not occur in some obscure academic journal but in the most public of venues: the *New York Times Magazine*. The December, 1969, issue included an article by historian Carl Degler, entitled "The Negro in America: Where Myrdal Went Wrong." Degler unleashed a barrage of criticisms:

- Myrdal underestimated the depth and virulence of Northern racism.

- Myrdal erred in thinking that change would come from labor unions, and underestimated the depth and virulence of racism in the ranks of organized labor.

- Myrdal had a top-down perspective on politics, and failed to recognize that the greatest pressure for change would come from blacks in the South. He particularly underestimated the potential of the black church as an instrument for change.

- Myrdal's "greatest weakness," according to Degler, was his optimism. *[As I commented at the outset, Myrdal's exuberance was his charm, but it is easy to see that, in the context of the racial crisis, optimism could be an intellectual liability as well.]* Myrdal's reverence for American democracy, and his belief that Americans were conscience-stricken over their treatment of blacks prevented him from grasping the extent to which racism was entrenched and reform would be fiercely resisted. The proposition that racism could be remedied by changing people's beliefs suddenly appeared untenable, even facile.

• Myrdal's model of change did not envision the need for compensatory programs. Indeed, when the idea of compensatory programs for blacks was broached in the early 1960s, Myrdal opposed them, opting instead for "universal programs" aimed at poor people generally.

The net effect of Degler's critique was to suggest that Myrdal's opus and its intellectual framework were obsolete. The time was ripe for a paradigm shift, as sociologists and others groped for a new framework that might shed light on the nation's escalating racial crisis.

What gradually emerged in the place of the old paradigm was what I have elsewhere called "a scholarship of confrontation."[139] This began with an outpouring of books, not by learned scholars, but by movement leaders and activists who suddenly found themselves with a massive white audience eager to engage their writing. The best sellers included King's autobiographical *Stride toward Freedom*, *The Autobiography of Malcolm X*, Huey Newton's *To Die for People*, and Angela Davis's autobiography. By 1969 Mel Watkins declared in the *New York Times Book Review* that there was a "Black Revolution in Books," citing such writers as James Baldwin, Richard Wright, Ralph Ellison, Lorraine Hansberry, and Julius Lester.[140] Alas, the very minority and radical voices that had long been relegated to the periphery were now at the center of both academic and popular discourses.

Scholars are chronically slow to respond to new events or to churn out their erudition. In Part 1 I noted the esoteric topics on the program of the annual meetings of the American Sociological Association in 1963, at a time that the society was reeling from nearly a decade of protest. Interesting enough, one of the first books to bridge the chasm between activism and academe was a collaborative work between Stokely Carmichael, a grassroots activist, and Charles Hamilton, a political science professor at Lincoln University. In *Black Power* they advanced a bold, new conception of racism, by drawing a distinction between individual and institutionalized racism:

Racism is both overt and covert. It takes two, closely related forms: individual whites acting against individual blacks, and acts by the total white community against the black community. We call these individual racism and institutionalized racism. The first consists of overt acts by individuals, which cause death, injury or the violent destruction of property. This type can be recorded by television cameras; it can frequently be observed in the process of commission. The second type is less overt, far more subtle, less identifiable in terms of *specific* individuals committing the acts. But it is no less destructive of human life. The second type originates in the operation of established and respected forces in the society, and thus receives far less public condemnation than the first type.[141]

They followed with this poignant example:

When white terrorists bomb a black church and kill five black children, that is an act of individual racism, widely deplored by most segments of society. But when in that same city—Birmingham, Alabama—five hundred black babies die each year because of the lack of proper food, shelter and medical facilities, and thousands more are maimed physically, emotionally and intellectually because of poverty and discrimination in the black community, that is a function of institutionalized racism.

Here was a truly revolutionary conception that saw racism as vastly greater than the beliefs and acts of misguided individuals, but rather as something that was embedded in institutions, so much so that it could be perpetuated through routine institutional practices without racist intent. Carmichael and Hamilton were giving theoretical exposition to the movement's slogan that the United States was "a racist society," in that it engendered and tolerated deep inequalities along racial lines. The implication was that the remedy for racism did not lie in countering racist stereotypes, but rather required a drastic overhaul of major institutions. It is remarkable that the sociological lexicon was so bereft of a construct that it required ingenious coinage on the part of a collaboration between a scholar and an activist. In any event, with a single phrase—institutionalized racism—Carmichael and Hamilton provided the conceptual apparatus for rethinking racism. Years later, the concept of institutionalized racism would provide the theoretical linchpin for affirmative action policy.

Gradually, a new canon of scholarly work began to emerge. Some of this came from an older generation of stalwarts with Marxist tendencies who, like Blauner, were committed to the black struggle long before it coalesced into a movement.[142] In time, a younger generation, steeped in the politics of the sixties, came on stream. Collectively, their work constituted a "scholarship of confrontation," whose hallmark, like that of the movement itself, was to confront American society and its major institutions for their complicity in racism.[143]

If there is a single work that meets Kuhn's definition of "an exemplar study" that is representative of a paradigm, it is Robert Blauner's *Racial Oppression in America*.[144] The title itself, which invoked the "o" word, signaled a challenge to the venerable race relations model. Blauner made no secret of his disenchantment with mainstream sociology. In the preface he writes: "My own developing framework probably owes more to the social movements of the oppressed than to standard sociology."[145] And in less polite language a few pages later: "Virtually all the new insights about racism and the experience of the oppressed have been provided by writers whose lives and minds were uncluttered by sociological theory."[146]

As is true of virtually any author of a book that is a singular success, Blauner was the right person in the right place at the right time. In an autobiographical essay, Blauner reveals that he was a student radical at the University of Chicago where, in addition to taking courses with Everett Hughes and Herbert Blumer, he joined the Communist Party.[147] Subsequently, he earned his Ph.D. in sociology at the University of California, Berkeley, went on to teach for a year at the University of Chicago, and then was hired as an assistant professor at Berkeley in 1963. *[Full disclosure: I was enrolled in Blauner's first graduate seminar. I well remember the disheveled and self-effacing neophyte who appeared at the first class. His personal manner already signaled that he was not one of those self-important professors who ruled the classroom. The Third World and Left students on campus gravitated to him, like bees to pollen. I was not one of Bob's inner circle, and did not realize until years later just how much his teaching and his example influenced my own thinking. I was a neophyte myself, and it was inspiring to have a professor who had the courage to flout the orthodoxies of our shared discipline.]*

Blauner's radical politics allowed him to bring a unique conceptual lens to the issue of race, though he was not a doctrinaire Marxist by any means. The Marx in him recognized racial oppression as oppression, and did not flinch from invoking that forbidden word. But in the tradition of Du Bois, Blauner was also a "race man" who refused to subsume race to class.

Blauner challenged the tendency in sociology, inherited from the Chicago school of race relations, to place racial and ethnic minorities in the same framework of analysis. This was the significance of his rejection of the immigrant analogy. Blauner stressed what was different about the condition of people of color, beginning with the fact that Native Americans and African Americans were not immigrants, but entered American society through conquest and slavery. Even more important was "the colonial labor principle": immigrants were rapidly absorbed into the nation's burgeoning industries, whereas racial minorities were mostly restricted to the preindustrial sectors of the national economy. Thus, whereas immigrant enclaves functioned as temporary way stations, preparing immigrants for social and geographical mobility, racial minorities were consigned to live permanently in isolated ghettos and barrios, in what amounted to a system of "internal colonialism." As is readily apparent, Blauner adopted the language and politics of anticolonialism to challenge the prevalent race relations model.

These were bold and revelatory conceptions that cut through layers of obfuscation and shed merciful light on the forces tearing American society apart. But a maverick scholar does not a paradigm make! When Myrdal wrote *An American Dilemma*, he did so with a massive grant from a prestigious foundation, and his book was published with much fanfare and became an instant classic, acclaimed in the general press as well as in academic circles. Blauner's book, by his own account, found an enthusiastic audience among minority scholars and students, and sold some 50,000 to 60,000 copies in the college market before going out of print in the late 1980s.[148] But Blauner acknowledged that is was not well received among mainstream sociologists. Not only that, but as he recalls with bitterness in his autobiographical essay, he was turned down twice for a promotion to full professor by his own colleagues.[149]

Blauner may have been the "exemplar" of the scholarship of confrontation, as I have suggested, but he was not alone, and a cohort of younger scholars with radical tendencies was coming on stream. Several of them were invisible staffers on the National Advisory Commission on Civil Disorders, better known as the Kerner Commission. The commission was appointed by President Johnson in the wake of the spiral of violence that began in Newark and Detroit in the summer of 1967 and spread like wildfire to scores of cities across the nation in the aftermath of King's assassination in 1968. In a behind-the-scenes article on the commission, Andrew Kopkind uncovers the internecine conflict that took place between radicals, conservatives, and moderates, which ultimately led to a mass firing of staff who were seen as too radical. According to Kopkind, disgruntled black staffers saw the report as "a white document written by white writers and aimed at a white audience—*about* black people." Yet in some ways the final report was a remarkably radical document that created a sensation. It was first on the *New York Times* paperback best-seller list in 1968 and sold almost two million copies.[150]

Unlike the earlier McCone Commission, which investigated the 1965 Watts "riot," the Kerner Report explicitly rejected the notion that the "disorders" stemmed from mindless violence on the part of aberrant ghetto youth. Studies conducted by the commission found that the typical rioter was somewhat better educated than those who did not actively participate in the riot, and had the sympathy of a broad segment of the ghetto community. The commission concluded that the riots constituted a form of protest.

What was especially momentous about the Kerner Report was its declaration that "white racism is essentially responsible for the explosive mixture which has been accumulating in our cities since the end of World War II."[151] This was an astonishing and unprecedented declaration. At the time, American society was reeling from a seemingly endless spiral of violence, replete with daily television coverage of looting, burning, and sniping. Yet a "moderate" presidential commission minced no words in placing the ultimate blame on white racism. It also made clear that the problem of segregation was far from solved by the passage of civil rights legislation a few years earlier. The first page of the report issued its famous admonition that "our nation is moving toward two societies, one black, one white—separate and unequal."

The Kerner Report concluded with seventy-three pages of policy recommendations, though it had no illusions about the prospects that they would be implemented. The last paragraph of the report quotes Kenneth Clark's testimony before the commission:

I read that report . . . of the 1919 riot in Chicago, and it is as if I were reading the report of the investigating committee on the Harlem riot of '35, the report of the investigating committee on the Harlem riot of '43, the report of the McCone Commission on the Watts riot.

I must again in candor say to you members of this Commission—it is a kind of Alice in Wonderland—with the same moving picture re-shown over and over again, the same analysis, the same recommendations, and the same inaction.[152]

Clark's cynicism was borne out by events. The report never became the basis for legislative action or other public policy initiatives. A few months after its publication, Richard Nixon was elected, partly on the basis of a racial backlash that was manipulated to advantage. Hubert Humphrey lost virtually the entire South, and George Wallace carried the Deep South states of Louisiana, Mississippi, Alabama, Georgia, and Arkansas. Furthermore, there was serious erosion of the traditional Democratic base among blue-collar families outside the South. This was indeed an ominous development. It meant that white flight was not just something that happened when blacks moved into white neighborhoods. White flight was also occurring within the Democratic Party.

The result was the end of the Second Reconstruction. As happened at the end of the First Reconstruction, the liberal forces gradually abandoned the cause of racial justice. Fearing the reactionary backlash, the thrust of liberal thought was to get "beyond race," calculated in large part to restore the electoral prospects of Democrats. This was the historical context for a liberal retreat from race. Unlike the racial backlash on the political Right that was explicitly and unabashedly antagonistic to blacks, the liberal backlash took an idiosyncratically liberal cast. It continued to profess concern for the plight of blacks, but it portrayed the race problem as one that was anchored in "class" rather than "race" per se. In short, the liberal retreat from race was predicated on that habitual tendency of the Left to subsume "race" to "class."

THE SCHOLARSHIP OF BACKLASH

In 1973 Joyce Ladner published a book whose title declared *The Death of White Sociology*. Indeed, the sheer force of the scholarship of confrontation, the unprecedented ascendancy of radical and minority voices that had long been relegated to the fringes, and the relentless trouncing of mainstream social science encouraged an intoxicating sense of intellectual triumph. It was to be short lived, however. In retrospect, it should have been obvious that the assertion of voices "from below" did little to transform the powerful institutions "from above." Notwithstanding grossly inflated claims about "the Left academy," the liberal establishment withstood all too well the fierce challenge from within. Leftists and minorities made inroads only in some universities, and even then, mainly in a few disciplines within the social sciences and humanities.[153] The power elite, to use C. Wright Mills's construct, remained intact. I have in mind the web of power represented by elite universities, professional associations, journals, publishing houses, think tanks, and "dream teams," plus those governmental agencies and foundations that provide the indispensable grants on which all of these entities, as well as research and publication, ultimately depend. There is also what might be called the reward-tocracy, an elaborate system of rewards that confers honors, awards, sinecures, and lavish grants on the chosen. One honor, reward, or grant begets others, and the cumulative result is to create iconic figures—an academic priesthood—who command respect and wield influence, and whose ideas are vested with reverential importance. We see here the process whereby a reigning paradigm is invested with regal qualities.

This is not to deny that there was a large stratum within the ranks of sociology that ardently embraced the emergent radical and minority discourses that challenged establishment sociology. However, as any sociologist should know, without power and without resources, these movements are destined to remain weak. We can only wonder how different it might have been had Bob Blauner been showered with grants from foundations and governmental agencies, as happened with Park and Myrdal, and as we will see, with William Julius Wilson only six years later upon the publication of his landmark book, *The Declining Significance of Race.* What if, instead of being denied promotion, Blauner (like Wilson) had been bestowed with a MacArthur "genius grant," or any of a number of prestigious awards, memberships in honorary societies, or trusteeships at this or that foundation? But no benefactor stepped forward to commission our erstwhile Communist to establish an Institute for the Study of Racial Oppression. *[Laughable, I know, but that's the point!]* What if Blauner had bagged a fat grant from one or another of the fourteen foundations and grantors that Wilson acknowledges in his 1996 book, *When Work Disappears?* With those resources he might have been able to train a cadre of students who might have gone on to develop a canon of research, building on his seminal ideas.[154] What if these students (like those of Park and Wilson) also secured positions in leading universities, thus advancing the mission of Berkeley's school of racial oppression? In short, we might have seen the emergence of a new paradigm. Contrary to Kuhn, paradigms don't just happen when cerebral men and women of science change their minds, but are contingent on institutional support and, to be blunt, the money that greases the academic wheel.[155]

In retrospect, Ladner's declaration of the death of white sociology was sadly premature. Indeed, even as she wrote, a political backlash was gaining momentum that would succeed in dismantling many of the policy gains of the post–civil rights era. As Alyson Cole has shown in *The Cult of True Victimhood*, scholars launched an intellectual crusade, largely funded by conservative foundations, that systematically challenged the discourses of feminism and civil rights, and made "the victim," so valorized by the movements of the 1960s, an object of derision and shame.[156]

A major turning point was the 1978 publication of *The Declining Significance of Race*. Wilson charts three major shifts in the pattern of American race relations that, he postulates, were related to underlying shifts in the national economy. In postindustrial cities, Wilson observed, there has been a growing bifurcation between a black middle class, which was positioned to take advantage of expanding opportunities in the post–civil rights era, and the lower classes, which were falling into deep and seemingly permanent poverty. His oft-quoted thesis is stated in the opening sentence of his first chapter: "Race relations in America have undergone fundamental changes in recent years, so much so that now the life chances of individual blacks have more to do with their economic position than with their day-to-day encounters with whites."[157]

Others had advanced this argument without notoriety. Wilson was a modern incarnation of "a class man," in that he subsumed race to class. Indeed, the idea that "race" has been transmuted into "class," was first advanced by none other than Robert Park in a 1939 essay on "The Nature of Race Relations." Park speculated that global forces in the modern world were reconstituting the social order in such a way that "diversities will be based in the future less on inheritance and race and rather more on culture and occupation." As a result, "race conflicts in the modern world . . . will be more and more in the future confused with, and eventually superseded by, the conflicts of class."[158] This same refrain is found in a 1939 article by Charles Johnson, Park's prize student, entitled "The Economic Basis of Race Relations." Johnson's opening sentence reads: "Race relations, as we conceive them today, may in many respects be said to be only incidentally racial." And Johnson's concluding sentence reads:

"Urbanization and industrialization will continue to shift the basis of relations from a caste to a class structure. In the end there will be *less emphasis on the significance of race difference than upon the solidarity of class interests.*"[159]

What then made Wilson's book such a sensation? Much of the controversy centered on its provocative title. According to Wilson, he planned to entitle his book *The Transformation of Race Relations*, essentially reiterating the old refrain about a shift from caste to class. But according to his account, in an epiphanic moment at two o'clock in the morning in a hotel in New York City, Wilson came up with his celebrated title.[160] As Neil McLaughlin has suggested, had Wilson entitled his book *The Increasing Significance of Class*, he would have escaped controversy *[and probably fame as well!]*.[161] However, "declining significance" were fighting words in 1978, a period of escalating racial backlash that threatened to blunt and even reverse many of the hard-won gains of the black protest movement. In this context, a book by an African American scholar with the claim that race was of "declining significance" emblazoned in its title, evoked a torrent of criticism. Actually, the book was written for an academic audience and published by an academic press, but thanks to an op-ed by Wilson in the *New York Times* timed with the publication of his book, "the declining significance of race" was thrust into the public arena, making Wilson and his book an instant sensation.

Wilson came under particularly heavy fire from black scholars. The Association of Black Sociologists passed a resolution stating that Wilson's book "obscures the problem of the persistent oppression of blacks."[162] Kenneth Clark, never one to mince words, wrote:

The belief that class has now supplanted race in the life chances of American blacks remains a pitiful delusion. This is a dangerous delusion because it drains energy and diverts attention from the stark fact that racial injustices perpetrated against all blacks—middle-class and underclassed blacks—remain the unfinished business of American democracy.[163]

Ironically, the criticism heaped on Wilson only played into the hands of his defenders, who extolled Wilson for his "courage" in standing up against militants and ideologues. Through Wilson's book, the genie of racial confrontation was placed back in the bottle, and over time Wilson emerged as the heir to Myrdal. The coronation came in 1994 with the announcement that Wilson

had been selected as the first non-economist to receive the Seidman Award in
Political Economy. Along with this prestigious award, he received the follow-
ing encomium from Robert Solow, M.I.T. economist and former Nobel Prize
winner, who served on the selection committee: "If anyone is a successor to
Gunnar Myrdal in the study of black society in the U.S., it's Bill Wilson."[164]
[The plot thickens: Myrdal was the first recipient of this award, in 1974.]

    Part of the impetus for Wilson's elevation into an icon came from white
elites who, as Derrick Bell often points out, need a black cover for their regressive positions on race. Indeed, Daniel Patrick Moynihan gloated publicly over
the fact that Wilson had taken up positions for which he had been vilified years
earlier. As he commented in his Godkin lectures at Harvard in 1984: "The family report had been viewed as mistaken; the benign neglect memorandum was
depicted as out-and-out racist. By mid-decade, however, various black scholars
were reaching similar conclusions, notably William Julius Wilson in his 1978
study, *The Declining Significance of Race.*"[165]

    To make sense of Wilson's ascent from relative obscurity to "the most in-
fluential sociologist of his generation," according to the *Washington Post*,[166] we
need to draw a distinction between Wilson the man and what can only be called
"Wilson mania." The contours of Wilson's remarkable and dizzying ascent can
be gleaned from his bio on the website of the Kennedy School.[167] In 1978 Wilson
published his now-famous book. At that time he was a lone scholar, laboring
without benefit of grants or patronage from foundations or other sources, though
he did receive a year off from the University of Chicago to rework a manuscript
that had been languishing for several years.[168] As we have seen, upon publication of *The Declining Significance of Race* in the context of the racially polarized
1970s, black scholars pilloried Wilson, but he emerged unscathed. By 1981–82 our
budding icon was named as a Fellow at the Center for Advanced Studies in the
Behavioral Sciences at Stanford. Then in 1987 he won the prestigious MacArthur
award, a five-year grant with no strings attached. In due course he was elected
to the National Academy of Sciences, the American Academy of Education,
the American Philosophical Society, the British Academy, and the Institute of
Medicine *[don't ask]*. In 1996 *Time Magazine* selected him as one of America's 25
Most Influential People *[pity the twenty-sixth!]*. Then came the National Medal
of Science in 1998, the highest scientific honor, followed by the Talcott Parsons
Prize in the Social Sciences by the American Academy of Arts and Sciences in

2003. Not only that, but no fewer than forty-one honorary degrees, plus numerous honors granted by various professional organizations. Finally, according to Wilson's published bio, he is currently a member of numerous national boards and commissions, and was previously the chair of the Board of the Center for Advanced Study in the Behavioral Sciences and of the Russell Sage Foundation.[169] Indeed, Wilson's trophy cabinet is a veritable catalog of the entities that constitute the power elite in American higher education! *[I say this in case my earlier claim of a power elite in academia struck you as political hyperbole.]*

If I have made sport of Wilson's laurels, it is not to disparage him personally. It is not Wilson's doing that his phone has rung off the hook ever since publication of his book declaring that race is of "declining significance." Rather, my intention is to illustrate the powerful influence of a power elite in canon formation.

If this were merely a case of a scholar catapulted to celebrity status, it would scarcely be worth our attention. But Wilson's message, notwithstanding its pretense of detached scholarship, had dire ramifications politically (which arguably is why he was elevated in the first place). In due time Wilson found himself on President Clinton's radar screen, and during the 1992 campaign, whenever Clinton was asked about race, he would cite the work of "the brilliant African-American sociologist William Julius Wilson" whose book *The Truly Disadvantaged* argued for a class-based policy that would expand the economy and generate jobs.[170] In his autobiography, Clinton writes: "I had become a convert to William Julius Wilson's argument, articulated in his book *The Truly Disadvantaged,* that there were no race-specific solutions to hard-core unemployment and poverty. The only answers were schools, adult education and training, and jobs."[171] Clearly, Clinton was invoking the Wizard of Harvard to justify his do-nothing policies when it came to the inner city or black people. Wilson can disavow responsibility for how his ideas are misrepresented by politicians, but as Adolph Reed has pointed out, "despite his prominence and visibility as a Democratic policy advisor, and the ease with which he can gain access to all main public forums, Wilson has never deigned to object publicly to the way his wrong-headed theories are borne out on the backs of poor people."[172]

The most devastating critique of Wilson's political entanglements came, not from a scholar or an activist, but from a journalist, Gretchen Reynolds, in a profile of Wilson in *Chicago* magazine. Reynolds wrote: "In the five years since the publication of his most famous book, *The Truly Disadvantaged*, Wilson has become the darling of centrist politicians for one reason: because he declared, in effect, that the best way to deal with racial issues was not to." Later she adds: "Wilson's prescriptions were of the grand-scale, society-wide variety. They began with a call for full employment. But what endeared Wilson to many national politicians—what turned Bill Clinton into an acolyte—was his de-emphasis of affirmative action."[173]

Wilson would subsequently demur that his advocacy of class-based politics and policy did not mean that he was opposed to affirmative action, and he joined the camp who contended that affirmative action should be based on class rather than race. Clearly, it was not Wilson's intention to undercut the black protest movement. On the contrary, the whole point of his "hidden agenda" was to provide political camouflage for programs that would benefit blacks. Nor can Wilson be blamed for the misappropriation of his ideas, whether by Clinton or by the enemies of affirmative action. However, Wilson did not use the leverage he had as one of the twenty-five most influential people in America to publicly denounce the appropriation of his "declining significance" argument for ends that he repudiated, like the dismantling of affirmative action. At times, furthermore, he advocated policies that were tantamount to "Negro removal" from coveted real estate in Chicago and New Orleans, all in the name of countering the putative "concentration effects" of poverty and moving these families, evicted from their homes and neighborhoods, "to opportunity."[174] One wonders if Wilson has ever questioned the political motives behind the accolades and grants that were showered on him. Wilson the man may be pure of heart, but the political function of Wilson mania was to provide intellectual legitimation, with a necessary black imprimatur, for the liberal retreat from race during the post–civil rights era.

The epitome of the scholarship of backlash came with the publication in 1995 of Dinesh D'Souza's *The End of Racism*. Alas, "declining significance" had been carried to its ludicrous extreme, to a claim that racism is a thing of the past. To deny the obvious, of course, requires some feats of intellectual jujitsu on D'Souza's part. Yes, inequalities exist, but these are not because of white racism, but rather because the black community is so riddled with cultural pathology that blacks are unable to grab the ladder of success. Yes, cab drivers won't pick up black fares, but this is because whites fear black crime. Yes, white employers or homeowners shun blacks, but it is because they are ineffectual workers or untrustworthy neighbors. D'Souza's message to blacks is to stop whining about racism and blaming whites for their problems, and to get their own cultural house in order. Invoking Booker T. Washington, D'Souza argues that it is up to blacks to close "the civilizational gap" with whites. As he writes: "The supreme challenge faced by African Americans is the one that Booker T. Washington outlined almost a century ago: the mission of building the civilization resources of a people whose culture is frequently unsuited to the requirements of the modern world."[175] [Give D'Souza some credit: he has an accurate "take" on Booker T. Washington, and by extension, Robert Ezra Park and the Chicago school of race relations!]

Liberal scholars have had a field day trashing The End of Racism. But how do we explain the canonization of the man who averred "declining significance," and the excommunication of the man who declared "the end of racism"? Granted, these two scholars arrive at their truths through different avenues. Wilson aligns himself with the struggle for racial and class justice, and on occasion has come out of the political closet and declared himself a social democrat. D'Souza is a right-wing ideologue who has no interest in race except to tweak the noses of his ideological enemies. He even goes so far as to advocate repealing those sections of the 1964 Civil Rights Act that curtail the right of individuals to freely discriminate against people whom they find objectionable. Let me be clear: Wilson and D'Souza are in antithetical political camps. Nevertheless, if we subject their writing to close scrutiny, it becomes clear that the reason that both writers arrive at the conclusion that racism is on the wane is because their books rest on the same theoretical underpinnings. To wit:

1 INSTITUTIONALIZED RACISM. D'Souza dismisses institutionalized racism as "a nonsense phrase," and criticizes civil rights activists "who have radicalized the definition of racism to locate it in the very structures of the American workplace."[176] Indeed, it is his rejection of the entire notion of institutionalized racism that allows him to reach the preposterous conclusion that "the end of racism" is at hand. But the same can be said of Wilson's The Declining Significance of Race. When one looks up "racism" in the index of Wilson's landmark study, the reader is referred to the entry on "racial

belief systems." Nor does the term "institutionalized racism" appear in the
index of Wilson's *When Work Disappears*, which purports to be a comprehensive study of the plight of the black underclass in Chicago.[177] This is
why Wilson can immerse himself for years of research on Chicago's South
Side—one of the most segregated cities in the United States—and fail to
see racism. It is a startling failure of sociological imagination, an inability
to see the forest for the trees.

2 OPPOSITIONAL CULTURE. Long before notions of biological inferiority came
on stream at the end of the nineteenth century, it was argued that Africans
were heathen and uncivilized, and this was used to give moral legitimacy
to slavery. As we have seen, the idea that culture, not genes, explains black
subordination, was central to Park's Weltanschauung. Over the decades it
has gone through a series of iterations, beginning with the "cultural depri-
vation" school in the 1950s, the "culture of poverty" theorists in the 1960s
and 1970s, and the "underclass" discourse of the 1980s. In recent years yet
another cultural theory has come on stream, this time with a Left twist.
Influenced by such theorists as Pierre Bourdieu and Paul Willis, it is now
argued that the poor develop an "oppositional culture," born out of resistance to oppression.

   The pitfalls of this theoretical position become apparent when Wilson
and D'Souza deploy the idea of oppositional culture. Wilson calls it "ghetto-
specific behavior," and asserts, "Through cultural transmission, individuals
develop a cultural repertoire that includes discrete elements that are relevant
to a variety of respective situations."[178] Now sounding like the leftist that
Wilson claims to be, D'Souza writes, "Black culture emerged out of the
crucible of racism and historical oppression directed specifically at blacks."
But he goes on to say that "what we have now is a downward spiral produced
by dysfunctional cultural orientations and destructive social policies."[179]
Thus, for all their political differences, both D'Souza and Wilson end up
locating the blame for black problems, not in external structures of class
or race, but in the cultural systems of blacks themselves.

3 RATIONAL DISCRIMINATION. According to D'Souza, when taxi drivers refuse
to pick up black patrons, they are responding to a fear of being mugged,
based on hard experience. He calls this "rational discrimination." In Chicago, Wilson found that many employers, including some black employers,

were reluctant to hire blacks and preferred Mexicans or other immigrants. Like D'Souza, Wilson concludes that these employers are not motivated by racism, but are acting rationally, based on negative experiences or perceptions of black workers.

But this position effectively defines racism out of existence! To counter this argument I retrieved my copy of Gordon Allport's 1954 classic, *The Nature of Prejudice*, from a dusty bookshelf. Allport defines prejudice as "an avertive or hostile attitude toward a person who belongs to a group, simply because he belongs to that group, and is therefore presumed to have the objectionable qualities ascribed to the group."[180] Employers in Wilson's study are acting on the basis of categorical distinctions, and hapless individuals are being denied employment not on the basis of their personal lack of qualifications, but on the basis of their group affiliation. It is a case of discrimination, plain and simple. To fail to recognize this, and to give credence to blanket stereotypes, is a stunning example of an epistemology of ignorance.

In a review of *When Work Disappears* in the *New Republic*, Joe Klein derides Wilson's use of such terms as "concentration effects" and "ghetto-related behavior." To quote Klein: "These, of course, are desperate euphemisms for the 'culture of poverty' that Wilson considers a neoconservative slur." Unlike D'Souza, Wilson may advocate jobs programs for the unemployed, but he has left himself wide open to Klein's counterpunch: "It would be a fantasy to believe that even a rigorous, lavishly funded jobs program would have much impact on the doom and devastation of the inner cities. The cultural forces pulling in the opposite direction are simply too powerful."[181]

Thus does Wilson hang himself by his own petards. As Joe Klein was shrewd to see, Wilson's "ideology is at war with his data." His liberal policy prescriptions are contradicted by the essentially conservative assumptions that undergird his study, allowing him to conclude that race is of "declining significance." D'Souza's principal transgression, which makes him a whipping boy of liberals, is that he blatantly violates the protocol of an epistemology of ignorance, by stating up front, in bold and unapologetic terms, messages that pervade liberal discourse but are cloaked in more circumspect and devious language. D'Souza is pummeled for his consistency and his bluntness, rather than engaging in the equivocation and self-contradiction of those who profess support for the black struggle, but blunder their way into positions that affirm or nourish racism or subvert antiracist policies.

PRESIDENT CLINTON'S RACE INITIATIVE: BACK TO THE FUTURE

Nowhere is the liberal retreat from race and the restoration of the antiquated and discredited race relations paradigm more evident than in President Clinton's race initiative. To arrive at this judgment, however, one has to cut through layers of fatuous and deceptive rhetoric, made all the worse because it was buttressed with good intentions. In the summer of 1997, Clinton launched his race initiative on this righteous note:

Will we become not one, but many Americas, separate, unequal and isolated? Or will we draw strength from all our people and our ancient faith in the quality of human dignity, to become the world's first truly multiracial democracy? That is the unfinished work of our time, to lift the burden of race and redeem the promise of America.[182]

Responsibility for the initiative was vested in an Advisory Board headed by John Hope Franklin, the august African American historian. The board was charged with stage managing a national dialogue on race, culminating with a Report to the President on how to "bridge the racial divide" and "achieve racial reconciliation."

Clinton's missionary tenor was echoed in the board's ultimate report: "Board members have spent the last 15 months seeking ways to build a more united and just America. They have canvassed the country meeting with and listening to Americans who revealed how race and racism have affected their lives."[183] Indeed, Appendix C of their report lists nearly 300 Advisory Board Events and Activities; Appendix D lists 175 One America Conversations and almost 1,400 dialogues on race that reached more than 18,000 people in 36 states and 113 cities; Appendix E lists nearly 600 schools and colleges across the nation that participated in a Campus Week of Dialogue with town hall meetings, lectures, film showings, and service events; Appendix F lists scores of states and cities that participated in Statewide Days of Dialogue events. Clearly, if racism could be talked to death, then we would have achieved Clinton's racial nirvana by now.

Adolph Reed has aptly described the national conversation on race as "a classically Clintonesque combo of psychobabble talk-show and televangelical faith-healing, dressed up as serious reflection on public issues."[184] That's not all. What about the "Race Initiative's initiator himself," Reed asks, "who has been so deeply implicated in the spread of corporate health care, pursuit of trade and investment policies that accelerate the global race to the bottom, who intensified the racist war on drugs and criminalization of inner-city minority populations, exponentially expanded the federal death penalty, eliminated the federal commitment to public assistance to the poor, led a retreat from the federal commitment to provide low-income housing, temporized about affirmative action, pandered to racist sensibilities ever since he capitalized on the execution of a poor, brain-damaged black Arkansan during his campaign for the 1992 presidential nomination"?[185] Was all this "yackety yack on race" merely a cover for Clinton's shoddy record on race? Or perhaps, as Clarence Lusane has suggested, another example of "Clinton's affliction for talking left and walking right"?[186]

The Advisory Board's Report to the President (hereafter "the Franklin Report," named after its venerable chairman, John Hope Franklin) was published under the title *One America in the 21st Century: Forging a New Future*. The authors of the report were clearly sensitive to the many skeptics who maintained that "we need action, not talk," and the report bulges with recommendations for bridging the racial divide and promoting harmony between the races. The problem, though, is that, at bottom, the race initiative was a throwback to the race relations model, with its Myrdalian reduction of racism to the level of individual beliefs and actions. It was as though the Civil Rights Revolution never happened! With all the good intentions that pave the road to hell, the Advisory Board effectively nullified the concept of institutionalized racism that, as I argued earlier, was the most important conceptual innovation that emerged from the decade of protest and that was central to the Kerner Commission report. As Claire Kim has written, "Exactly three decades after the Kerner Commission completed its work, the President's Initiative on Race dramatically reformulated the American race problem."[187]

Specifically, in lieu of the Kerner Commission's focus on structural racism, the Advisory Board reduced the problem of race to promoting tolerance and mutual understanding. The implications of this conceptual difference become crystal clear when one examines the respective action agendas of the two reports. The Kerner Commission concluded with seventy-three pages of policy recommendations that envisioned a comprehensive program of economic development and social reconstruction targeted at poverty areas and racial ghettos. Not only does the Franklin Report lack any such policy initiatives, but there is no sense of crisis that the three pillars of antiracist public policy—affirmative action, school desegregation, and racial districting—had all been eviscerated by actions of all three branches of government over several decades. Nor is there mention that Clinton signed the legislation that abolished welfare entitlements, which will inevitably widen the racial gap in income and living standards.

It is true that the Franklin Report includes an endorsement of affirmative action, albeit a tepid one, along with a litany of vague proposals for reforming housing, health care, education, and criminal justice. Its main thrust, however, is on bridging the racial divide through dialogue. Once again, the academic establishment failed to act while Rome burned, except that we are asked, not to fiddle, but to dialogue! To reach that dubious objective, the board's report provides us with a dazzling array of alternatives: One America Conversations, Campus Weeks of Dialogue, Statewide Days of Dialogue, meetings, forums, conferences, public service announcements, and visits to the One America Website.

The Franklin Report reaches its inane epitome in its concluding section, entitled "Ten Things Every American Should Do to Promote Racial Reconciliation." Here we see a breathtaking betrayal of the sociological tradition. It is as though Durkheim concluded his masterpiece with Ten Things Everybody Should Do to Avoid Suicide. Or Weber offered Ten Tips For Succeeding in Business. Or Marx proposed a WPA-style Jobs Program for the Lumpen Proletariat. But if the president's Advisory Board on Race has displayed an abysmal failure of sociological imagination, who are we to blame but the sociologist of "race relations" who has perennially reduced social facts down to the level of individual predispositions? What can we hope of a presidential commission or the public at large if so-called race experts, despite their assiduous labors, still do not see that good race relations are unattainable—indeed inconceivable—unless there is a basic parity of condition between the black and white citizens of this nation?

In effect, the Clinton race initiative represented the restoration of an epistemology of ignorance, marked far more by its opacities and omissions than by any acts of commission. Therefore, it is not surprising that the board's report was assailed by critics on the Left—"race men" and "class men" alike. They spoke the unpalatable truths that experts of race relations have so long suppressed:

- Frances Fox Piven: "The Board compliments the nation lavishly on our racial progress—and there has been progress—but it does not frontally address the growing and deep divide that compounds race differences with class differences. Obviously, this new racial and class configuration is the result of the rapid polarization of income and wealth of the past 25 years which, given persistent racism together with educational disadvantage, hits racial minorities harder. The working and middle classes are more diverse, to be sure. But the poor are poorer, and the welfare rolls are increasingly composed of Blacks and Hispanics."[188]

- Clarence Lusane: "There is no call for massive social intervention on the part of the state similar to the 1930s Works Progress Administration or the 1960s War on Poverty efforts. A substantial, multi-year domestic Marshall Plan is minimally needed if there is to be a significant advance in ending the class dimensions of racism."[189]

- Manning Marable: "A real conversation about race must examine critically the institutional barriers that have been erected to subordinate people of color, denying them an equal voice in society. Such a conversation would interrogate white politicians and government officials who push for so-called 'race-blind' initiatives, which only buttress white racial privilege. As W.E.B. Du Bois knew, the struggle to uproot racism requires 'race-conscious solutions.' Only by talking honestly about the institutions and policies that perpetuate white power and privilege can we begin the long and difficult journey toward reconciliation."[190]

- Chester Hartman: "[Is] the President's Initiative any more or other than yet another largely time-buying, windowdressing move to give the impression that Something Is Being Done about the country's historic, deeply grounded racism?"[191]

In his article in *The Progressive*, aptly entitled "Yackety-Yak about Race," Adolph Reed delivered the coup de grâce to the race initiative:

> The problem isn't racial division or a need for healing. It is racial inequality and injustice. And the remedy isn't an elaborately choreographed pageantry of essentializing yackety-yak about group experience, cultural difference, pain, and the inevitable platitudes about understanding. Rather, we need a clear commitment by the federal government to preserve, buttress, and extend civil rights *and* to use the office of the Presidency to indicate that commitment forcefully and unambiguously. As the lesson of the past three decades in the South makes clear, this is the only effective way to change racist attitudes and beliefs.[192]

Against the backdrop of the homilies and placebos that fill the Franklin Report, one has to be struck by the acuity of these dissident voices, steeped as they are in a paradigm that substitutes "oppression" for "race relations," that does not treat racism as an anomaly that can be remedied through a national program of group therapy, and that does not shirk from impugning major political and economic institutions for their complicity in producing and reproducing the racial inequalities that rend American society. The fact that such voices were not represented on the board, or even the staff, of the president's commission is stark evidence of the politics that pervaded the commission—its constitution, proceedings, and reports.[193] It is also proof of the continuing marginalization of radical and minority voices within an academic establishment that welcomes dissent, so long as it is safely contained on the margins.

The slogan hurled by protestors—NO JUSTICE, NO PEACE—contains an elemental truth: that we are faced with an ultimate choice between peace and justice. The root problem with "white sociology"—indeed, what makes it "white"—is that it has been far more concerned with peace than with justice. Here we arrive at the crucial insight: that the famed "race relations" model, in its ideology and praxis, was a system of racial pacification, one that was willing to forgo racial justice for the sake of racial peace. This was the driving force behind the genesis of the race relations paradigm, and its transmission to generations of sociologists down to the present.

Blacks, on the other hand, have abundant reason to put more weight on justice than on a peace that, from their standpoint, does not feel like peace. In his famous "Letter from a Birmingham Jail," Martin Luther King drew a distinction between "a negative peace which is the absence of tension" and "a positive peace which is the presence of justice."[194] He also argued that polarization and conflict are sometimes necessary to shake white society out of its apathy and intransigence. This is what stirs in the gut of the protestor who, whether out of determination or despair, bellows: NO JUSTICE, NO PEACE. But the overall thrust of mainstream sociology, from Park down to the present, has been to devise ways to reduce tension rather than to promote justice. It has been a project of pacification rather than reparation.

Stripped bare of the necessary conceptual tools for grasping the meaning of conflict, Everett Hughes and his minions were at a loss when black insurgency unexpectedly erupted and threw the entire society into crisis. Indeed, "insurgency" was not a word that existed in the sociological lexicon.[195] Eventually, as we have seen, the seismic changes that shook American society at its foundations forced sociology to open its canon to radical and minority voices that had long been kept on the margins, and the result was "a scholarship of confrontation" that, for the first time, reflected the sensibilities and interests of the oppressed, and championed justice over peace. This, as we have also seen, was short lived, and a scholarship of backlash, bolstered by a general racial backlash in the larger society, gradually reinstated the victim-blaming discourses that anteceded the civil rights era.

To be sure, there are legions of scholars in the academic trenches who valiantly endeavor to forge what Edward Said called "an antithetical scholarship" that opposes hegemonic discourses and reflects the interests and viewpoints of subaltern groups. They are modern incarnations of the black radical tradition and the Marxist tradition that have challenged the main currents of sociology ever since the establishment of the first department of sociology at the University of Chicago a century ago. A case could be made that these insurgent scholars have more leverage and influence in the profession than ever before, at least judged by the politics of the individuals who have been elected to the presidency of the American Sociological Association in recent years. In his presidential address in 2001, Joe Feagin cited the views of Albion Small and other of sociology's founders who held that sociology should not be an end in itself, but should also improve society. Feagin proposed an ambitious "social justice agenda" for the twenty-first century.[196] Similarly, in his presidential address in 2004, Michael Burawoy implored sociologists to broaden the scope of the discipline beyond "professional sociology," and "to recognize the legitimacy and value of a normative sociology that engages in advocacy and activism in pursuit of progressive ideals."[197]

The larger issue, however, concerns intellectual hegemony: which viewpoints prevail, which are influential in major intellectual and political discourses, which shape public policy, which are represented on presidential commissions, which are represented on the boards of foundations and those other organizations that determine, through their grants and subsidies, knowledge production. By these criteria, it is difficult to avoid the conclusion that Stanford Lyman's rebuke still holds: "Sociology . . . has been part of the problem and not part of the solution."[198]

What would an affirmative epistemology on race entail? In the first place, an affirmative epistemology would dispense with the façade of value-free social science, a posture that only privileges the racial status quo. It would commit itself to antiracism, whether in the realm of ideas or public policy. This is the starting point for *not* ignoring the ugly realities of race, for *not* trivializing racism as disembodied beliefs and attitudes, for *not* shifting the focus of analysis and blame away from structures of oppression and onto people who are the living legacy of slavery. A perspective that conceives of race as structure would expose the extent to which the United States and its major institutions are still stratified by race. It would show that the much-ballyhooed progress of the black middle class is a result, not of a deracialization of labor markets, but on the contrary, of affirmative action policies whose purpose was to override racist barriers. Instead of the standard cant about "progress," we would see that this is a period of backlash when the hard-won gains of the civil rights protest era have been eviscerated or lost altogether. Instead of using past atrocities as the baseline for measuring progress, we would insist on total parity, after three centuries, between the black and white citizens of this nation.

The choice ultimately is between a sociology that, despite its liberal pretensions, is wedded to a liberal variant of the racial status quo, or a sociology that lives up to the emancipatory promise of its classical tradition by putting social structure at the center of sociological inquiry, and committing itself unequivocally to the antiracist struggle. It would be a sociology that does not trade justice for a negative peace.

PART THREE

ETHNICITY: THE EPISTEMOLOGY OF WISHFUL THINKING

> I warn the US that if you think you are going to get tacos and
> nachos from me, you are going to be very surprised. I want
> the United States of America. I want to swallow you up. I
> have already swallowed your language and now it is mine.
>
> *Richard Rodriquez, "La Raza Cosmica"*[1]

"EVERY SOCIETY, EVERY NATION, AND EVERY civilization has been a kind of melting pot and has thus contributed to the intermingling of races by which new races and new cultures eventually emerge."[2] So wrote Robert Ezra Park in 1937. It is a testament to Park's prescience that he was able to imagine the melting pot at a time when the United States was ethnically more diverse, and more fragmented, than every before. During the previous half century, the nation had absorbed over twenty-five million immigrants, mostly from Eastern and Southern Europe. These "new immigrants"—Italians, Greeks, Poles, Russian Jews, Ukrainians, Hungarians and others, far removed geographically and culturally from the people who settled the United States during its first century—were widely believed to be "unassimilable." In Chicago, for example, 70 percent of the population consisted of immigrants and the children of immigrants, and the city was divided into a patchwork of ethnic neighborhoods. When Park assumed his position at the University of Chicago in 1914, the backlash against the immigrant "invasion" was at its peak. Finally, in 1921 Congress passed legislation that drastically cut back the volume of immigration and instituted nationality quotas based on the representation of a given nationality in the 1910 census. Not satisfied, three years later the restrictionists passed a law that not only further reduced the volume of immigration, but also pegged nationality quotas to the 1890 census, before the influx from Eastern and Southern Europe. Effectively this meant that future immigration would be restricted mainly to the nations in Northern and Western Europe, thus preserving the purity of the old Anglo-American stock.

Against this background, Park's dictum that "every nation, upon examination, turns out to have been a more or less successful melting-pot" provided reassurance that the intermingling of peoples was a universal process and that America's ethnic discord would resolve itself over time.[3] This evolutionary optimism had paradoxical consequences with respect to immigrant as opposed to colonized minorities. In the first instance, it undercut nativism and projected a future where immigrants would be successfully incorporated into the body politic. In the case of colonized minorities, however, Park's evolutionary optimism was his fatal flaw. It elided the extent to which Indians, Africans, Mexicans, and "Orientals" were imperial subjects, identified by an indelible mark of color, deprived of rights of citizenship, ruthlessly exploited, and relegated to live in reservations, ghettos, barrios, and Chinatowns encircled by barriers of discrimination. All groups endured "prejudice" and "discrimination," but Park's fatal elision was his failure to theorize the difference in the systems of bigotry that befell immigrant as opposed to colonized minorities. In the case of immigrants, the message was one of incorporation: You will be one of us, whether you want to or not. But in the case of the nation's colonized minorities, the message was one of exclusion: No matter how much you are like us, you will remain apart.

As much as Park's evolutionary optimism was a detriment when it came to the nation's colonized minorities, it was the source of his perspicacity when it came to immigrants. It allowed him to look beyond the messy and chaotic events on the ground, and to imagine a future where these immigrants, though degraded and maligned, would eventually be fused culturally and even biologically with the dominant group, forming a new nationality. Thus the political paradox: the implications of Park's race relations cycle were liberatory when it came to immigrant minorities—in that it belied the fears and allegations of nativists. But when it came to colonized minorities, the race relations cycle amounted to a form of epistemic violence. It turned a blind eye to the horrific crimes visited against these peoples, and fostered complacency by projecting an optimism that the problems of the moment would be resolved with the sheer passage of time.

One caveat is necessary: the line between colonized and immigrant minorities was not drawn entirely on the basis of color difference. Nativists equated "Anglo Saxon" with whiteness, and therefore uncertainty about the "whiteness" of immigrants abounded. At least this is the contention of a recent genre of "whiteness studies" whose central tenet is that when they first arrived, the Irish, Poles, Hungarians, Hebrews, and especially those swarthy Italians faced the possibility of being lumped together with the nation's racial pariahs.[4] Perhaps so. After all, these groups were hardly embraced fraternally as kinfolk! Rather, they were seen as distinct races, defined by biology and culture alike.

In making their point, however, scholars of whiteness repeat Park's conceptual error: they obscure what was fundamentally different between "the races of Europe" and colonized minorities. Although the term "race" was broadly applied to European immigrants and they were denigrated and abused, they were hardly subjected to the all-encompassing system of domination and exploitation that was the destiny of colonized minorities. Unlike colonized minorities, immigrants were rapidly absorbed into the center of an expanding industrial economy. Moreover, bigotry against immigrants was never sanctioned by law and enforced by the state, as was the case for Native Americans and African Americans, Mexicans in the Southwest, and Chinese on the West Coast. To say this is not to engage in a frivolous "comparative suffering," as is often alleged. On the contrary, it affirms a crucial historical fact: that colonized minorities were subject to a unique oppression, different in kind as well as degree. Unless this is fully grasped, it becomes impossible to explain the divergent trajectories of colonized and immigrant minorities throughout American history, down to the present. And once grasped, it is no longer surprising that "the races of Europe" were ultimately accepted into the fraternity of whiteness.

To repeat, Park's fundamental error was lumping racial and ethnic groups within the same theoretical framework, and this explains why Park could be so mistaken when it came to race and so prescient when it came to ethnicity.

To the nativists who feared that the nation's open-door immigration policy amounted to "race suicide," Park had a compelling rejoinder: "The modern Italian, Frenchman, and German is a composite of the broken fragments of several different racial stocks."[5] Park understood more completely than anybody else that what we were observing in the United States was more than the making of a new nation. It was the making of the first truly global people—an amalgam of literally all of the peoples on the planet.

At the time that Park wrote, the idea of the United States as a melting pot was very much a part of popular discourse, thanks in large measure to Israel Zangwill's 1908 play, *The Melting-Pot.*[6] At the end of the drama, Zangwill's hero cries out triumphantly:

Ah, what a stirring and seething! Celt and Latin, Slav and Teuton, Greek and Syrian,—black and yellow . . . East and West, and North and South, the palm and the pine, the pole and the equator, the crescent and the cross—how the great Alchemist melts and fuses them with his purging flame![7]

For Zangwill and Park alike, the melting pot had positive, almost messianic, connotations of regeneration and rebirth. It represented the triumph of the cosmopolitan ideal over narrow parochialism.[8]

Park's optimism about the outcome of immigration was shared by the next generation of Chicago sociologists. When W. Lloyd Warner and Leo Srole conducted field studies of immigrant communities in the 1940s, they held firm to the assimilation model. They recognized that the ethnic enclave, though it seemed to nurture separatism and isolation, actually functioned as a decompression chamber, allowing immigrants to adjust to their new surroundings and preparing the next generation to venture forth into the mainstream. Contrary to appearances, the ethnic community functioned as an instrument of assimilation.[9]

The assimilation paradigm ruled supreme during the period bracketed by the two World Wars. The prevailing view was that ethnicity was a relic of the past, destined to wither away with the advance of industrialization and modernity.

After World War II, however, a new generation of sociologists came on stream who vehemently rejected the idea of the melting pot. Many of these scholars were children of immigrants who clawed their way up the academic ladder. Their revisionist view of the melting pot can be seen as part of a broader trend among the partially deracinated progeny of immigrants: assimilation breeds nostalgia. Thus, we are left with the irony: immigrants who are most authentically steeped in ethnic culture tend to throw it away, often with both hands, as they doggedly pursue the opportunities that led them to immigrate in the first place. Decades later, their largely assimilated children and grandchildren engage in desperate, but usually futile, efforts to recover the very culture that their parents relinquished. As children of immigrants entered the ranks of social science, they brought this same nostalgia to their analysis of ethnic trends. Assimilation came to be viewed, not as rebirth, but as obliteration.

The turning point came with the publication of *Beyond the Melting Pot* in 1963. Nathan Glazer and Daniel Patrick Moynihan, each of whom had ascended from immigrant poverty to the ivory tower, conducted a broad study of ethnic groups in New York City, and concluded that "the point about the melting pot is that it did not happen."[10] The syntax of this much-quoted passage warrants a moment's reflection. To say that the melting pot "did not happen" is not the same as saying that it was not happening. Indeed, Glazer and Moynihan's core argument was that ethnic groups had shed much of their original culture and had evolved new identities in the United States. Thus, their famous title was at odds with their own contentions, as historian Philip Gleason has shrewdly observed:

Glazer and Moynihan invited an oversimplified reading by the title they chose and by the statement, made twice, that "the point about the melting pot is that it did not happen." For, despite this seemingly categorical assertion, they did not deny the reality of assimilation. On the contrary, they regarded assimilation as a powerful solvent that washed out immigrant languages, customs, and "the specifically *national* aspect." For that reason they looked upon "the dream of 'cultural pluralism,'" as no more realistic than "the hope of a 'melting pot.'" Glazer and Moynihan might therefore have said with equal justice that cultural pluralism "did not happen" either.[11]

However, it was not Glazer and Moynihan's core argument, but their enticing title, that took hold in the canon. Aside from selling over 300,000 copies, *Beyond the Melting Pot* marked a paradigm shift in the study of ethnicity. For Glazer and Moynihan and their legions of readers, there was clearly a sense of relief and vindication that the melting pot did not happen.

This claim, though pregnant with self-contradiction, fit perfectly into the emerging Zeitgeist. By the early 1970s other books appeared that trumpeted the survival of ethnicity over the sinister forces of assimilation. Their titles celebrated *The Decline of the WASP* and *The Rise of the Unmeltable Ethnics*.[12] In 1972 an article in the *New York Times Magazine* proclaimed in bold letters, "America Is NOT a Melting Pot."[13] Indeed, these writers contended that the United States was undergoing an "ethnic revival" that would resuscitate immigrant cultures. Again, there is a striking historical irony. When ethnic groups were intact and cultural differences pronounced, leading sociologists held that assimilation was inevitable. Several decades later, when these groups had undergone profound transformation, forsaking major elements of their ancestral cultures and comfortably embracing identities as Americans, the prevailing view was that the melting pot "did not happen."

But such attempts to "wish assimilation away" would prove difficult to sustain intellectually. With the exception of Native Americans and Chicanos in territories annexed from Mexico, ethnic groups in the United States are transplanted peoples, far removed in time and space from their original homelands. The necessity of adapting to life in the United States made assimilation, in Park's words, "progressive and irreversible."[14] Herbert Gans was one of the first to cast a skeptical eye on the ethnic revival. In 1974 he wrote: "Even the raw materials for an ethnic cultural revival in America are unavailable, and despite the claim of some ethnic intellectuals, so is the interest for such a revival."[15] In that same year Gunnar Myrdal dismissed the ethnic movement as "upper-class intellectual romanticism."[16] In *The Ethnic Myth*, published in 1981, I contended that the ethnic revival was actually a symptom of decline, "a dying gasp" of ethnic consciousness on the part of groups already at an advanced stage of assimilation.[17]

The long-term trends all suggested that the melting pot was working just as the Chicago sociologists had predicted. The grandchildren of immigrants had largely forsaken their ancestral language and culture. To be sure, they clung with pride to shards of their cultural past, but they had been transformed into Americans by the schools, by the tentacles of mass culture, and by the sheer passage of time. The closer the grandchildren of immigrants came to fulfilling the immigrant dream of mobility and success, the further they drifted from the *World of Our Fathers*, to use Irving Howe's lyrical title. Geographical mobility—to the suburbs—followed economic mobility, and assimilation owed far more to the centrifugal effects of the suburbs than it did to the centripetal effects of the city, where ethnicity thrived in distinctive ethnic enclaves. More recently, the gender revolution dealt another blow to ethnicity, if only because women were liberated from the kitchen and the laborious food preparation that literally nurtured ethnicity. And the upshot of all these changes—the acid test of assimilation—was a soaring rate of intermarriage across ethnic and religious lines. Richard Alba used 1990 census data to document marriage patterns among the current generation of adults (born between 1956 and 1965). The percent whose spouse's ancestry was different from their own was as follows: Germans, 52 percent; English, 62 percent; Irish, 65 percent; Italians, 73 percent; French, 78 percent; Scots/Scots-Irish, 82 percent; Polish, 84 percent.[18] Overall, 56 percent of U.S.-born whites were married to spouses whose ancestry differed from their own, and only a fifth had spouses with an identical ethnic background.[19] Clearly, for the descendents of the great waves of European immigration in the nineteenth and early twentieth centuries, the marital melting pot is a reality.

Nevertheless, the main current of thought in sociology during the 1960s and 1970s was to steadfastly reject the assimilation model and, following Glazer and Moynihan's lead, to celebrate ethnicity's triumph over the dreaded melting pot. To reach this implausible conclusion, however, sociologists had to engage in tortuous mental gymnastics. Let me postulate five "rules of sociological method" that sustain an epistemology of wishful thinking. *[Dear Reader: Were you hoping that I went away for good? There has been less to carp about since wishful thinking on ethnicity is less pernicious and far less lethal than willful ignorance on race. In both cases science is deployed to validate cherished beliefs, though with this difference: In the case of an epistemology of ignorance, to avoid the incrimination and dissonances of racism, sociologists engaged in denial, evasion, and as a final resort, obfuscation. They had to deny a reality before their eyes: an oppressed people whose very presence made a lie of their cherished assumptions about American democracy and decency. In the case of ethnicity, however, a different set of impulses and defenses kicked in. Now it was a matter, not of denying a reality before their eyes, but rather of imagining a reality that they yearned for—an ethnicity that, like a Phoenix, could rise from its own ashes.]*

Rule 1: Defining Assimilation Out of Existence. Epistemological trouble begins with the metaphor of "the melting pot." It conjures up an image of a bubbling cauldron into which immigrants descend—whether they jump or are pushed is another matter—and are quickly dissolved into oblivion. With this as a benchmark, one can declare triumphantly: The melting pot did not happen.

The language and the imagery of a "melting pot" totally obscure the evolutionary logic that was central to Robert Park's theory. For Park, assimilation is a process that occurs incrementally across generations. Thus, Glazer and Moynihan's declaration that the melting pot "did not happen" is little more than a rhetorical diversion from the question they wished to avoid: was assimilation happening? Was ethnicity becoming *less* significant as a basis for personal identity and group cohesion? Indeed, one could take the facts as presented in *Beyond the Melting Pot*, add some that were left out, and arrive at a new title: *The Declining Significance of Ethnicity*. Now, ask yourself: would a book with this title have become an instant classic? Would it have sold over 300,000 copies? How are we to explain the fact that, as a rhetorical frame, "declining significance" was irresistible when applied to racism, but unpalatable when applied to ethnicity? What does this say about the canon on ethnicity? Are our "classics" nothing more than a hit parade of books that are ideologically congenial?[20]

Rule 2: The Ethnic Academy. Paradigm shifts with regard to ethnicity have coincided with an ethnic succession in the profession itself.[21] The first generation of Chicago sociologists, like Park, were mostly old-stock Americans from small-town, Protestant backgrounds.[22] While this is also the soil that gave rise to nativism, these scholars envisioned a liberal alternative whereby immigrants would be assimilated. Essentially, "assimilation" was a circumlocution for "Americanization," in that it substituted the language of biology for the language of politics. However, the image of being digested and disgorged was hardly pleasing to immigrants, though some did embrace the trope of rebirth. For example, Mary Antin began her autobiography *The Promised Land* on this rhapsodic note: "I was born, I have lived, and I have been made over."[23]

An early dissenter from the assimilation model was Horace Kallen, a young philosopher of German-Jewish extraction who was also an early Zionist. Kallen coined the term "cultural pluralism" and promoted it as a societal ideal in a 1915 article in *The Nation*, "Democracy Versus the Melting Pot: With Special Reference to the Jewish Group."[24] The subtitle is noteworthy because it raises the question: Was cultural pluralism a specifically Jewish project, at least insofar as it was embraced and advanced by self-identified Jewish scholars? Did it entail an ideology and a politics that were particularly congenial to Jews, given their experiences as a perennial minority that wrestled with the dilemma of maintaining ethnic loyalties while demanding full rights of citizenship? Kallen's conception of nations within a nation seemed to strike that delicate balance, thus providing an ideological alternative to the melting pot.

Several caveats are necessary. Needless to say, all minorities grapple with the quandary of living in two worlds and not fully belonging to either, and thus have existential reason to embrace the idea of cultural pluralism. It was also the case that some of the early advocates of cultural pluralism, such as Hutchins Hapgood and Randolph Bourne, were from old American stock. Hapgood looked with admiration on "the spirit of the ghetto," to cite the title of his book.[25] Bourne looked to immigrants to provide a cosmopolitan alternative to the provincialism and materialism that, he believed, pervaded American society.[26] Finally, during the "ethnic revival" of the 1970s, some of the most ardent advocates of cultural pluralism were not Jewish. For example, Andrew Greeley, who is both a sociologist and a priest, wrote *Why Can't They Be Like Us? America's White Ethnic Groups*, and Michael Novak, in *The Rise of the Unmeltable Ethnics*, championed the cause of white ethnics who clashed with the racial liberalism of that period.[27] Even so, as R. Fred Wacker observes in his paper on "Assimilation and Cultural Pluralism in American Social Thought," "the development of the ideology [of cultural pluralism] was shaped by the universalistic yet paradoxically particularistic goals and assumptions of Jewish intellectuals."[28]

Indeed, Zangwill and Kallen can be seen as representing two opposing strands of modern Jewish thought. One reacts against pariah status and is willing to forsake ties to the past for the promise of full integration into the surrounding society. The other seeks to have it "both ways," and to insist on full participation in the public sphere at the same time that ethnic solidarities are preserved in the private sphere. Against Zangwill's "melting pot," Kallen invoked the metaphor of an "orchestra" where each instrument contributed to the symphony of civilization.

Kallen was also reacting to the coercive tactics of the Americanization movement that sought to make Americans of the children of immigrants. He imported the idea of "a federation of nationalities" from Central Europe, where minority leaders proposed this as a democratic alternative to monistic regimes that did not recognize the rights of minorities.[29] It made its way into sociological discourse in a 1920 book by another Jewish scholar, Isaac Berkson, *Theories of Americanization*.[30] Berkson posited three "theories" of ethnic adjustment: "the Americanization theory," "the melting pot theory," and "the federation of nationalities theory." His personal position was clear: he feared the melting pot as amounting to the erasure of group identities, and regarded cultural pluralism as a more palatable alternative.

However, the idea of cultural pluralism withered on the academic vine for several decades until it was resurrected by Nathan Glazer, in an article he wrote for *Commentary* in 1953 under the title "America's Ethnic Pattern: 'Melting Pot' or 'Nation of Nations'?" Glazer's core argument was essentially the same as the one he would expound a decade later in *Beyond the Melting Pot*: that ethnic groups in the United States did not retain much of the language and culture of their countries of origin, but existed as "ghost nations, built around ideologies of support of the home countries, and drawing their real strength from experiences in America which make their elements feel less than full Americans."[31]

Clearly, the rhetorical position that "the melting pot never happened" was congenial to Jewish intellectuals and activists at *Commentary*, a publication of the American Jewish Congress that reached a broader audience of intellectuals, thus exemplifying that delicate blend of universalism and particularism. In 1952 *Commentary* disinterred and published an obscure speech that Marcus Hansen had delivered to the Augustana Historical Society in 1938, in which he advanced his now-famous thesis of "third-generation return," postulating that "what the son wishes to forget the grandson wishes to remember."[32] Oscar Handlin, the son of Jewish immigrants and the first self-identified Jew to be granted tenure in the History Department at Harvard, wrote a foreword in which he contended that Hansen's thesis had broad application to Jews and non-Jews alike. Thus, *Commentary* again served as the venue for the projection of this seminal idea into academic discourse, and Glazer cited and amplified Hansen's thesis in his article a year later on "America's Ethnic Pattern." Here was an optimistic counterpoint to the assimilation thesis: if there was a third-generation return, there was hope, still, of avoiding the ethnic apocalypse.

In 1964 (a year after the publication of *Beyond the Melting Pot*), the cultural pluralist position got another boost with the publication of Milton Gordon's *Assimilation in American Life*.[33] Gordon refurbished Berkson's tripartite schema with new terminology: Anglo-American conformity, the melting pot, and cultural pluralism. Gordon's book was hugely influential, thanks to a more favorable Zeitgeist in 1964 for the idea of cultural pluralism. Unlike 1920, when Berkson published *Theories of Americanization*, ethnic groups had demonstrated their loyalty to the nation during World War II and had traveled far down the road of assimilation. In this historical context, the call for cultural pluralism seemed more a plea for tolerance than a radical revisioning of the nation as a federation of nationalities.

Another reason why Kallen's idea and Berkson's schema were more palatable in 1964 was that sociology had been transformed. Not only did the discipline expand exponentially during the decades following World War II, but its ranks were increasingly populated with the children of immigrants, many of whom were Jewish.[34] This was especially true in the nascent field of "race and ethnic relations," and therefore it is reasonable to pose a taboo question: To what extent were the ethnic allegiances and sensibilities of Jewish scholars inflected on the canon?[35] Was the cultural pluralism model, as theory and as ideology, particularly compatible with their ideals, experiences, and perceived interests?

The dominant position that scholars of Jewish origin enjoyed in the field of race and ethnic relations waned during the post–civil rights era. Two things happened. One was the entry of blacks and other racial minorities who previously had little representation in the field. The other development was a gradual influx of the children of post-1965 immigrants. In both cases a contributing factor has been the establishment of ethnic studies programs that provide institutional anchorage, including those all-important professorial lines. The result has been an outpouring of research on both race and immigration, much of it—though certainly not all—conducted by ethnic insiders. And the cultural pluralism model of the older generation morphed into a new school of thought under the banner of multiculturalism, again reflecting group ideals, experiences, and interests.

Rule 3: Knowing Where to Fish. In *What Is History?* Edward Carr compares the historian to the fisherman who knows where to go for the fish he wants, and in an allusion to method, what kind of tackle to use.[36] Sociologists of ethnicity know where to go to find ethnicity: in the multiplicity of ethnic communities, urban enclaves, neighborhoods, religious and cultural institutions, or informal settings where ethnicity not only persists, but thrives. The result has been a plethora of studies that provide much fodder for their contention that the melting pot is a myth. The problem is that the most assimilated members of these groups are outside the survey researcher's sampling frame or the ethnographer's purview, and consequently these studies yield an exaggerated picture of ethnic persistence.[37] If assimilation rather than ethnicity were the focal point of inquiry, researchers would fish in different waters and come up with drastically different results.

Another problem with the discourse on assimilation is that it presents two stark alternatives: ethnic persistence or assimilation. In reality, this is a false dichotomy: both occur simultaneously in different segments of the ethnic population. Historian John Higham had it right when he wrote that this is a situation of smaller and stronger cores and larger and weaker fringes.[38] However, the smaller and stronger cores have commanded far more attention in the social sciences than the larger and weaker fringes. Thus, we are left with the question: Which is the better barometer of the future—the smaller and stronger cores or the larger and weaker fringes?

Rule 4: Defining Ethnicity Down. I noted earlier how sociologists have made it semantically difficult to assimilate. At the same time, they have made it semantically easier to pass the test of ethnicity. One can trace the defining down of ethnicity across generations of sociologists who, confronted with increasing evidence of assimilation, have had to engage in artful hairsplitting to defend their position that the melting pot was a myth.

Thus, one generational cohort contended, along with Glazer and Moynihan, that ethnic groups exhibit a pattern of "accommodation without assimilation," implying that immigrant groups successfully adapted to their new circumstances. When later studies turned up compelling evidence that these reconfigured cultures were themselves breaking down, sociologists retreated to the position that cultural pluralism may be on the decline, but "structural pluralism"—parallel communities based on subjective identities—persisted.[39] A next position conceded that structural pluralism was also breaking down, but insisted that assimilation does not lead to amalgamation. When subsequent research showed that the rates of exogamy were soaring, even among Jews where exogamy was historically low, sociologists launched meticulous studies to determine whether the non-Jewish partner converted and whether the children of these hybrid couples retained the ethnicity of the Jewish parent.[40]

For example, Calvin Goldscheider, a leading scholar of American Jewish life and a consummate demographer, acknowledges that the rate of intermarriage among American Jews has risen to between 40 and 50 percent, but declares that this "does not necessarily mean erosion of the Jewish community." Indeed, according to Goldscheider, "intermarriage may even imply strength when significant proportions of the intermarried are actively involved in being Jewish and practicing Judaism."[41] With this flurry of wishful thinking, fears about "the vanishing Jew" are allayed, and exogamy, once thought to be the death knell of collective existence, magically becomes "a new basis for optimism about the future of Jewish communities around the world."[42]

With these shifting definitions, scholars of ethnicity keep moving back the goalposts of assimilation, assuring that few people will ever pass through.

Rule 5: Redefining Assimilation as Ethnogenesis. In an influential paper published in 1976, "Emergent Ethnicity: A Review and Reformulation," William Yancey, Eugene Ericksen, and Richard Juliani accused melting pot theorists of employing "a static view of culture." On the premise that that culture is always changing, they cast doubt on the relevance of "the portable heritage" that immigrants carry over with them. Thus, they concede that Italian Americans, for example, bear little resemblance to their distant cousins in Italy, but contend that Italian Americans have developed a distinctive ethnic culture tailored to their circumstances on American soil.[43] The implication is that this reconstituted ethnicity, far from signifying social death, is proof of the persistence and resiliency of ethnic cultures. From the vantage point of the country of origin, this may look like assimilation, but is actually an example of ethnogenesis, the successful adaptation of cultures to their new circumstances. Thus, with this rhetorical sleight of hand, the melting pot is defined out of existence.

The problem is that this argument does not withstand scrutiny. It may be true, as Kathleen Neils Conzen and her colleagues point out, that "ethnic groups in modern settings are constantly recreating themselves in response to changing realities both within the group and the host society."[44] However, this theoretical position only raises doubt about the ethnic future. What is the ultimate endpoint of this process of incessant change? When does cultural change stretch to the point that there is an irreparable breach with that "portable heritage," and people tell the probing census taker: "I'm just plain American"? Besides, it is wrong to portray assimilation theory as "static" since

it, too, presumes cultural change—in the direction of assimilation and ultimate amalgamation! Thus, the key question remains: Does this reconstituted
ethnicity provide the basis for a stable and enduring ethnicity? Or is it merely
a transitional phase in a long-term assimilation process? In other words, are
we observing ethnogenesis or assimilation itself?

Notwithstanding the artful hairsplitting in the realm of theory, and the
cherry picking in the realm of data, the evidence is overwhelming that the descendants of the great waves of immigration during the nineteenth and early
twentieth centuries are at an advanced stage of assimilation. Indeed, they are
now referred to as "Euro-Americans" by the latest generation of ethnic sociologists. As far as these writers are concerned, the melting pot *did* happen—for
whites! On the other hand—or so the argument goes—the new immigrants
who bear the mark of racial difference, need not fear the melting pot since
their race renders them immune to the potent solvents that lie within.

MULTICULTURALISM: BACK TO THE FUTURE[45]

"Euro-Americans." With a single word, the debate that raged for decades over the
fate of European ethnic groups was settled: the melting pot was a reality, but for
whites only. This amounted to a paradigm shift as the idea of "cultural pluralism" was resurrected and refurbished with a new name: "multiculturalism."

The social context for this paradigm shift, as mentioned above, was yet
another great wave of immigration that was triggered by the 1965 Hart-Cellar
Act. Passed on the heels of the Civil Rights Revolution, this legislation revoked
the national origins quotas instituted in 1924 that effectively restricted immigration, not just to Europe, but to Northern and Western Europe. Though
unanticipated by its advocates, the reform precipitated a tidal wave of immigrants, mostly from Asia, Latin America, and the Caribbean—totaling over
30 million by 2006. Not only did this change "the face of America"—to use
the vaguely racialist construction bandied about in the popular press—but it
changed the face of sociology as well. As in the past, a number of the progeny
of these new immigrants gravitated to the field of race and ethnic relations.

The mantra of this new generation of ethnic sociologists is: Assimilation
for thee but not for me. They assert flat out, "assimilation theory is dead,"
dismissing it as a Eurocentric construct that has little or no relevance to the

new immigrants who are not white.[46] In this view, even though European immigrants were different from one another in nationality and language, in religion and culture, these differences were ultimately trumped by their common whiteness. And at the very same time that these groups were moving into the mainstream of American life, the nation's racial minorities—"people of color"—were relegated to reservations, ghettos, barrios, and Chinatowns. The result was a process of ethnic formation that has resulted in a racial division between Native Americans, African Americans, Hispanic Americans, Asian Americans, and, alas, Euro-Americans. David Hollinger has dubbed this as "the ethno-racial pentagon."[47]

Hollinger has been a lonely critic of this new lexicon, and in *Postethnic America* he asks some tough questions: When we strip away the rhetorical gloss of the ethno-racial pentagon, aren't we left with the all too familiar division between black, yellow, white, red, and brown?[48] Is the ethno-racial pentagon the progressive conception it pretends to be, or is it a reversion to old and discredited racial categories? In a democratic society, is this the way we should classify people or organize a polity?

We also need to ask whether these categories are merely the imposition of faceless bureaucrats at the Census Bureau, under the sway of ethnic scholars and activists, reflecting *their* worldview. Or does the ethno-racial pentagon reflect the understandings and aspirations of ordinary people as they grapple with the questions that preoccupy immigrants everywhere: Who am I? How do I reconcile past, present, and future? What do I want for my children, and what, realistically, can I expect?

According to Min Zhou, "privately, few Americans of Asian ancestry would spontaneously identify themselves as Asian, and fewer still as Asian American. They instead link their identities to specific countries of origin, such as China, Japan, Korea, the Philippines, India or Vietnam."[49] Much the same can be said of "Latinos," who identify primarily as Puerto Ricans, Mexicans, Dominicans, Cubans, Salvadorans, Columbians, Peruvians, and so on.[50] A large-scale study of both Asian and Latino adolescents found "an overwhelming preference for same-ethnic peers" (in terms of nationality). The authors concluded, "There is little evidence of panethnicity among Asian and Latino youth."[51] Even more telling, most Asians who marry outside their nationality, do not marry Asians of some other nationality: they marry whites.[52] Again, it behooves us to ask whether panethnicity reflects the realities on the ground, or is only wishful thinking on the part of a self-selected group of ethnic scholars and activists.

On the other hand, it may be premature to draw any firm conclusions. It is said of Italians that they became "Italian" in the United States, since as immigrants they identified primarily with region—as Sicilians, Milanese, Calabrians, Romans, and so on. In the case of Jews, divisions between Germans and Russians once ran deep, not to speak of intra-group distinctions between Poles, Litvaks, Romanians, and so on. The lesson of history is that these nationality and regional divisions were erased as identities coalesced around more generic categories of race or religion. It is entirely possible that in the future identities will coalesce along the lines of the ethno-racial pentagon. However, this would still leave us with Hollinger's complaint that, at bottom, the pentagon is predicated on crude, racialist notions about "color." Thus we cannot escape the thorny question: If these distinctions do take root, will they constitute a multiculturalism worthy of its name? Where is the "culture" that Euro-Americans supposedly share? Isn't it the case that "European" is merely rhetorical gloss for "white," just as "Asian" is for "yellow," and "Latino" is for "brown"? Or is it the case that these categories, however much they originate in racialist assumptions, paradoxically engender the institutional and cultural forms that sustain identity and community?

Thus the question remains: Is American society evolving into a quintuple melting pot, drawn along immutable racial lines, or is it the destiny of these latest hyphenated Americans to repeat the experience of the "races of Europe" and to melt into a common mainstream? Indeed, anxieties over this issue have led to fierce debates over whether or not a hyphen should be placed, for example, between Asian and American.[53] Critics object that the hyphen implies that the Asian is not fully American, or that the Asian-American is less Asian. On the assumption that these are autonomous identities—that the sum of their values is not 100 but 200 percent—it has become conventional to dispense with the hyphen. Fierce debates have also been waged over the term "Hispanic," with its referent to Spain, versus "Latino," which lays claim to multiethnic and multiracial identities forged in the Spanish diaspora. The problem though is that the ethnic future will not turn on these linguistic niceties or on whether we add or subtract a hyphen.

Thus, the crucial question: Are the new immigrants destined to follow in the footsteps of earlier immigrants, which is to say, footsteps leading into the melting pot? Or are they developing the institutional structures and cultural materials that will assure ethnic continuity for the foreseeable future? And what about those racist barriers that are assumed to prevent assimilation? Is it true that race is an insurmountable barrier? Or will Asians and Latinos surmount persistent racist barriers, and melt into the mainstream? And if Asians and Latinos are destined for the melting pot, where do African Americans and Native Americans stand in relation to the evolving configuration of American nationality?

The thrust of research and writing by the new ethnic pluralists rejects assimilation even as a theoretical possibility, much less an imminent reality. Scores of studies have been conducted that document the process of ethnic formation that has resulted in the emergence of highly integrated immigrant communities, replete with population concentrations, commercial districts, churches, fraternal organizations, publications, and a host of other organizations that provide an institutional basis for identity and community. As noted earlier, Warner and Srole observed a similar scenario half a century ago, but they were less inclined to take appearances at face value. Rather, they contended that the ethnic subsociety had a paradoxical function: "to nurse their members through a period of transition until these members 'unlearn' what they have been taught and successfully learn the new way of life necessary for full acceptance into the host society."[54] Is history repeating itself? Do these ethnic communities constitute the ecological basis for an enduring ethnicity, or are they merely latter-day versions of ethnic constellations that paradoxically facilitate assimilation? In short, is the ethnic subsociety a transitional stage in a long-term assimilation process?

The main current of thought in the immigrant literature, as we have seen, has been to reject the past as a barometer of the future, and to emphasize the differences rather than the similarities between past and present immigrants. Aside from the factor of race, multiculturalists cite several other factors that, they argue, make their situation different:

- Today's immigrants enter a society that is far more tolerant of diversity, thanks to the civil rights movement. Indeed, the ideology of multiculturalism extols ethnic difference and provides institutional mechanisms, such as bilingual education, for the preservation of immigrant language and culture. As a result, the Asians, Latinos, and Caribbeans have formed cohesive ethnic communities with flourishing economies and foreign-language media, including cable television, that provide institutional anchorage for preserving language and culture.

- Compared to European immigrants, most new immigrants have easy access to their homelands, thanks to telecommunications and cheap airfare, allowing transnational identities to flourish.[55]

- Many new immigrants arrive with education and skills, and often capital as well, and therefore are not forced to compromise their ethnic identities for the sake of economic survival. Indeed, in today's global economy it is not a handicap, but an asset to be multilingual and multicultural.

These are compelling points. The question, though, is whether they add up to the conclusion that "the assimilation model is dead," and that the new immigrants will not "melt" as did their predecessors from Europe. It must be conceded that this is a plausible scenario, given what we know about racism as a divisive force in American history. On the other hand, we also know that race qua African Americans has always translated into a racism that is more virulent and more pervasive than the brands of racism endured by other "people of color."[56] Therefore, history should caution us that the "race" of Asians and Latinos might pose obstacles that are less formidable than those that exist for African Americans and immigrants of African descent. The question is whether the racism that Asians and Latinos encounter today has greater affinity with the xenophobia and prejudices experienced by Eastern and Southern Europeans when they arrived than with the system of oppression experienced a century ago by the nation's colonized minorities.

This raises another semantic issue of some consequence. Throughout this book, I have embraced Blauner's concept of "colonized minorities" as it applied historically to the cases of Mexicans in the Southwest, Chinese contract laborers, and the anti-Asian bigotry that led to the atrocious internment of 120,000 citizens of Japanese descent during the Second World War. Are multicultural theorists correct, however, in conflating these historical situations with that of today's immigrants from Asia and Latin America, notwithstanding some resonance with the past? It hardly makes sense to lump Taiwanese college students who overstay their student visas with the "coolie labor" that was mercilessly exploited and abused. Nor can we ignore the sharp social class divisions within the immigrant population. Many post-1965 immigrants were professionals or business entrepreneurs in their countries of origin, and hardly fit the image of the "huddled masses" of yore. Indeed, their immigration sometimes amounts to a brain drain from these poorer nations.[57] Furthermore, as David Hollinger points out, "today's immigrants are more prepared for a measure of assimilation by the worldwide influence of American popular culture; most are more culturally attuned to the United States before they arrive here than were their counterparts a century ago."[58] Although these immigrants certainly encounter prejudice and discrimination in the United States, their situation is in no way comparable to that of Asians and Latinos 150 years ago, or for that matter, the poorer segments of the Asian and Latino populations today, who come under very different circumstances and confront formidable obstacles of both race and class.[59] Given these discontinuities, it makes little sense to invoke "history" to make a blanket claim that the melting pot is "for whites only."

In point of fact, this proposition receives little support from the very large body of research on the new immigration. On the contrary, the weight of evidence leads to the conclusion that, notwithstanding their racial difference, today's Asian and Latino immigrants are not only assimilating but are doing so at an even faster rate than did earlier immigrants from Europe.

In retrospect, an early indicator of the eventual assimilation of European immigrants was the rapidity with which they lost their native languages. A pattern emerges with stubborn consistency. Immigrants, of course, retained their native tongues; their children were bilingual; and by the third generation, the overwhelming majority were monolingual in English.[60] The virtual eradication of languages in only two generations shows just how fragile culture is, at least once it loses its "survival value" and is severed from the institutions that nourish it. The loss of language has far-reaching implications. As Ronald Schmidt observes: "Because of its own characteristics and potential importance in the constitution of identities (individual, ethnic, national), language has the capacity to engage people's interests and political imaginations on a deeply emotional level."[61] Indeed, this is why immigrants all through history have dispatched their children to language schools in an attempt to preserve their native tongues. But the harsh lesson of history is that sentiment—even passionate loyalty—is not enough to protect culture from the powerful forces of assimilation. Indeed, the United States has been aptly described as "a language graveyard."[62]

This process is being reenacted—if anything, at an accelerated pace—among the new immigrants. In a study of Los Angeles, based on 1990 census data, David López found that, among Asians, the shift to monolingualism was nearly universal by the third generation.[63] Consider what this means for family dynamics. Unless the immigrant grandparents acquire a basic fluency in English, which often is not the case, then grandchildren cannot converse with their grandparents except through the mediation of their bilingual parents.

The picture is more complex among Latinos, though the overall pattern is still one of rapid language loss. If retention of Spanish were to occur anywhere in the United States, it would be in Los Angeles. Not only do most L.A. Latinos live in predominantly Latino neighborhoods, but the city also has a thriving ethnic press and electronic media. Furthermore, Los Angeles has had an official policy of promoting multiculturalism, including bilingual education and bilingual ballots. Yet López found that 57 percent of third-generation Latinos spoke only English at home.[64] Spanish was retained mainly in households where a foreign-born person—presumably that all-important immigrant grandparent—was present. Among Mexican American youth living in households with no immigrants, only 20 percent spoke Spanish at home.

In his recent best seller *Who Are We?* Samuel Huntington frets that there is a danger that the massive influx of Mexican immigrants will not only Latinize the Southwest, but raises the specter of reconquista—of Mexico or Mexicans claiming the area of the Southwest that was conquered and annexed in the 1840s. Clearly, in light of the precipitous rate at which young Latinos are substituting English for Spanish, it would appear that Huntington has little to worry about! Indeed, he cites data himself showing that only 12 percent of the children of Mexican-born immigrants speak only Spanish or more Spanish than English at home,[65] yet he continues to rant against policies that protect language minorities and mandate bilingual ballots and school programs. Geoffrey Nunberg has stated the matter well: "Considered in the light of the actualities, then, English-only is an irrelevant provocation. It is a bad cure for an imaginary disease."[66]

A study of Cubans in South Florida also found that most young people prefer to speak English at home, even when they are bilingual.[67] Nor was this true only of the middle classes. Among second-generation youth who classified themselves as working class or poor, three-quarters preferred to speak English. The weight of the evidence is clear: regardless of social class, the children of immigrants are far down the road to monolingualism. If Spanish is the cultural glue that is supposed to fasten the otherwise disparate Spanish-speaking nationalities into a panethnic whole, then it is difficult to avoid the conclusion that the prospects for Latino panethnicity are bleak.

A recent national study confirms a pronounced tendency toward English monolingualism by the third generation. In the case of Japanese, Filipinos, Chinese, and Koreans, the percentage of third-generation children (aged six to fifteen) who speak only English at home is over 90 percent. For Cubans, the figure is 78 percent. For Mexicans and Dominicans, the figures are 64 and 52 percent, respectively.[68] Clearly, even though today's society is nominally more conducive to language retention, the new immigrants, including those who are economically marginal, are moving very rapidly to English monolingualism.

Perhaps the earliest indicator of assimilation is the first names that parents choose for their newborn children. After all, a parent who chooses an ethnic name is literally inscribing ethnicity on the child for life, whereas parents who choose an "American" name clearly have made a major concession to the melting pot, whether they do so consciously or not. A study of baby names in New York City found that in 2005 the five most popular names for Hispanic girls were Ashley, Emily, Isabella, Jennifer, and Mia. For Hispanic baby boys, it was Angel, Anthony, Christopher, Justin, and Joshua. Clearly, Samuel Huntington does not have much to fear from Latinos with names like Ashley and Angel![69] Actually, Angel is a crossover name, pronounced AHN-hel in Spanish.

In the case of Asians, the five most common baby names for girls were Emily, Sophia, Nicole, Michelle, and Rachel. For boys, it was: Ryan, Jason, Kevin, Daniel, and Justin. By passing up distinctively Asian names for their newborn children, these parents are engaged in an act of anticipatory socialization. Indeed, this finding throws into question one of the most dominant themes in the immigrant literature, that generational conflict occurs as the more assimilated children break away from the constraints of their immigrant parents. The naming practices suggest otherwise—that many immigrant parents are implicated in the assimilation of their own children, and are more willing than one would ever know from the social science literature to release their children to the melting pot. As Irving Howe wrote about Jewish immigrants at the turn of the twentieth century: "In behalf of its sons the East Side was prepared to commit suicide; perhaps it did."[70]

If the naming practices among immigrants and loss of a native language mark the beginning of the assimilation process, marriage across ethnic lines represents its fateful last stage. Here again, the data do not support either the assumptions or the hopes of the multiculturalists. A study based on the 1990 census found that 40 percent of Asians born in the United States married non-Asians—and these are mostly the children, not the grandchildren, of immigrants. The figures ranged from 22 percent among Vietnamese to 31 percent among Japanese, 38 percent among Asian Indians, 46 percent among Chinese, 65 percent among Filipinos, and an astounding 72 percent among Koreans.[71] These figures are so high that they call into question whether "race" is the immutable mark of color that is generally assumed. Furthermore, the level of marriage between Asians of different nationalities is strikingly low, contradicting assumptions of a shared or evolving panethnicity. Rather, most Asians who intermarry do so with whites, giving rise to speculation that Asians are in the process of "becoming white."[72] Mary Waters found that in the vast majority of cases where the father is white and the mother is not, these parents identify their children as "white."[73]

Despite overwhelming evidence, ethnic scholars have been loath to accept the verdict that assimilation is "happening." A recurrent theme in the literature on Asian Americans is that in the white mind the image of Asians as "foreign" persists no matter how many generations they have been in the United States and no matter their level of success.[74] There is another way of looking at this, however. At the present about 60 percent of the Asian-origin population are foreign-born and another 28 percent are the children of immigrants. Only 12 percent are third-generation.[75] Obviously, there is a time lag before Asians attain visibility in the media and other spheres of public life, and perceptions catch up with shifting realities. We can safely predict that the day is rapidly approaching when the perception of Asians as "forever foreign" will be a thing of the past.[76]

Rates of intermarriage for Latinos are lower than for Asians, but they are high nevertheless. Overall, almost one-third of U.S.-born Latinos between the ages of twenty-five and thirty-four are married to non-Latino whites. When nationality and race are taken into account, the levels are much higher. The following figures are based on the 1990 census and pertain to persons with the following characteristics: (1) born in the United States, (2) male, (3) aged twenty to thirty-four, (4) identify as white, and (5) married. Among Mexicans with these characteristics, 32 percent are married to non-Latino whites. The comparable figure for Puerto Ricans is 54 percent; for Cubans, 59 percent; for Central Americans, 79 percent.[77]

Indeed, marriage across racial lines has become so commonplace that some commentators have raised the possibility of a "mestizo America"—a racial mixture, like that in South American nations, which blurs the boundaries among ethnic groups. In this view, it is not a question of minorities being absorbed into a white majority, but rather of a fusing of these diverse peoples into a new amalgam. We even know how this new American will look, thanks to an artist's computer-generated portrait (through a process called "morphing") that was featured on the cover of *Time* in 1993. What better personification of Robert Park's observation that every nation is "a more or less successful melting-pot"? Equally significant is the sea change in attitudes toward interracial marriages. A century ago the idea of "race mixing" was condemned as "mongrelization," whereas today it is accepted with virtual equanimity. *Time*'s editor explained dispassionately that the purpose of their graphic was to "dramatize the impact of interethnic marriage, which has increased dramatically in the US during the latest wave of immigration."[78]

The tendency among sociologists has been to regard the upsurge in racial intermarriage as signifying the extension of "the boundaries of whiteness"—in other words, the incorporation of whole groups that previously were regarded as racial "other." True enough, but one day we may come to the realization that whiteness itself has been permanently transformed. In his autobiography *The Accidental Asian*, Eric Liu arrives at this epiphany: "America is white no longer, and it will never be white again."[79]

Like it or not—and the dissent of the multiculturalists is clear—assimilation is the wave of the future, the inexorable byproduct of forces put into motion by the act of immigration itself.

THE AFRICAN AMERICAN EXCEPTION

Admittedly, this is a sweeping conclusion. While I believe that it captures the main thrust of American ethnic history, it does not tell the whole story. In particular, it does not account for the African American exception.[80] Here we speak of a group that came to America in slave galleys, not immigrant vessels. While successive waves of immigrants flowed into the country, first to settle the land mass and later to provide labor for burgeoning industries, blacks were trapped in the South in a system of feudal agriculture. Even in the North, a rigid color line excluded them from the manufacturing sector, except for a few dirty, backbreaking, and dangerous jobs that whites spurned. In effect, the industrial revolution was "for whites only," depriving blacks of the jobs and opportunities that delivered Europe's huddled masses from poverty.

This was the historic wrong that was supposed to be remedied by landmark civil rights legislation in the 1960s. However, by the time large numbers of blacks arrived in Northern cities, the manufacturing sector was undergoing a long-term decline, reflecting the impact of laborsaving technology and the export of jobs to low-wage countries. Not only did blacks encounter a far less favorable structure of opportunity than did immigrants, not only did they suffer from the economic consequences of past discrimination, not only did they continue to encounter pervasive racism in the world of work, but they also encountered intense labor competition from yet another huge wave of immigrants. Ironically, most of these immigrants would not be here but for the civil rights movement that led to the overhaul of immigration policy in 1965.

The standard cant is that immigrants take jobs that blacks don't want, but this is a partial truth at best. Immigrants have made inroads into every segment of the workforce, including coveted jobs in the health care industries, construction, building maintenance, light manufacturing, and even government service, which has long been the staple of the black middle class. Nor are immigrants any longer restricted to a few gateway cities. Increasingly, they are penetrating all regions of the nation and all segments of the American economy, as is their aspiration and their right. Without doubt the continuing flow of immigrants has been a boon to the national economy, but it has also dealt a blow to African Americans who were poised for progress in the wake of the Civil Rights Revolution.[81]

Notwithstanding their "racial" differences and the many impediments that they confront, the new immigrants have been able to bypass blacks on the proverbial road to success. As I have argued above, this is also a road that ultimately leads into the melting pot. It is a mark of the melting pot's failure that African Americans, whose roots on American soil go back to the founding of the nation, are today more segregated than recent immigrants from Asia and Latin America. According to Douglas S. Massey, "No other ethnic or racial group in the United States has ever, even briefly, experienced such high levels of residential segregation."[82] What clearer manifestation of African American exceptionalism could there be?

All the while that Zangwill's melting pot was "roaring and bubbling," and Europe's races were amalgamating into whites, thirty states had antimiscegenation laws proscribing marriages between blacks and whites. Sixteen of these states still had these laws on the books when the Supreme Court declared them unconstitutional in 1967. Even today, at a time when marriage across racial lines has been soaring for Asians and Latinos, it has inched up only slightly for blacks (to 6 percent for males and 2 percent for females).[83]

Not only do blacks bear the brunt of exclusion, but there is also evidence that many blacks actively reject the melting pot. At least this can be inferred from baby naming practices. A study found that black and white naming conventions were similar early in the century, but diverged sharply after the rise of black nationalism in the 1960s.[84] Blacks developed a custom of finding unique names, often derived from African languages, or coining entirely new names. A recent study based on California's birth data found that "more than 40 percent of black girls were given names that were not given to even one of the more than 100,000 white girls born in the state the same year."[85] In New York City, the five most popular names for black girls in 2005 were Kayla, Jada, Madison, Destiny, and Brianna. For boys they are Joshua, Elijah, Justin, Jayden, and Isaiah.[86] With the exception of Justin, which is popular among Asians and Latinos, these names have little currency among other groups.[87] If it is true, as I contended earlier, that the naming practices among Asians and Latinos indicate that these groups are on a path into the melting pot, then the naming practices among blacks suggest the opposite: that blacks are defiantly running away from the melting pot. Not without penalty, however. Recent studies report that employers often discriminate against applicants who have conspicuously "black" names.[88]

There are other ways in which it can be said that, unlike immigrants, blacks are "running away from the melting pot." At the same time that immigrants were losing their ancestral languages, blacks were forging an African American dialect, one that, according to sociolinguists, has all of the defining attributes of a legitimate language.[89] Another example is the emergence of Kwanzaa as an African American variant of Christmas. As Elizabeth Pleck has shown, this was the invention of black nationalists in the 1970s, but over time has evolved into a celebration of family and blackness.[90] By themselves, these developments may not be all that important, but they are important insofar as they reflect deeper trends of identity, culture, and community.

Here we confront the major point of difference between African Americans and immigrants so far as the issue of culture is concerned. For immigrants, the ethnic community was a transitional phenomenon that facilitated their movement, geographically and socially, into the mainstream of society. To be sure, economically mobile immigrants exhibited a pattern of resegregation, as Louis Wirth observed, as they attempted to rebuild churches and other institutions that were essential to their collective survival.[91] They did not, to repeat, flop into the melting pot and melt into oblivion. However, we now have the verdict of history, though some will still deny it: these ethnic communities were destined to a gradual and inexorable decline across generations.

For African Americans it was another matter altogether: the ghetto was a permanent fact of life. And here we confront a great historical paradox—for these ghettos, the enforced home of the nation's racial pariahs, also spawned and nourished a vibrant African American subculture. Again, the contrast with immigrants is striking, as Bob Blauner has argued:

Whereas the immigrant ghettos allowed ethnic cultures to flower for a period, in the long term they functioned as way stations on the road to acculturation and assimilation. But the black ghetto has served as a central fixture of American racism's strong resistance to the assimilation of black people. Thus the ghetto's permanence has made it a continuing crucible for ethnic development and culture building.[92]

Thus, the supreme paradox: precisely because of its permanence, the ghetto functions as "a continuing crucible for ethnic development and culture building." It is precisely because no other ethnic or racial group in the United States has ever experienced such prolonged levels of residential segregation that the ecological and social prerequisites did not exist for ethnic persistence and renewal.

Other differences ensue from the simple fact that blacks were not immigrants. Unlike immigrants, who clung to vestiges of cultures ripped from their moorings in distant places, black culture evolved out of the lived experience of black people on American soil. Instead of isolated fragments selected precisely because they did not interfere with mainstream American culture, black culture is an integral part of the everyday lives of black people. In short, it is a *living* culture, one that displays a vitality and dynamism that is generally lacking among the atrophying cultures of the nation's immigrant groups.

Ironically, generations of sociologists have taken the opposite position, on the one hand valorizing the rich cultures of the nation's immigrants, and on the other, holding that blacks were "only white men with black skin, nothing more, nothing less," as Kenneth Stampp wrote in the preface to *The Peculiar Institution*.[93] The further irony is that this position had liberal intentions. It was the way that white liberals avowed that blacks are "just like us" but for the happenstance of skin color. It was meant as a compliment, however much it was predicated on myopia and condescension.

This is how Glazer came to commit a major gaffe. In the same book where he and Moynihan declared that ethnic groups survived the melting pot, Glazer wrote: "It is not possible for Negroes to view themselves as other ethnic groups viewed themselves because—and this is the key to much in the Negro world—the Negro is an American and nothing else. He has no values and culture to guard and protect."[94] This was 1963, before the upsurge of black militancy and the eruption of the "soul movement" that celebrated and rejuvenated black culture. By 1970 Glazer came under fierce attack, and in the second edition, he confessed, albeit in fine print, that his statement had given him "considerable pain."[95] All that he meant, he now explained, was that blacks have no *foreign* culture to guard and protect. However, this only compounds the error! These foreign cultures—precisely because they were foreign—were destined to a gradual but inexorable decline. In contrast, black culture is a bona fide example of ethnogenesis—literally, the genesis of new cultural forms that evolved through interaction with American culture, a far cry from the fraught attempts of immigrants to cling to shards of the past. Moreover, as an indigenous product of the American experience, black culture continues not only to thrive in segregated black communities but also to exert a powerful influence on mainstream American culture.

In an edited collection, *Signifyin(g), Sanctifyin', and Slam Dunking*, Gena Dagel Caponi and her collaborators make a powerful case that there is—always has been—a distinctive African American aesthetic that runs through music, dance, sport (hence the inclusion of slam dunking), and oral expression.[96] The vitality and dynamism of this aesthetic derives, not from tutelage, but from the lived experience of ordinary people. This is captured in an evocative passage from an autobiographical book by Johnny Otis, a white rhythm and blues artist who grew up in a black neighborhood in Berkeley, California:

I never had to instruct my horn players how to phrase a passage. . . . The music grew out of the African American way of life. The way mama cooked, the Black English grandmother and grandfather spoke, the way daddy disciplined the kids—the emphasis on spiritual values, the way Reverend Jones preached, the way Sister Williams sang in the choir, the way the old brother down the street played the slide guitar and crooned the blues, the very special way the people danced, walked, laughed, cried, joked, got happy, shouted in church. In the final analysis, what forms the texture and adds character to the music is the African American experience.[97]

Clearly, none of this was within Nathan Glazer's orbit of experience when he wrote that blacks have "no values and culture to guard and protect," or when he amended this to imply, contradicting his own analysis of white ethnics, that the only "real" culture is a foreign culture.

In contrast to Glazer's vacuity, consider the account of the writer John Edgar Wideman: "Our stories, songs, dreams dances, social forms, style of walk, talk, dressing, cooking, sport, our heroes and heroines provide a record . . . so distinctive and abiding that its origins in culture have been misconstrued as rooted in biology."[98] Indeed, Robert Park speculated that blacks had a distinctive temperament that was transmitted biologically, and accounted for their "genial, sunny, and social disposition."[99]

From Park through Glazer, white sociology failed to apprehend—indeed, could not know—that there is a distinctive African American culture that has roots in Africa and evolved on American soil, first under slavery and later in those very ghettos that white sociology portrayed mainly as sites of social disorganization and cultural pathology.[100] "That an African American aesthetic not only survives but thrives and has been the vanguard of American cultural expression," Caponi writes, "is a powerful testament to its vitality and power."[101]

The contemporary manifestation of this vibrant African American aesthetic is the emergence of hip hop culture, and its florescence into a cultural phenomenon that embraces music, dress, and graphic art. The profound impact of hip hop culture on white youth has aroused consternation, however. "What are we of make of a young white man from the suburbs," Charles Gallagher asks, "who listens to hip-hop, wears baggy hip-hop pants, a baseball cap turned sideways, unlaced sneakers and an oversized shirt emblazoned with a famous NBA player who, far from shouting racial epithets, lists a number of racial minorities as his heroes?"[102] It is tempting to see this as an important cultural exchange, one that marks a bridging of the racial divide, as white youth identify with black performers and emulate the black idiom of dress and self-presentation. Are white youth in a sense "becoming black"? Does it imply a breach of the color line, potentially with political consequences as these youth identify with the racial "other" and with the black cause?

Critics think otherwise. In an incisive article entitled "Blackophilia and Blackophobia: White Youth, the Consumption of Rap Music, and White Supremacy," Bill Yousman contends that the white dalliance with hip hop culture is about consumption and self-gratification, and hardly makes whites allies in the struggle for racial justice. On the contrary, it reinforces the "otherness" of blacks, and like black minstrelsy in past generations, provides white youth with a template for projecting their own sexual anxieties and illicit desires. To quote Yousman: "The images that White youth consume most voraciously are images of Black violence, Black aggression, and Black misogyny and sexism. These are the very same images that both mainstream conservative politicians and far-right White supremacists invoke to justify regressive social policies or violent 'reprisals.'"[103]

Another astute critic, Robin Kelley, writes that gangsta rap "is a place of adventure, unbridled violence, erotic fantasy, and/or an imaginary alternative to suburban boredom."[104] For blacks this culture may represent a form of political resistance and protest against the ravages of life in the hood. But for whites it amounts to voyeurism from the safe distance of white privilege. As Yousman writes, "it is far too easy for White youth to adopt the signifiers of Blackness when they do not have to deal with the consequences of Blackness in America."[105] Nor can it be assumed that these white youth even hear the same music, or rather derive the same meaning from it. Consider Richard Wright's penetrating observation some sixty-five years ago: "Our music makes the whole world dance. . . . But only a few of those who dance and sing with us suspect the rawness of life out of which our laughing-crying tunes and quick steps come; they do not know that our songs and dances are our banner of hope flung desperately up in the face of a world that has pushed us to the wall."[106]

Wright's eloquence provides a conceptual lens for examining ongoing debates about the impact of hip hop culture on black youth. Some commentators go so far as to place the blame for the myriad of problems that confront black youth on hip hop culture. A recent example is Orlando Patterson's op-ed piece in the *New York Times* under the self-contradictory title, "A Poverty of the Mind." Reacting to a number of recent studies documenting the crisis among black youth in terms of schooling and jobs, Patterson asserts that the "standard explanatory fare" of structural factors fails to explain the poor school performance of black men, who also, or so he alleges, pass up low-wage jobs that immigrants are willing to take. He locates the blame in black subculture, specifically the "cool-pose culture" that is "simply too gratifying to give up." According to Patterson, "For these young men, it was almost like a drug, hanging out on the street after school, shopping and dressing sharply, sexual conquests, party drugs, hip-hop music and culture, the fact that almost all the superstar athletes and a great many of the nation's best entertainers were black." Patterson calls this "the Dionysian trap," an erudite spin on obsolete culture-of-poverty theory.[107]

Instead of realizing that gangsta rap is a culture of alienation, a wail against the hopelessness and degradation of the inner-city poor, "our banner of hope flung desperately up in the face of a world that has pushed us to the wall," Patterson, from his ivory tower, inverts cause and effect, and posits hip hop culture as a source of the overwhelming problems that beset poor black youth.[108] The effect is to blame these powerless people for their own degradation, and even to begrudge our nation's youthful outcasts the ingenuity and creative energy that drive hip hop culture, providing some outlet and solace for what the legacy of slavery has wrought.

The conclusion is unavoidable: America's melting pot has been inclusive of everybody *but* blacks. Or to put it another way, we have a *dual melting pot*: one for blacks, and the other for everybody else. This should come as no surprise. Dualism has always been the ruling principle of race in the United States: it began with the dualism between slave and free labor, which itself was predicated on an ideological dualism between civilized and primitive man. The dualism of Jim Crow. The dualism of segregated housing, schools, cultural institutions, and the health care system. The dualism in the sphere of everyday life, where blacks and whites live in different worlds. Not to speak of the internal duality that Du Bois wrote about so luminously—the double-consciousness of being both an American and a Negro, "two souls, two thoughts, two unreconciled strivings; two warring ideals in one dark body."[109] The visionaries who imagine getting "beyond race," "beyond ethnicity," "beyond multiculturalism" are sadly out of touch with the events on the ground in the here and now. Perhaps the day will come when their books will be lauded for their prescience, but at this moment they seem strangely removed from the world we inhabit.[110]

A number of recent writers contend that there is an evolving "black" melting pot that will absorb all of those groups who are phenotypically "black," including African Americans, Caribbean immigrants, Afro-Latinos, and African immigrants.[111] To be sure, these groups resist being lumped together, and insist on being defined by nationality or ethnicity. This was Mary Waters's finding in her study of West Indian immigrants and their children in New York City, but to her surprise Waters also found that "hardly anyone saw any problems with intermarrying with American blacks."[112] Afro-Latinos are marrying along racial lines as well. As indicated earlier, among U.S.-born Puerto Rican males aged twenty-five to thirty-four, 54 percent of those who self-identified as white married non-Latino whites. The figure for those who identified as non-white was only 27 percent, suggesting a tendency to "melt" along racial lines.[113]

If this analysis is right, and groups that are phenotypically black are destined to merge through intermarriage, the other melting pot will include everybody *but* blacks, including Asians and light-skinned Latinos. This means that the ballyhooed American melting pot is actually a racist formation, divided along racial lines. It is a testament to the unremitting impact of racism, of a nation that has stubbornly refused to confront its legacy of slavery and to include African Americans in the circle of "we." I am tempted to say that the dual melting pot reflects a failure of American democracy, but when we remember that two centuries of slavery and a century of Jim Crow were sanctioned by all three branches of our government, it should come as no surprise that our vaunted democratic institutions have failed to forge the basis for genuine racial reconciliation.

Just think: it required a long and bloody grassroots struggle in the second half of the twentieth century just to attain the rights of citizenship that were

supposedly secured by the Reconstruction Amendments and the Civil Rights
Act of 1875 that guaranteed blacks equal treatment in all public accommoda-
tions. If this is "progress," it is progress of a people on a historical treadmill.

CONCLUSION

In *The Melting-Pot*, Zangwill wrote: "There she lies, the great Melting-Pot—
Listen! Can't you hear the roaring and the bubbling?"[114] Yet two generations
of social scientists have turned a deaf ear to the melting pot. My contention is
that the melting pot roars and bubbles still, and the whole point of the epistemology of wishful thinking has been to evade, to elide, and to gloss over this
unwelcome development. Of course, in doing so, these self-appointed arbiters of
the ethnic future presumptuously disregard the sensibilities and choices of the
very constituencies that they claim to represent. These are people who, judged
by their actions, do not share the apocalyptic dread of the melting pot that runs
through the social science literature. As a result, these scholars have produced
a body of research and writing that is deeply flawed by wishful thinking.

    On the other hand, the metaphor of a melting pot is misleading insofar as
it suggests that assimilation occurs with the speed of instant oatmeal or mol-
ten iron. Rather, assimilation must be seen, as Park saw it, as an incremental
process that occurs across generations. To be sure, these transitional cultural
formations have a vitality and integrity all their own. As George Lipsitz writes
about Puerto Ricans: "Puerto Rican 'assimilation' is not into the dominant
culture and does not entail the disappearance of distinct national backgrounds,
but rather involves a fusion of diverse working-class cultures shaped by marginalization and exclusion in order to create 'a healthy interfertilization of
cultures.'"[115] The nagging question, though, is whether these hybrid cultures
are only transitional stages in a long-term assimilation process.

    Then again, even if Park is correct in his basic tenets and his prophecy
of ultimate assimilation, the simple fact is that we live in the present, not the
future. It may be our national destiny to become a melting pot, but today the
United States is a remarkably polyglot society in which ethnicity flourishes.
Despite an overriding trend toward assimilation, ethnic loyalties and attachments remain strong even among segments of older immigrant groups. New
immigrants, freshly arrived on American soil, are only at the early stages of the

assimilation process. To ignore these realities by focusing only on long-term trends runs the risk of eclipsing the lives and sensibilities of entire communities who define themselves, still, by their biological lineage and cultural heritage.

Nor does this warning apply only to ideologues on the political Right who, in the name of the melting pot, have waged a remorseless crusade against bilingualism, multicultural education, and affirmative action. In recent years, a Left discourse has emerged that impatiently looks "beyond race" and "beyond ethnicity," imagining a post-ethnic future where people are not defined by genes or ancestry. Indeed, some writers go so far as to promote the idea of intermarriage across racial and ethnic lines as a way of eliminating, once and for all, the dissonances and conflicts attending racial and ethnic diversity.

For example, Gary Nash, one of the pioneers of multicultural education, has published an essay titled "The Hidden History of Mestizo America," in which he argues that we "need new ways of transcending America's Achilles' heel of race, now that a certain amount of progress has been achieved in living up to our credo."[116] Like Nash, Orlando Patterson advocates miscegenation as the ultimate solution to our supposedly intractable race problem.[117] Never mind that African Americans—not to speak of other ethnic groups—may not wish to miscegenate themselves out of existence. Never mind that it would take generations, if not centuries, to actually produce the hybrid nation that they envision. Never mind that blacks are *already* a hybrid people, but for the nefarious "one drop of blood rule" that consigned Homer Plessy to the railroad car for Negroes, although he was only one-eighth black ("an octoroon," in the hideous racist lexicon of the time). Instead of confronting the urgent problems of race in America and addressing the challenges of the multicultural society that we are, these visionaries betray their progressive values and use a utopian vision of the melting pot as a façade for moral capitulation. Again, Stanford Lyman's reproach of the evolutionary assumptions that pervade sociological thought apply to these new visionaries: "Since the time for teleological redemption is ever long, blacks might consign their civic and egalitarian future to faith in the ultimate fulfillment of the inclusion cycle's promise."[118]

The vision of a multicultural society is also appropriated by writers on the political Right as a façade for moral capitulation. This is the reason that Nathan Glazer's *We Are All Multiculturalists Now* should be read with skepticism. Glazer has garnered praise for "changing his mind," but on closer examination he has only resurrected the schema that he proposed in his 1953 article on "America's Ethnic Pattern," in which he championed cultural pluralism and predicted that pluralism would increasingly be drawn along racial and religious lines. Glazer has hardly been won over to the cause of using multiculturalism as a rallying cry for advancing the rights of minorities and attacking structures of inequality. On the contrary, he has thrown in the towel with respect to African Americans, and any hope of achieving significant racial integration in the foreseeable future. Granted, there are grounds for pessimism. But this is the man who contributed to the defeat of the civil rights agenda by spearheading the battle against affirmative action policy with his 1975 book, *Affirmative Discrimination*. Now, thirty years later, when the crusade against affirmative action has achieved its nefarious objective—the effective dismantling of affirmative action policy, whose entire purpose was to *integrate* blacks into jobs, schools, and housing—Glazer declares that his sin was that he was too optimistic in assuming that racial segregation and inequality "were anomalies that would in time be swept aside."[119] Alas, he now comes to the realization that "the castelike character of American blacks" has not changed, and therefore, in resignation he concludes that "we must pass through a period in which we recognize difference, we celebrate difference, we turn the spotlight on the inadequacies in the integration of our minorities in the past and present."[120] In Glazer's hands multiculturalism becomes a respectable cover for racial apartheid.

The fatal flaw in Glazer's thinking was pointed out by Oliver Cox half a century ago: treating caste as a reified given, rather than confronting its roots in political economy. Glazer does not throw himself on the figurative sword for his complicity in eviscerating affirmative action policy, which was hugely successful in integrating blacks into jobs and schools where they had been excluded all through America's history. Nor does he propose joining the battle against the structural racism that accounts for the racial isolation and inequality he laments. Instead, he takes refuge in multiculturalism, as providing ideological justification for benign neglect. *["It seems we must pass through a period in which we recognize difference, we celebrate difference . . ." blah, blah, blah].* As Cox wrote about Myrdal: "The author relies finally upon time as the great corrector of all evil."[121] Glazer has abused the logic and intentions of multiculturalism to sanction racial inequality and isolation, all in the name of "difference."

It is quite another matter for David Hollinger when he advances a vision of a postethnic society where people are not defined by ancestry or genes. Like others in the "beyond race" school, Hollinger is impatient to get on with the postmodern project, to break out of the trap of racial and ethnic classification, to unleash the creative energies that come with shedding old skin and exploring new possibilities, and to acquire new and unexpected identities that are not defined by ancestry and genes. These are laudable goals, for sure. The trouble is that these new melting-pot theorists not only fail to take the black exception into account, but they promulgate their ideas at a time when millions of new immigrants are only recent arrivals, and when their ethnic solidarities are indispensable for advancing their struggles against the intertwined oppressions of race and class. Nor are these freshly arrived immigrants ready to forsake their ethnic identities and sign on to Hollinger's postethnic project. Hollinger may well be proved correct by history. But don't we have to wait for history to catch up with prophecy?

Let me be clear. There is compelling evidence that the United States will one day become a melting pot, and that this day is approaching faster than the multiculturalists are willing to acknowledge. From a moral standpoint, however, it is imperative that this melting pot evolve through the operation of historical forces rather than through public policy interventions. It is wrong—to continue the metaphor—to turn up the temperature under the melting pot, or to nudge, cajole, or push people into the bubbling cauldron. Any use of state power to undermine ethnicity or to force assimilation is incompatible with democratic principles and violates the rights of ethnic minorities to hold onto their languages and cultures.

The irony of the matter is that, like earlier waves of immigrants, today's newcomers will find their way to the melting pot in due course. So, presumably, will African Americans, but not until the structures of American apartheid are thoroughly dismantled. Not until "the ideal of human brotherhood has become a practical possibility," as Du Bois wrote in his 1897 essay "On the Conservation of Races."[122] When that condition is met—when the ideal of human brotherhood has become a practical possibility—people will have reason to embrace the personal and social integration that is the promise of the melting pot.

[Dear Reader: We've come to the end of our shared intellectual journey. I hope you leave, as I do, with a deeper and more honest reckoning of the stark realities

of race and ethnicity in American society. Above all, I've labored to subject the race relations model, the intellectual legacy of the Chicago school of race relations, to critical scrutiny. It is clear, I hope, that on matters of both race and ethnicity, this model has failed to confront realities that went against the belief systems, the cherished values, and the interests of successive generations of scholars who have used the tools of science, with its mystique of objectivity, to defend white supremacy and to advance their own ethnic projects. The result has been epistemologies that ultimately are self-serving and fail intellectually.

Let me share my authorial dilemma with you. I asked myself whether it is fair to leave the prevailing paradigm in tatters, as I hope I have, without at least attempting to point the way to a new paradigm. Is it enough to play the role of critic, to heap criticism on others and disparage their paradigm without offering anything positive in its place? I was tempted to add a chapter entitled "Toward a New Paradigm," but decided against it for two reasons.

First, the credo of the critic is that arriving at critical consciousness is a precondition for political transformation. It is scarcely possible to contemplate an alternative to hegemonic discourses on race and ethnicity until we extricate ourselves from the strictures of the old paradigm. Thus, it is not the responsibility or the mission of the critic to know the remedy for the diagnosed affliction. Moreover, if I were to presume to delineate the contours of "a new paradigm," I would contradict a central assumption of my critique: that hegemonic discourses prevail precisely because they serve powerful interests. It is not as though one only has to point out intellectual error in order to prevail intellectually! There is nothing I have said in my book that has not been said, with far more profundity and eloquence than I can muster, by Cox, Du Bois, and Marx, and their acolytes across generations. The point is that there is much political work that must be done before the received wisdom is relegated to the cold storage of history.

The second reason I do not venture down the path of "a new paradigm" is that there are others, better equipped than myself, who have taken on this challenge. Their work constitutes a canon of "antithetical scholarship," to use Edward Said's apt term, that goes against the prevailing discourses and represents the interests and viewpoint of subaltern groups.[123]

These scholars enter the fray with full knowledge that they are swimming against the current, and their chances of success are slim at best. Why, then, do they persevere? First of all, because there is the moral obligation to speak truth, to resist hegemony in all of its multifarious forms, and to develop the intellectual and political framework that might, at some unforeseeable time, be called into action. But there is another reason, which sustains intellectual warriors who stubbornly fight losing battles. This was the spirit of the civil rights movement, captured by Godfrey Hodgson, in his chapter on "The Black Uprising." As he wrote of the courageous activists in SNCC (the Student Non-Violent Coordinating Committee) who took on the dangerous mission of registering blacks to vote in Mississippi: "Success is not the only test . . . in the end, since failure is the fate of most human endeavors, what matters is with what enterprise and in what spirit one fails. For an ethic of success, they substituted an ethic of honesty and courage."[124]

Then again, we can take hope in the fact that SNCC ultimately triumphed and changed history.]

ACKNOWLEDGMENTS

LIKE ALL BOOKS, MINE IS A PRODUCT OF history and biography. I was born in 1940, came of age in the 1950s, and became politically conscious in the 1960s. Thus, I experienced very personally and acutely the collision between the bland uniformity of the 1950s and the proud aberration of the 1960s, which called into question the assumptions of my youth and early education, and put me on a path to eventually challenge the orthodoxies of my discipline. Many people along this life's journey have influenced me intellectually and politically—sometimes directly, more often in subtle and intangible ways that I realize only in retrospect.

My mother had a mock violin that she played whenever my father, as he was wont to do, lapsed into bombast or sanctimony. This was early tutelage in separating the wheat from the rhetorical chaff. Alas, I now realize that I have been playing her mock violin in my capacity as a sociologist.

Coming out of a public high school in the 1950s, I'm not sure I knew what a critical idea was when I enrolled as a student at Brown University. In registration line I was nudged into an experimental "IC" course taught by Dennis Wrong. The acronym stood for the "Identification and Criticism of Ideas." It was essentially a great books curriculum, and we read such luminaries as

Freud, Fromm, Durkheim, Veblen, and Reisman. I was blown away by their iconoclasm, and welcomed their implicit challenge to my assumptions and worldview. Marx was notably absent from Dennis's pantheon, but hey, this was 1958! I remember that Dennis's voice and entire body would quiver with nervous excitement whenever ideas clashed around the seminar table.

I wish I could say that I chose Berkeley for its intellectual ferment, but in truth I chose it for its reputation as "the best department of sociology." The month after I arrived, the Cuban missile crisis shattered any illusion of monastic tranquility, and I found myself attending mass meetings organized by self-proclaimed socialists. In 1962 the Berkeley campus was already a political hotbed. When classes broke for lunch at noon, Sproul Plaza was crowded with tables, and activists—some of them fresh from civil rights battles in the South—distributed literature and recruited members. It was the university's attempt to banish the tables to the lower plaza that triggered the Free Speech Movement in 1964. I wish I could say that I was on the front lines during the years of protest that ensued, but that was not the case either. I was cloistered at the Survey Research Center, busy crunching numbers for a survey of anti-Semitism in American society. It was my good fortune to work with Gertrude Jaeger Selznick, a philosopher of science who introduced me to the sociology of knowledge. Gertrude relentlessly extracted meaning from the raw facts spewed from the computer, and was riveted on the logic of inquiry, including the tacit assumptions embedded even in terms of discourse.

Of course, it was impossible not to be swept up in the political culture and revolutionary ethos that was Berkeley in the 1960s. Two friends, David Wellman—who was a red diaper baby—and Gary Marx—who was an activist in the Congress of Racial Equality—provided personal links to race and radicalism, two strands of thought that run through this book. Dave and I were both enrolled in Bob Blauner's first doctoral seminar in the fall of 1963. At the time I was not fully cognizant of how deeply I was influenced, not only by Blauner's teaching, but also by his example. Here was a young professor who was more than a purveyor of knowledge, but who also challenged the orthodoxies in his field.

In 1971 I took my first teaching job in the Ph.D. Program in Sociology at the CUNY Graduate Center, and was assigned to teach an undergraduate course on Race and Ethnic Relations at the City College of New York. The campus had just gone through a convulsive struggle leading to the adoption of an open admissions policy at CUNY, and tensions ran high. I assigned the hot new book, *Beyond the Melting Pot*, pleased that it dealt with the five major ethnic groups in New York City. My class consisted mostly of African American students, and I stumbled upon the principle of standpoint epistemology. I found myself refracting *Beyond the Melting Pot*, and other standard texts of sociology, through the eyes of my black students (or rather how I would read the texts if I occupied their position in the social universe). It was in this classroom that my disenchantment with "white sociology" began to take root.

I want to acknowledge flat out that I am very much a part of "the sociological establishment" that I criticize throughout this book. I cherish my life within the University, and have benefited enormously from many colleagues (too many to mention by name) in the Department of Urban Studies at Queens College and the Ph.D. Program in Sociology at the Graduate Center. I have benefited as well from the wonderfully diverse students who provided me with vicarious access to their worlds, as well as other "standpoints" from which to examine the world of race, ethnicity, class, and gender.

I have also benefited from another aspect of the institutional life of the university: the occasional invitation to speak on a college campus. Three such events were particularly useful in the development of this book.

First, thanks to Wahneema Lubiano, in 1993 I was invited to give a paper at the Race Matters Conference at Princeton University. Over the years I have given many papers at academic conferences, and I am used to being received (in some quarters) as a "contrarian," "a curmudgeon," and worse! But at the Race Matters Conference, my paper on "The Liberal Retreat from Race" galvanized the audience and elicited approbation that I never received, before or since. Could it be that I'm not a "contrarian" after all, but that it is the world we inhabit that is upside down or inside out?

Second, thanks to Mitch Duneier and Erik Olin Wright, in 1999 I was invited to participate in the Visiting Scholars Program at the Havens Center at the University of Wisconsin, Madison. The two public lectures that I delivered—one on race, the other on ethnicity—provided the embryo for this book.

Third, thanks to Njia Porter-Lawrence and Neil Kraus, in 2005 I was invited to give a lecture at the University of Wisconsin, River Falls. Realizing that most students came from old German and Scandinavian stock, and that the Twin Falls area has had a recent influx of Hmong, Somalis, and other immigrants, I decided to speak on "The Melting Pot: Past and Future." This lecture evolved over time into the third part of this book.

In New York I had the good fortune, thanks to Gertrude Ezorsky and Bill Kornblum, to hitch my academic wagon to *New Politics*, a radical journal that is free of cant and that bridges the chasm between the university and a wider community of intellectuals and activists. The editors, Phyllis and Julius Jacobson, became dear friends as well as compatriots in the struggle for a just society. It has meant everything over the past eighteen years to have an outlet for my writing in a journal that liberated me from the straitjacket of academic discourse.

Bill Kornblum, who has personal roots in Chicago sociology, read the first two parts of the book and gave me the benefit of his multifaceted perspective on race and class in America. Alyson Cole also gave me the benefit of her scrupulously critical eye, and her feedback was enormously helpful during the revision process. As my e-buddy, Alyson provided an unfailing sounding board, plus cheer and distraction.

Heartfelt thanks to many others who have been helpful at various stages of this project: Alan Aja, Stanley Aronowitz, Michael Burawoy, Rod Bush, Martin Eisenberg, Barry Finger, Ron Hayduk, Herbert Hill, Mike Hirsch, Rose Kim, Micaela di Leonardo, Seymour Leventman, Stanford Lyman, Neil McLaughlin, Jeff Maskovsky, Patricia Mathews-Salazar, Setsuki Nishi, Tom Pettigrew, Valli Rajah, Adolph Reed, Michelle Rief, Benjamin Ringer, Greg Robinson, Stephen Shalom, Edward Snajdr, Roberta Spalter-Roth, Gregory Squires, Jonathan Tilove, and David Wellman. Heartfelt thanks as well to my editors at Stanford University Press. To Kate Wahl, for her confidence in this project, and for her sound judgment and innovative spirit. Her magic wand transformed an idea into a book. To Richard Gunde, for his meticulous copyediting. To Judith Hibbard, who is both wordsmith and deft quarterback. And to Nicholas Koenig, whose work as an indexer went beyond the call.

Finally, my family. More than ever, biography and history come together. I met Sharon Friedman at a time when "the political is personal" was both mantra and credo. I have relied on her these many years for honest and critical feedback and ultimate support. Our children, Danny and Joanna, have been a source of inspiration, as they passed through Piaget's four stages and went on to become independent and critical thinkers. What offers inspiration and hope is that they transcend the inculcated obsessions and phobias that made the civil rights revolution necessary and liberating for us all.

NOTES

PROLOGUE

1. Jean-Paul Sartre, Introduction to Albert Memmi, *The Colonizer and the Colonized* (Boston: Beacon Press, 1965), xxii.

2. The project never came to fruition. According to Myrdal's biographer, the two giants had trouble establishing a collaborative relationship. Walter Jackson, *Gunnar Myrdal and the American Conscience* (Chapel Hill: University of North Carolina Press, 1990), 354. It is likely that there were intellectual disagreements between them as well. As Jackson also notes, Clark was "focused on increasing black political and economic power" (307), a far cry from Myrdal's brand of colorblind liberalism.

3. Oliver Cromwell Cox, *Caste, Class, & Race: A Study in Social Dynamics* (New York: Modern Reader, 1970), 510.

4. Ibid., 531.

5. Herbert Aptheker, *The Negro People in America: A Critique of Gunnar Myrdal's* An American Dilemma (New York: International Publishers, 1946), 19.

6. Edward Hallett Carr, *What Is History?* (New York: Knopf, 1965), 26.

PART ONE

1. Stanford M. Lyman, *The Black American in Sociological Thought* (New York: G. P. Putman's Sons, 1972), 15.

2. This chronology is adapted from Lester A. Sobel, ed., *Civil Rights, 1960–1966* (New York: Facts on File, 1967), 109–230.

3. Donald R. Matthews, "Political Science Research on Race Relations," in *Race and the Social Sciences,* Irwin Katz and Patricia Gurin, eds. (New York: Basic Books, 1969), 113.

4. Carol Polsgrove, *Divided Minds: Intellectuals and the Civil Rights Movement* (New York: W. W. Norton, 2001), xviii.

5. Quoted in ibid., 28. Orig. source: Lawrence Dunbar Reddick, "Whose Ordeal?" *New Republic* (September 24, 1956), 9–10.

6. Stanford Lyman, "Race Relations as Social Process: Sociology's Resistance to a Civil Rights Orientation," in *Race in America*, Herbert Hill and James E. Jones, eds. (Madison: University of Wisconsin Press, 1993), 394, 397.

7. Everett C. Hughes, "Race Relations and the Sociological Imagination," Presidential address read at the annual meeting of the American Sociological Association, Los Angeles, August 1963, and published in the *American Sociological Review* 28 (December 1963). Reprinted in Everett Hughes, *The Sociological Eye* (Chicago: Aldine-Atherton, 1971), 478.

8. Charles W. Mills, *The Racial Contract* (Ithaca, NY: Cornell University Press, 1977), 18.

9. Hughes, "Race Relations," 493–94.

10. Ibid., 494.

11. W.E.B. Du Bois, "Address to the Nation," delivered at the Second Annual Meeting of the Niagara Movement, Harpers Ferry, West Virginia, August 16, 1900, www.wfu.edu/~zulick/341/niagara.html.

12. Oliver Cromwell Cox, *Caste, Class, & Race* (New York: Modern Reader, 1948), 463.

13. C.L.R. James, "The Revolutionary Answer to the Negro Problem in the U.S.A.," speech at the Socialist Workers Party in 1948, www.marxists.org/archive/james-clr/works/1948/revolutionary-answer.htm.

14. See Cedric Robinson, *Black Marxism: The Making of the Black Radical Tradition* (Chapel Hill: University of North Carolina Press, 1983).

15. *Phylon* 10:2 (1948), 171.

16. Ibid., 61.

17. In 1936 Atlanta, Fisk, and Howard employed more than 80 percent of all black Ph.D.s. Anthony M. Platt, *E. Franklin Frazier Reconsidered* (New Brunswick, NJ: Rutgers University Press, 1991), 23; Michael R. Winston, "Through the Back Door: Academic Racism and the Negro Scholar in Historical Perspective," *Daedalus* 100:3 (Summer 1971), 695.

18. Quoted in James E. Conyers and Edgar G. Epps, "A Profile of Black Sociologists," in *Black Sociologists: Historical and Contemporary Perspectives*, James E. Blackwell and Morris Janowitz, eds. (Chicago: University of Chicago Press, 1974), 247.

19. C. Wright Mills, *The Sociological Imagination* (New York: Oxford University Press, 2000), 8.

20. Howard Winant, in *The Bubbling Cauldron: Race, Ethnicity, and the Urban Crisis*, Michael Peter Smith and Joe R. Feagin, eds. (Minneapolis: University of Minnesota Press, 1995), 31–49.

21. Bob Blauner, *Racial Oppression in America* (New York: Harper & Row, 1972).

22. Martin Luther King, Jr., *I Have a Dream*, James M. Washington, ed. (San Francisco: Harper Collins, 1992), 16. Orig. source: *Phylon* 28 (April 1957), 24–34; italics added.

23. In a recent study of Booker T. Washington, Michael Rudolph West arrives at the same understanding concerning the language and politics of "race relations." As he writes: "The idea of race relations is a form of analytic segregation. The great import of the race relations idea lies not only in what it helps clarify for many Americans in the Age of Washington, but also because it survives Washington, remaining in force down to the time of the civil rights movement as the main ideological buttress sustaining antidemocratic practices and proscription in a nation elsewhere aggressively proclaiming its democratic creed and institutions. . . . Americans, as a general matter, have hesitated to embrace in a straightforward way the idea of racial oppression." Michael Rudolph West, *The Education of Booker T. Washington: American Democracy and the Idea of Race Relations* (New York: Columbia University Press, 2006), 16.

24. Thomas Kuhn, *The Structure of Scientific Revolutions* (Chicago: University of Chicago Press, 1985).

25. Ibid., 77.

26. Interview, October 2005.

27. Hughes, "Race Relations," 879–90; Hughes, *The Sociological Eye*, 478–95. The *Social Science Citations Index* indicates that Hughes's paper was cited twenty-five times between 1963 and 2005.

28. James B. McKee, *Sociology and the Race Problem: The Failure of a Perspective* (Urbana: University of Illinois Press, 1993), 9.

29. Hazel Rowley, *Richard Wright: The Life and Times* (New York: Henry Holt, 2001), 250.

30. This tag, "father" of the race relations school, runs throughout the canon on race and ethnicity. In the estimate of Everett Hughes: "Park probably contributed more ideas for analysis of racial relations and cultural contacts than any other modern social scientist." Introduction to *Race and Culture* (New York: Free Press, 1950), xiii. This has been Park's enduring reputation. In 1967 Ralph Turner, a leading scholar of social movements, wrote: "Probably no man has so deeply influenced the direction taken by American empirical sociology as Robert E. Park." Quoted in Blackwell and Janowitz, *Black Sociologists*, 197. In his recent book, *Charles S. Johnson: Leadership beyond the Veil in the Age of Jim Crow* (Albany: State University of New York Press: 2003), Patrick J. Gilpin writes: "With all due respect to the European scholar Georg Simmel, under whom Park studied, and to W.E.B. Du Bois, whose pioneering work *The Philadelphia Negro* (1899) was an early scholarly work on race relations, Robert E. Park was the father of the study of race relations" (32). In "Black Belts and Ivory Towers: The Place of Race in U.S. Social Thought, 1892–1948," *Critical Sociology* 30:2 (2004), Davarian Baldwin writes of "white scholar Robert Park, the 'father' of urban sociology and race relations in the U.S. He challenged fixed genetic visions of social relations with a theory of cultural evolution informed by the idea that race is a dynamic and changing product of socio-historical conditions" (400).

31. According to Morris Janowitz, the "Green Bible" was the leading textbook in the discipline for two decades, selling over 30,000 copies until it went out of print in 1943. Janowitz, introduction to the 3rd edition of *Introduction to the Science of Sociology* (Chicago: University of Chicago Press, 1969), xi. According to Lewis Coser, *Introduction to the Science of Sociology* was "by far the most important textbook-reader in the early history of American sociology." *Masters of Sociological Thought* (New York: Harcourt Brace Jovanovich, 1971), 371.

32. Winifred Raushenbush, *Robert E. Park: Biography of a Sociologist*, with a foreword and an epilogue by Everett C. Hughes (Durham, NC: Duke University Press, 1979), 371.

33. Ibid., 105. This point is also echoed by Lewis Coser: "Park was, above all, a great teacher who managed to inspire his students with his own enthusiasm for the study of urban phenomena and race relations. He wrote relatively little himself; his main contributions consist of journal articles and introductions to the books of his students." "American Trends," in Tom Bottomore and Robert Nisbet, eds., *A History of Sociological Analysis* (New York: Basic Books, 1978), 315. Among Park's students were an astonishing number of people who gained prominence in the field of race and ethnic relations, including E. Franklin Frazier, Emory Bogardus, Everett Stonequist, Andrew Lind, Everett Hughes, Helen Hughes, and William Carlson Smith. Stow Persons, *Ethnic Studies at Chicago, 1905–45* (Urbana: University of Illinois Press, 1987), 33. Coser also writes: "There is no better testimony to the impact of Park's teaching than the imposing roster of his students. Everett C. Hughes, Herbert Blumer, Stuart Queen, Leonard Cottrell, Edward Reuter, Robert Faris, Louis Wirth, and E. Franklin Frazier all became presidents of the American Sociological Society. Helen McGill Hughes, John Dollard, Robert Redfield, Ernest Hiller, Clifford Shaw, Willard Waller, Walter C. Reckless, Joseph Lohman and many other students of Park became leading social scientists." Coser, *Masters*, 372. By the same token, this impressive list is an indication of the impact of Park's ideas on the discipline.

34. Park, "An Autobiographical Note," *Race and Culture*, v.

35. Paul J. Baker, "The Life Histories of W. I. Thomas and Robert E. Park," *American Journal of Sociology* 79 (September 1973), 257.

36. The reverberations of Belgium's "rape of the Congo" continue even today. See Adam Hochschild's excellent essay on Belgium's halfhearted attempt to confront its imperial past in "In the Heart of Darkness," *New York Review of Books* 52:15 (October 6, 2005), 39–42.

37. Raushenbush, *Robert E. Park*, 36.

38. Robert E. Park, "A King in Business," in Stanford M. Lyman, *Militarism, Imperialism, and Racial Accommodation* (Fayetteville: University of Arkansas Press, 1992), 210, 212, 217.

39. Robert E. Park, "The Terrible Story of the Congo," ibid., 221.

40. Robert E. Park, "The Blood-Money of the Congo," ibid., 234.

41. Park, "An Autobiographical Note," vii.

42. Booker T. Washington, *Up from Slavery* (New York: W. W. Norton, 1966; orig. pub. 1901), 13.

43. Booker T. Washington, "Cruelty in the Congo Country," *The Outlook* 78 (October 8, 1904).

44. Fred Matthews, *Quest for an American Sociology: Robert E. Park and the Chicago School* (Montreal: McGill-Queens University Press, 1977), 61.

45. W.E.B. Du Bois, *Souls of Black Folk* (New York: Penguin, 1996), 43.

46. Matthews, *Quest*, 61

47. Quoted in ibid., 62.

48. Ibid., 63.

49. Kevin K. Gaines, *Uplifting the Race: Black Leadership, Politics, and Culture in the Twentieth Century* (Chapel Hill: University of North Carolina Press, 1995), 1.

50. According to Washington's biographer, Louis Harlan, Max Bennett Thrasher, a white journalist from Boston, was the ghostwriter for *Up from Slavery*. Washington dictated autobiographical notes to Thrasher or wrote a rough sketch of chapters that Thrasher then revised. When Thrasher died suddenly of peritonitis in 1903, one of the smaller buildings on the Tuskegee campus was named Thrasher Hall. Louis R. Harlan, *Booker T. Washington: The Making of a Black Leader, 1856–1901* (New York: Oxford University Press, 1972), 246.

51. Matthews, *Quest*, 63.

52. St. Clair Drake, introduction to *The Man Farthest Down: A Record of Observation and Study in Europe*, by Booker T. Washington with the collaboration of Robert E. Park (New Brunswick, NJ: Transaction Books, 1984; orig. pub. 1912).

53. Booker T. Washington, *The Story of the Negro*, vol. 1 (New York: Peter Smith, 1909), 15. In his acknowledgment, Washington writes of Park: "Without his constant and painstaking assistance I could not have accomplished the object which I have had in view" (iv).

54. Raushenbush, *Robert E. Park*, 49.

55. John H. Stanfield, *Philanthropy and Jim Crow in American Social Science* (Westport, CT: Greenwood, 1985), 38.

56. Raushenbush, *Robert E. Park*, 67.

57. Dinesh D'Souza, *The End of Racism* (New York: Free Press, 1995), 554.

58. In *Uplifting the Race*, Kevin Gaines provided a riveting historical account of the political flip side of "uplift ideology." As he writes: "Although uplift ideology was by no means incompatible with social protest against racism, its orientation toward self-help implicitly faulted African Americans for their lowly status, echoing judgmental dominant characterizations of 'the Negro problem'" (4). Michael Rudolph West makes very much the same point in his recent study of Booker T. Washington: "The prevalence of Washington's ideas enabled Americans to isolate African America's just claims from those democratic values they elsewhere proudly proclaimed. Its beauty lies in the way it allows an evasion of the question of costs: the consequences of this injustice visited upon these Americans." West, *The Education of Booker T. Washington*, 17.

59. Raushenbush, *Robert E. Park*, chap. 8.

60. Ibid., 67.

61. Ibid., 68.

62. Ibid., 68–69. According to Martin Bulmer, "From 1913 to 1918, Park and Thomas worked side by side in the department, and their collaboration continued after Thomas's dismissal, when he worked with Park on the Americanization studies for the Carnegie Corporation. Later in the 1920s, Park organized a group of Chicago sociologists to nominate Thomas, successfully, for the presidency of the American Sociological Society and thus restore him to professional respectability." *The Chicago School of Sociology* (Chicago: University of Chicago Press, 1984), 62.

63. Raushenbush, *Robert E. Park*, 72.

64. Matthews, *Quest*, 57.

65. Morris Janowitz, introduction to *W. I. Thomas on Social Organization and Social Personality* (Chicago: University of Chicago Press, 1966), liv.

66. Raushenbush, *Robert E. Park*, 77.

67. Ibid.

68. Platt, *E. Franklin Frazier Reconsidered*, 21.

69. Noel A. Cazanave and Darlene Alvarez Maddern, "Defending the White Race: White Male Opposition to a 'White Racism' Course," *Race and Society* 2:1 (1999), 25–50.

70. Matthews, *Quest*, 81.

71. Drake, introduction to *The Man Down Farthest Down*, xxxvi.

72. Robert Ezra Park, "Racial Assimilation in Secondary Groups, With Particular Reference to the Negro," *Race and Culture*, 204–20. Orig. publication: *Publication of the American Sociological Society* 8 (1913), 66–83.

73. Park, *Race and Culture*, 204

74. Ibid., 206.

75. Du Bois, *Souls*, 44.

76. According to Martin Bulmer, "W. I. Thomas was the most productive and original scholar in the department in its first two decades." Bulmer, *The Chicago School*, 37. See also, Persons, *Ethnic Studies*, 45.

77. Mary Jo Deegan, *Jane Addams and the Men of the Chicago School, 1892–1918* (New Brunswick, NJ: Transaction Publishers, 2005), 2; Persons, *Ethnic Studies*, 10.

78. William Julius Wilson, *The Declining Significance of Race* (Chicago: University of Chicago Press, 1978), 153.

79. John Stanfield, "The 'Negro' Problem within and beyond the Nexus of Pre–World War I Sociology," *Phylon* 43:3 (1982), 201. "In his [Park's] model, groups assimilate not through biological amalgamation and political economic equality but through gradual change from caste relations to parallel class relations within racial groups—a feat achieved through members of subordinate groups internalizing the values of the dominant group." Wilson also contends that racism has morphed from caste to class, as suggested by the title of his first chapter, "From Racial Oppression to Economic Class Subordination," *Declining Significance*, 1.

80. Max Weber, "Science as a Vocation," in *From Max Weber: Essays in Sociology*, H. H. Gerth and C. Wright Mills, eds. (New York: Oxford University Press, 1958), 129–50.

81. Albion Small, "Scholarship and Social Agitation," *American Journal of Sociology* 1:5 (March 1896), 569.

82. Richard Weiss, "Racism in the Era of Industrialization," in *The Great Fear: Race in the Mind of America*, Gary B. Nash and Richard Weiss, eds. (New York: Holt, Rinehart & Winston, 1970), 142.

83. Walter P. Metzger, *Academic Freedom in the Age of the University* (New York: Columbia University Press, 1955), 139.

84. Mary O. Furner, *Advocacy & Objectivity: A Crisis in the Professionalization of American Social Science, 1865–1905* (Lexington: University of Kentucky Press, 1975), 205. Unfortunately, this fine book is out of print.

85. Dorothy Ross, *The Origins of American Social Science* (New York: Cambridge University Press, 1991), 102–3; Furner, *Advocacy*, 176.

86. Ross, *Origins*, 116.

87. Ibid.

88. Ibid.

89. Furner, *Advocacy*, 165.

90. Ibid., 177.

91. Ibid. Professionalization swept other social sciences as well, but sociology had an additional problem: in the popular mind it was confused with socialism, which would not have sat well with donors and university governors. Matthews, *Quest*, 96.

92. As Mary Jo Deegan shows in *Jane Addams and the Men of the Chicago School, 1892–1918*, "Male sociologists were expected to be abstract thinkers," whereas "female sociologists were expected to be 'practical' thinkers, capable of reaching out to strangers in a hostile world and in this way mimicking the female roles of wife, mother, and daughter in the home" (2). Indeed, Park insisted that his interest in sociology was "theoretical rather than practical." Coser, "American Trends," 382. When he wrote that the sociologist "was to be a kind of super-reporter" preoccupied with the "Big News," he meant that his sociological eye was focused on "the long-time trends which recorded what is actually going on rather than what, on the surface of things, merely seems to be going on." Park, "An Autobiographical Note," x–xi.

PART TWO

1. Charles W. Mills, *The Racial Contract* (Ithaca: Cornell University Press, 1997), 19. Italics in original,

2. Richard Weiss, "Racism in the Era of Industrialization," in *The Great Fear: Race in the Mind of America*, Gary B. Nash and Richard Weiss, eds. (New York: Holt, Rinehart & Winston, 1970), 143. Also, see Nicholas Patler, *Jim Crow and the Wilson Administration* (Boulder: University Press of Colorado, 2004).

3. Chicago Commission on Race Relations, *The Negro in Chicago* (Chicago: University of Chicago Press, 1922), 606. The Hyde Park Improvement Protective Club had some 350 members, including some of the wealthiest people on the South Side. Allan H. Spear, *Black Chicago* (Chicago: University of Chicago Press, 1967), 22.

4. Quoted in Stow Persons, *Ethnic Studies at Chicago, 1905–45* (Urbana: University of Illinois Press, 1987), 28.

5. Quoted in Charles U. Smith and Lewis Killian, "Black Sociologists and Social Protest," in *Black Sociologists: Historical and Contemporary Perspectives*, James E. Blackwell and Morris Janowitz, eds. (Chicago: University of Chicago Press, 1974), 197. Orig. source: Ernest W. Burgess, "Social Planning and Race Relations," in *Race Relations: Problems and Theory*, J. Masuoka and Preston Valien (Chapel Hill: University of North Carolina Press, 1961), 17.

6. This is how Emory Bogardus, a collaborator of Park, described the philosophical dispassion that Park brought to his 1920s Race Relations Survey of Asians on the West Coast. Fred Matthews, *Quest for an American Sociology: Robert E. Park and the Chicago School* (Montreal: McGill-Queens University Press, 1977), 113.

7. Persons, *Ethnic Studies*, 30.

8. Quoted in David Levering Lewis, *W.E.B. Du Bois, 1868–1919* (New York: Henry Holt, 1994), 479.

9. Matthews, *Quest*, 176.

10. Ibid., 96

11. Persons, *Ethnic Studies*, 38.

12. According to Matthews, Thomas even gave Park sartorial advice on his attire (Matthews, *Quest*, 86). Park's intellectual debts to Thomas were many. According to Persons, "in the area of ethnic and racial studies the dominant influence in determining the point of view and frame of reference of the group came from William Isaac Thomas" (Persons, *Ethnic Studies*, 45). In *Introduction to the Science of Sociology*, Park and Burgess, both neophytes to sociology, acknowledge that W. I. Thomas had suggested the general plan of the volume. When Thomas was sent into exile after the scandal over his sexual liaison with a married woman, authorship for *Old World Traits Transplanted* was transferred from Thomas to Park and Herbert Miller. According to Persons, Thomas provided the key theoretical ideas that went into Park's famous paper, "Human Migration and the Marginal Man" (Persons, *Ethnic Studies*, 45). Finally, according to Persons, Park "adopted Thomas's belief that immigrants and blacks could both be studied profitably in the same frame of reference" (ibid., 79).

13. Robert E. Park, "Negro Home Life and Standards of Living," *Annals of the American Academy of Political and Social Science*, vol. 49 (special issue), The Negro's Progress in Fifty Years (September 1913), 147–63. This article was written during the hiatus between Park's affiliation with Tuskegee and his arrival at the University of Chicago, and under the title he lists his address: Wollaston, Mass.

14. This article was discretely excluded from the posthumous volumes that Everett Hughes and his collaborators compiled of Park's writings. The clothbound volume was published under the title *The Collected Papers of Robert Ezra Park*, vol. 1 (New York: Free Press, 1950) which morphed into *Race and Culture* in the 1964 paperback edition (New York: Free Press, 1964). In addition to Hughes, the editors included Charles S. Johnson, Jitsuichi Masuoka, Robert Redfield, and Louis Wirth.

15. Park, "Negro Home Life," 147.

16. Ibid., 149; italics added.

17. Ibid., 163; italics added.

18. Quoted in Persons, *Ethnic Studies*, 11.

19. Erving Goffman, *Stigma* (New York: Simon & Schuster, 1963), 5.

20. W.E.B. Du Bois, "To the Reader," *Black Reconstruction* (New York: Harcourt, Brace, 1935).

21. Park, "Negro Home Life," 163

22. Matthews, *Quest*, 76

23. Chicago Commission on Race Relations, *The Negro in Chicago: A Study of Race Relations and a Race Riot* (Chicago: University of Chicago Press, 1922). According to Johnson's biographers, "although Johnson's authorship of the commissions report was never fully acknowledged, it was widely understood that the two-volume monograph . . . was largely his work." Patrick J. Gilpin and Marybeth Gasman, *Charles S. Johnson: Leadership beyond the Veil in the Age of Jim Crow* (Albany: State University of New York, 2003), 12. According to Martin Bulmer, "Johnson, with the advice of Park, was the architect of its [the commission's] research program." Martin Bulmer, *The Chicago School of Sociology* (Chicago: University of Chicago Press, 1984), 75.

24. Arthur Waskow makes this point forcefully in his book *From Race Riot to Sit-In* (New York: Doubleday, 1966), chap. 5.

25. Chicago Commission on Race Relations, *The Negro in Chicago*, 195

26. Ibid., 433.

27. Stanford M. Lyman, "Race Relations as Social Process: Sociology's Resistance to a Civil Rights Orientation," in *Race in America: The Struggle for Equality*, Herbert Hill and James E. Jones, Jr., eds. (Madison: University of Wisconsin Press, 1993), 370.

28. Ralph Turner, as quoted in *The Black Sociologists: The First Half Century*, John H. Bracey, Jr., August Meier, and Elliott Rudwick, eds. (Belmont, CA: Wadsworth, 1971), 6.

29. Robert Ezra Park, "Our Racial Frontier on the Pacific," in *Race and Culture*, 150.

30. Bracey, Meier, and Rudwick, *Black Sociologists*, 6–7. For an excellent synthesis of Park's race relations cycle, see Lewis Coser, *Masters of Sociological Thought* (New York: Harcourt Brace Jovanovich, 1971), 359–60.

31. Park, *Race and Culture*, 151.

32. Charlotte Perkins Gilman, "A Suggestion on the Negro Problem," *American Journal of Sociology* 14 (July 1908), 80. Gilman ends the quoted passage by noting that only the Japanese have benefited more from "contact" with European culture.

33. Herman Schwendinger and Julia R. Schwendinger, *The Sociologists of the Chair* (New York: Basic Books, 1974), 173–74.

34. I. A. Newby, *Jim Crow's Defense: Anti-Negro Thought in America, 1900–1930* (Baton Rouge: Louisiana University Press, 1930), 48. Orig. source: Lester F. Ward, *Pure Sociology, A Treatise on the Origin and Spontaneous Development of Society* (New York, Macmillan, 1903), 359.

35. American Sociological Association Online Bookstore, www.e-noah.net/asa/asashoponlineservice/ ProductDetails.aspx?productID=ASAOEDVDWARD.

36. Ward's acclaimed telesis including the idea that "war has been the chief and leading condition of human progress," and war is an instrument whereby "the master race of the planet has extended its dominion over inferior races." Schwendinger and Schwendinger, *Sociologists of the Chair*, 173–74.

37. Ibid., 173.

38. Ibid., 100.

39. R. W. Connell, "Why Is Classical Theory Classical?" *American Journal of Sociology* 102 (May 1997), 1516–17.

40. Ibid., 1517.

41. Ibid., 1530.

42. John Hope Franklin, "The Dilemma of the American Negro Scholar," in *Soon, One Morning: New Writing by American Negroes, 1940–1962*, Herbert Hill, ed. (New York: Knopf, 1963), 62.

43. Connell, "Why Is Classical Theory Classical?" 1519.

44. Park, *Race and Culture*, 151.

45. E. Berkeley Tompkins, *Anti-Imperialism in the United States: The Great Debate, 1890–1920* (Philadelphia: University of Pennsylvania Press, 1970), 10.

46. Ibid., 50.

47. Park's flight into abstraction, and his concomitant failure to confront the realities on the ground, were evident in his treatment of racial conflict involving Japanese Americans on the West Coast. During the early 1920s, racial tensions were rising, and Park was commissioned to conduct a study. As Stow Persons points out, "It was, in other words, to be a study of assimilation, for which previous work like that of Thomas and Znaniecki might serve as a model since 'the problems of the European and the Asiatic, though different in certain respects, are enough alike to be comparable.' . . . Park's faith in the progress of the interaction cycle was obviously great enough to permit him to minimize the severity of the racial conflict."

Alas, the study was barely underway when Congress passed the Japanese Exclusion Act of 1924, which barred all immigration from Japan. Protests were held in Japan declaring this as "a day of humiliation." Did Robert Park speak out against the travesty of this patently racist legislation? Did he reexamine the optimistic assumptions underlying the race relations cycle? Did he weigh the possibility that assimilation theory might not apply to racial minorities? None of the above. Once again, he maintained Olympian distance from the gritty facts on the ground, and averred that racial tension on the Pacific Coast was a byproduct of the westward expansion and the natural consequence of "a new intermingling of races." Persons, *Ethnic Studies*, 68–69.

48. In his article on "The Tradition of Sociology Teaching in Black Colleges: The Unheralded

Professionals," Butler A. Jones writes: "Even if exiled to one of the poorer white colleges or to one of the less affluent social welfare agencies, the white sociologist did not entirely lose his advantage. There were still many avenues (a network of friends and acquaintances in the profession, contacts made in social gatherings) open to him that were closed to blacks." In Blackwell and Janowitz, eds., *Black Sociologists*, 135.

49. Anthony M. Platt, *E. Franklin Frazier Reconsidered* (New Brunswick, NJ: Rutgers University Press, 1991), 41; Michael R. Winston, "Through the Back Door: Academic Racism and the Negro Scholar in Historical Perspective," *Daedalus* 100:3 (Summer 1971), 695.

50. Platt, *E. Franklin Frazier Reconsidered*, 66.

51. Jones, "The Tradition of Sociology Teaching in Black Colleges," 134.

52. Otto Klineberg: in *A History of Psychology in Autobiography* vol. 6, ed. Gardner Lindzey (Worcester, MA: Clark University Press, 1930), 166.

53. Anthony Platt, Introduction to 2001 edition of E. Franklin Frazier, *The Negro Family in the United States* (Notre Dame, IN: University of Notre Dame Press, 2001), xii–xiii.

54. Platt, *E. Franklin Frazier Reconsidered*, 21.

55. Ibid., 226.

56. Quoted in ibid., 43. Also see John Stanfield, *Philanthropy and Jim Crow in American Social Science* (Westport, CT: Greenwood, 1985).

57. Gordon L. Weil, *Roebuck, U.S.A.* (New York: Stein & Day, 1977), 50.

58. For a path-breaking exposition of this seminal idea, see Bob Blauner and David Wellman, "Toward the Decolonization of Social Research," in Bob Blauner, *Still the Big News* (Philadelphia: Temple University Press, 2001), 173–85.

59. Edwin R. Embree and Julia Waxman, "Julius Rosenwald: Philanthropist," *Phylon* 9:3 (1948), 227.

60. Cheryl Lynn Greenberg, *Troubling the Waters: Black-Jewish Relations in the American Century* (Princeton, NJ: Princeton University Press, 2006), 70.

61. Jones, "The Tradition of Sociology Teaching in Black Colleges," 136.

62. The term, "surrogate control" is Jones's (ibid., 135). Jones directed much of his fire at Charles Johnson, whom he denounces as the University of Chicago's prime "establishment nigger," and as "the new Booker T. Washington, exercising suzerainty over a more limited and specialized territory" (136).

63. Davarian L. Baldwin, "Black Belts and Ivory Towers: The Place of Race in U.S. Social Thought, 1892–1948," *Critical Sociology* 30:2 (2004), 418.

64. Jones, "The Tradition of Sociology Teaching in Black Colleges," 136.

65. Quoted in Adolph Reed, "Introduction," Oliver Cromwell Cox, *Race: A Study in Social Dynamics*, fiftieth anniversary edition of *Caste, Class, & Race* (New York: Monthly Review Press, 2000), xv.

66. Charles Sturgeon Johnson, *Shadow of the Plantation* (Chicago: University of Chicago Press, 1934), and *Growing up in the Black Belt* (Washington, D.C.: American Council on Education, 1941).

67. Matthews, *Quest*, 175.

68. G. Franklin Edwards, "E. Franklin Frazier," in Blackwell and Janowitz, eds., *Black Sociologists*, 66.

69. Platt, *E. Franklin Frazier Reconsidered*, chaps. 2–8.

70. Ibid., 33–34.

71. Ibid., 52.

72. E. Franklin Frazier, "The Pathology of Race Prejudice," in Bracey, Meier, and Rudwick, *Black Sociologists*, 83.

73. Ibid., 86.

74. Quoted in Platt, *E. Franklin Frazier Reconsidered*, 83.

75. Quoted in ibid., p. 83. Stanford Lyman writes: "One of Park's persistent themes is racial temperament, which, he wrote, 'consists in a few elementary but distinctive characteristics, determined by physical organizations and transmitted biologically.'" Stanford M. Lyman, *The Black American in Sociological Thought* (New York: G. P. Putman's Sons, 1972), 41.

76. E. Franklin Frazier, "The Pathology of Race Prejudice," *Forum* 77 (June 1927), 856–62.

77. Platt, *E. Franklin Frazier Reconsidered*, 83–84.

78. Frazier later acknowledged that his article was written in "a partly satirical vein." Ibid., 82.

79. Ibid.

80. Ibid., 78–79.

81. See Richard Herrnstein and Charles Murray, *The Bell Curve* (New York: Free Press, 1994), and Russell Jacoby and Naomi Glauberman, *The Bell Curve Debate* (New York: Times Books, 1995).

82. E. Franklin Frazier, *The Negro in the United States* (New York: Macmillan, 1949).

83. Platt, *E. Franklin Frazier Reconsidered*, 52.

84. E. Franklin Frazier, *The Negro in Harlem: A Report on Social and Economic Conditions Responsible for the Outbreak of March 19, 1935* (New York: Arno Press, 1968), 7.

85. Ibid., 129.

86. Christopher A. McAuley, *The Mind of Oliver C. Cox* (Notre Dame: University of Notre Dame Press, 2004), 2.

87. In *Race, Class, and the World System: The Sociology of Oliver C. Cox*, Herbert M. Hunter and Sameer Y. Abraham, eds. (New York: Monthly Review Press, 1987), xxxi.

88. Sean P. Hier, "Structures of Orthodoxy and the Sociological Exclusion of Oliver C. Cox," in ibid., 303.

89. Oliver Cromwell Cox, *Caste, Class, & Race* (New York: Modern Reader, 1948), 462.

90. Ibid., 463.

91. Ibid., 474.

92. Ibid., 470.

93. Ibid., 474.

94. Ibid., 462.

95. Again, I refer readers to R. W. Connell's astute analysis in "Why Is Classical Theory Classical?"

96. Schwendinger and Schwendinger, *Sociologists of the Chair*, 564; emphasis in original.

97. Mills, *The Racial Contract*, 19. The blindnesses and opacities were indeed structural. As Schwendinger and Schwendinger comment: "It would have been virtually impossible for the field to have been dominated by Park and Burgess' metatheory—or even the modern theoretical variations in liberal-functionalism—if it were not for the political repression of radical scholarship. As far as sociology in the United States is concerned, the long-term consequences of the systematic political repression of radical alternatives within the American academy cannot be overstated." *Sociologists of the Chair*, 490–91.

98. I first encountered this formidable construct in Robin Kelley's foreword to Cedric J. Robinson, *Black Marxism: The Making of the Black Radical Tradition* (Chapel Hill: University of North Carolina Press, 1983), xii. A check of Google Scholar yielded only eight hits for the term, spelled either in the singular or the plural.

99. Mills, *The Racial Contract*, 18.

100. W.E.B. Du Bois, "Note to the Reader," *Black Reconstruction* (New York: Russell & Russell, 1963; orig. pub. 1935).

101. Wilson Record, *Race and Radicalism* (New York: Cornell University Press, 1964), 37.

102. Karl Marx, *The Poverty of Philosophy* (Chicago: Charles H. Kerr, 1934), 121.

103. Cox, *Class, Caste, & Race*, 476.

104. Robert K. Murray, *Red Scare: A Study in National Hysteria, 1919–1920* (New York: McGraw-Hill, 1964).

105. Du Bois, *Black Reconstruction*, 727.

106. Robinson, *Black Marxism*, 186.

107. The origins of the historic contention between "race men" and "class men" is examined in historical detail in James O. Young, *Black Writers of the Thirties* (Baton Rouge: Louisiana State University Press, 1973).

108. This paragraph is based entirely on David Levering Lewis, *W.E.B. Du Bois: Biography of a Race* (New York: Henry Holt, 1994), 420–21. For an excellent analysis of the race/class problematic, as it played itself out in American history, see Rod Bush, *We Are Not What We Seem* (New York: New York University Press, 1999), chap. 1.

109. See Michael Goldfield, *The Color of Politics: Race and the Mainsprings of American Politics* (New York: New Press, 1997).

110. Quoted in Mark Solomon, *The Cry Was Unity* (Jackson: University Press of Mississippi, 1998), 70–71.

111. Quoted in ibid., 71.

112. Robin D. G. Kelley, *Hammer and Hoe* (Chapel Hill: University of North Carolina Press, 1990), 13.

113. Solomon, *The Cry Was Unity*, 75–76.

114. Quoted in Jonathan Scott Holloway, *Confronting the Veil* (Chapel Hill: University of North Carolina Press, 2002), 101–2.

115. Ibid., 98

116. In 1936 Bunche wrote: "The Negro is said to be a 'racial minority' group, but this is true only in a narrow and arbitrary sense. Economically, the Negro primarily is identified with the peasant and proletarian classes of the country, which are certainly not in the minority." Quoted in Young, *Black Writers*, 54.

117. Aldon Morris, *The Origins of the Civil Rights Movement* (New York: Free Press, 1984), 288.

118. "The Civil Rights Movement," www.socialistalternative.org/literature/malcolmx/ch3.html.

119. James B. McKee, *Sociology and the Race Problem: The Failure of a Perspective* (Urbana: University of Illinois Press, 1993), 109.

120. *The Collected Papers of Robert Ezra Park*, Everett Cherrington Hughes, Charles S. Johnson, Jitsuichi Masuoka, Robert Redfield, and Louis Wirth, eds. (Glencoe, IL: Free Press, 1950).

121. This phrase originated in Britain and was imported to the United States by Lewis Killian. See Lewis M. Killian, "'The Race Relations Industry' as a Sensitizing Concept," in *Research in Social Problems and Public Policy*, vol. 1, Michael Lewis, ed. (Greenwich, CT: JAI Press, 1979).

122. McKee, *Sociology*, 256.

123. Ibid., 283

124. This viewpoint was first advanced in 1966 by Thomas Pettigrew, who said: "I think one of the great fallacies we have had in the field of race relations for many, many decades has been to worry about attitudes rather than about conditions. It is a crude but, I think, generally correct statement to say that attitudes are more often a result than a cause of most of our race-relation situations." Of course, what is discouraging is that we are still having this conversation forty years later. Thomas F. Pettigrew, "Transcript of the American Academy Conference on the Negro American—May 14–15, 1965," in "The Negro American—2," *Daedalus* 95:1 (Winter 1966), 312.

125. McKee, *Sociology*, 272.

126. In his review of *The Race Problem*, John Rex criticizes McKee for neglecting works that

"problematize the relation between 'race' and class." *American Sociological Review*, 23:5 (September 1994), 647. Mckee gives passing mention to such writers as Du Bois, Cox, and Blauner, but there is no systematic attempt to examine the works that sought to compensate for precisely the failures that he highlights in his book ("Marx" and "Marxism" do not even appear in the index). The only time "oppression" appears in Mckee's index is to flag "oppression psychosis," which refers to a condition involving "persistent and exaggerated mental states which are characteristically produced under conditions where one group dominates another"(302). For a trenchant analysis of anthropological practice that *does* apply a robust critical perspective, and takes fire at studies that fail to anchor culture in political economy, see Micaela di Leonardo, *Exotics at Home* (Chicago: University of Chicago Press, 1998). For a critical analysis of the role of anthropology in the construction of race, see Lee D. Baker, *From Savage to Negro* (Berkeley: University of California Press, 1998).

127. Mckee, *Sociology*, 366.

128. Howard Zinn, *You Can't Be Neutral on a Moving Train: A Personal History of Our Times* (Boston: Beacon Press, 1994).

129. This section, together with the two that follow, borrows heavily from my previous study, *Turning Back: The Retreat from Racial Justice in American Thought and Policy* (Boston: Beacon Press, 1995 and 2001).

130. Stanfield, *Philanthropy*, 142.

131. Quoted in Walter Jackson, *Gunnar Myrdal and the American Conscience* (Chapel Hill: University of North Carolina Press, 1990), 21.

132. "After extended negotiations in the fall of 1937 and the spring of 1938, Myrdal managed to obtain an annual salary of $19,800 for two years. In depression dollars, this amount would be roughly equivalent to $152,000 in 1986 currency." David W. Southern, *Gunnar Myrdal and Black-White Relations* (Baton Rouge: Louisiana State University Press, 1987), 14. The $280,000 estimate adjusts for inflation since 1986.

133. F. P. Keppel, Preface to *An American Dilemma: The Negro Problem and Modern Democracy* (New York: McGraw-Hill, 1964; orig. ed. 1944), xlviii.

134. Jackson, *Gunnar Myrdal*, 34. Myrdal's letter is dated October 7, 1937.

135. Keppel, Preface, xlvii.

136. Gunnar Myrdal, *An American Dilemma: The Negro Problem and Modern Democracy* (New York: McGraw Hill paperback ed., 1964; orig. ed. New York: Harper, 1944), 1049.

137. Jackson, *Gunnar Myrdal*, xi.

138. Thomas Kuhn, *The Structure of Scientific Revolutions* (Chicago: University of Chicago Press, 1985), 92.

139. Steinberg, *Turning Back* (2001 ed.), chap. 3.

140. Mel Watkins, "The Black Revolution in Books," *New York Times Book Review* (August 10, 1969), 8ff.

141. Stokely Carmichael (later renamed Kwame Ture) and Charles V. Hamilton, *Black Power: The Politics of Liberation in America* (New York: Vintage Books, 1967), 4; emphasis in original.

142. One can discern three overlapping waves of race books that reflect a "scholarship of confrontation." The foundational "first wave" includes: Wilson Record, *Race and Radicalism* (Ithaca, NY: Cornell University Press, 1964); Harold M. Baron, *The Negro Worker in the Chicago Labor Market* (Chicago: Chicago Urban League, 1968); John Leggett, *Class, Race and Labor* (New York: Oxford University Press, 1968); Robert Allen, *Black Awakening in Capitalist America* (New York: Doubleday, 1969); James Boggs, *Racism and the Class Struggle* (New York: Monthly Review Press, 1970); August Meier and Elliott Rudwick, *From Plantation to Ghetto* (New York: Hill & Wang, 1970); James A. Geschwender, *The Black Revolt* (Englewood Cliffs, NJ: Prentice-Hall, 1971); William Tabb, *The Political Economy of the Black Ghetto* (New York: Norton 1971); Stanford

M. Lyman, *The Black American in Sociological Thought* (New York: G. P. Putman's Sons, 1972); Raymond Franklin and Solomon Resnik, *The Political Economy of Racism* (New York: Holt, Rinehart & Winston, 1973).

143. The "second wave of race books," written by the "children of the 1960s," overlaps to some extent with the first wave. What follows is a very partial list: Gary Marx, *Protest and Prejudice* (New York: Harper & Row, 1967); Harry Edwards, *The Revolt of the Black Athlete* (New York: Free Press, 1969); Joyce A. Ladner, ed., *The Death of White Sociology* (New York: Vintage, 1973); Michael Lipsky and David J. Olson, *Commission Politics: The Processing of Racial Crisis in America* (New Brunswick, NJ: Transaction Books, 1977); David Wellman, *Portraits of White Racism* (New York: Cambridge University Press, 1977). See the penultimate endnote in Part 3 for a list of "third wave race books" that build on the foundation of the scholarship of confrontation.

144. Bob Blauner, *Racial Oppression in America* (New York: Harper & Row, 1972).

145. Ibid., viii.

146. Ibid., 5.

147. Bob Blauner, "Race and Radicalism in My Life and Work," in John H. Stanfield II, ed., *A History of Race Relations Research: First-Generation Recollections* (Newbury Park, CA: Sage Publications, 1993), 7.

148. A revised and expanded edition was published by Temple University Press in 2001 under the title *Still the Big News: Racial Oppression in America*. It must be noted that Blauner backed away from some of his positions in the original edition. Even his laudable title, *Racial Oppression in America*, was relegated to the subtitle *[ouch!]*. His new title, *Still the Big News*, was derived from Robert Park *[ouch again]*, who saw the sociologist as a "superjournalist," focused on the big story. *[As we have seen, this often meant escape into abstractions that obfuscated the realities on the ground.]* It goes without saying that Blauner has a right to revise and update his thinking, but this doesn't mean that he didn't have it right the first time!

149. Blauner, "Race and Radicalism," 15.

150. Andrew Kopkind, "White on Black: The Riot Commission and the Rhetoric of Reform," in Anthony M. Platt, *The Politics of Riot Commissions* (New York: Macmillan, 1971), 378. Kopkind provides details of internal politics and conflicts between "radicals" and "moderates." Also, Gary T. Marx, "Two Cheers for the National Riot (Kerner) Commission Report," in *Black Americans: A Second Look*, J. F. Szwed, ed. (New York: Basic Books, 1970).

151. *Report of the National Advisory Commission on Civil Disorders* (New York: Bantam Books, 1968), 110.

152. Ibid., 265.

153. Everett Carll Ladd, Jr., and Seymour Martin Lipset, *The Divided Academy: Professors and Politics* (New York: McGraw Hill, 1975), chaps. 2 and 4.

154. William Julius Wilson, *When Work Disappears: The World of the New Urban Poor* (New York: Knopf, 1996), xi.

155. There has been some institutional support for critical scholarship at the University of California, Berkeley, that had its inception with a Third World Strike in 1969 by students demanding a School of Ethnic Studies. After strident protest, the administration finally acceded to the establishment of an Institute of Race and Community Studies *[note the circumspect language]*. This provided something of an institutional home for Blauner, who at the time had a grant from the National Institute of Mental Health for a study of Racism, Manhood, and Culture *[again, note what bagged the grant]*. Eventually the Institute of Race and Community Studies morphed into the Institute for the Study of Social Change *[sanitary language for revolution?]*, headed by Troy Duster. The center secured a large training grant targeted for minority students, thanks to the assistance of Eliot Liebow, who had a position at the National Institute of Mental Health *[again, note how grantsmanship is played to advantage]*. This

grant helped to support doctoral research for a score of minority students. A far cry from my imagined Institute for the Study of Racial Oppression, but one can see here the attempts to maneuver within the existing regime of foundation and government grants to secure financial resources for critical scholarship on race. (Thanks to David Wellman for providing this account in personal communication.)

156. Alyson Cole, *The Cult of True Victimhood: From the War on Welfare to the War on Terror* (Palo Alto, CA: Stanford University Press, 2006).

157. William Julius Wilson, *The Declining Significance of Race* (Chicago: University of Chicago Press, 1978), 1.

158. Park, *Race and Culture*, 116.

159. Charles Johnson, "The Economic Basis of Culture Conflict," reprinted in *When Peoples Meet: A Study in Race and Culture Contacts*, Alain Locke and Bernhard J. Stern, eds. (New York: Progressive Education Association, 1942), 217 and 231; italics added.

160. William Julius Wilson, "Dialogue," in *The Declining Significance of Race? A Dialogue among Black and White Social Scientists*, Joseph R. Washington, ed. (proceedings of a symposium held at the University of Pennsylvania under the sponsorship of the Afro-American Studies Program in March 1979), 117–18.

161. Neil McLaughlin, "Beyond Race Versus Class: The Politics of William Julius Wilson," *Dissent* (Summer 1993), 362–67.

162. Quoted in Hollie West, "Getting Ahead and the Man behind the Class-Race Furor," *Washington Post* (January 1, 1979).

163. Kenneth B. Clark, "Contemporary Sophisticated Racism," in Washington, ed., *The Declining Significance*, 105.

164. *Footnotes*, American Sociological Association (October 1994), 5.

165. Daniel Patrick Moynihan, *Family and Nation* (San Diego: Harcourt Brace Jovanovich, 1986), 42. Soon after the publication of *The Declining Significance of Race*, Nathan Glazer also commented: "These are not things that haven't been said before. It is the first time that a black social scientist said them with such strength." Quoted in West, "Getting Ahead."

166. www.asanet.org/page.ww?section=Awards&name=Award+1998+Citation+William+Julius+Wilson.

167. http://ksgfaculty.harvard.edu/william_wilson.

168. Wilson's book was originally intended for a book series aimed at undergraduates that Peter Rose was editing for Random House. According to Rose, the editors at Random House rejected Wilson's submission because it was "more treatise than text" and did not conform to the narrow guidelines for the series. The rest, as they say, is history. See Peter I. Rose, "White Liberal," in Stanfield, *A History of Race Relations Research*, 219. Wilson's slant is somewhat different: "The first title of the book was 'Black America.' I had a contract with Random House to write the book; I wanted to get out of that contract because they wanted me to write a simple-minded book for undergraduate students. My ideas were developing and I was concerned about certain kinds of issues, so I got out of that contract only after I agreed to write a textbook for them. The University of Chicago Press then moved in." Such are the birth pangs of a "classic." Wilson, in Washington, *The Declining Significance*, 117–18.

169. http://ksgfaculty.harvard.edu/william_wilson.

170. For example, an article in the *Atlantic Monthly* noted the following: "He [Clinton] repeatedly cited William Julius Wilson's 1987 book *The Truly Disadvantaged*, which says that today's ghetto social problems, such as crime, welfare dependency, and family disintegration, are primarily the result of the loss of good manufacturing jobs. Clinton seemed to be using Wilson's book as a kind of talisman. . . . Clinton seems to have filed away in his mind a sound-bite-like statement along the lines of 'the ghetto underclass was created by deindustrialization.'" *Atlantic Monthly* (October 1992), www.theatlantic.com/doc/199210/clinton/4.

171. Excerpted in *The Blueprint*, a publication of the Democratic Leadership Council, www.ppionline.org/ndol/ndol_ci.cfm?kaid=127&subid=173&contentid=252794.

172. Adolph Reed, "America Becoming—What Exactly? Social Policy Research as the Fruit of Bill Clinton's Race Initiative," *New Politics* 8 (Winter 2002), 6, www.wpunj.edu/newpol/issue 32/reed32.htm.

173. Gretchen Reynolds, "The Rising Significance of Race," *Chicago* 41 (December 1992), 82, 127.

174. Adolph Reed and Stephen Steinberg, "Liberal Bad Faith in the Wake of Hurricane Katrina," *Black Commentator*, www.blackcommentator.com/182/182_cover_liberals_katrina.html; Brod Bagert, Jr., "Hope VI and St. Thomas: Smoke, Mirrors, and Urban Mercantilism," Report, London School of Economics, September 2002, https://wa.gc.cuny.edu/exchange/SSteinberg1/Inbox/No%20Subject-41.EML/1_multipart_xF8FF_2_HOPEVIandStThomas.pdf/C58EA28C-18C0-4a97-9AF2-036E93DDAFB3/HOPEVIandStThomas.pdf?attach=1. Larry Bennett and Adolph Reed Jr., "The New Face of Urban Renewal: The Near North Redevelopment Initiative and the Cabrini-Green Neighborhood," in Adolph Reed Jr., *Without Justice for All* (Boulder, CO: Westview Press, 1999), 175–211.

175. Dinesh D'Souza, *The End of Racism* (New York: Free Press, 1995), 554.

176. Ibid., 289.

177. Wilson, *When Work Disappears*. Also see Stephen Steinberg, "Science and Politics in the Work of William Julius Wilson," *New Politics* 6:2 (Winter 1997), www.wpunj.edu/~newpol/issue22/steinb22.htm.

178. Wilson, *When Work Disappears*, 71.

179. D'Souza, *The End of Racism*, 482.

180. Gordon Allport, *The Nature of Prejudice* (New York: Anchor Books, 1958), 8.

181. Joe Klein, "The True Disadvantage," *The New Republic* 215 (October 28, 1996), 36. For a commentary on Klein's review, see Adolph Reed, Jr., "Dissing the Underclass," *The Progressive* 60 (December 1996).

182. Bill Clinton, "One America in the 21st Century," Commencement address, University of California, San Diego (June 14, 1997), http://usinfo.state.gov/journals/itsv/0897/ijse/clint11.htm.

183. *One America in the 21st Century: The President's Initiative on Race*, the Advisory Board's Report to the President (Washington, D.C.: Government Printing Office, 1998), 1.

184. Reed, "America Becoming," 1.

185. Ibid., 6.

186. Clarence Lusane, "Not a Word of Criticism of Clinton," *Poverty and Race* (November/December 1998), Poverty and Race Research Action Council, Symposium: President Clinton's Race Initiative, Part 2, www.prrac.org/full_text.php?text_id=323&item_id=3336&newsletter_id=36&header=Symposium:%20President%20Clinton's%20Race%20Initiative%20Part%20One.

187. Claire Jean Kim, "Clinton's Race Initiative: Recasting the American Dilemma," *Polity* 33 (Winter 2000), 186.

188. Frances Fox Piven, "No Surprises," *Poverty and Race* (November/December 1998), Poverty and Race Research Action Council, Symposium: President Clinton's Race Initiative, Part 2, www.prrac.org/full_text.php?text_id=221&item_id=1881&newsletter_id=41&header=Symposium:%20President%20Clinton%27s%20Race%20Initiative%20Part%20Two.

189. Clarence Lusane, "Six Precepts on Race in Pre-Millennium America," *Poverty and Race* (January/February 1998), Poverty and Race Research Action Council, Symposium: President Clinton's Race Initiative, Part 1, www.prrac.org/full_text.php?text_id=323&item_id=3336&newsletter_id=36&header=Symposium:%20President%20Clinton's%20Race%20Initiative%20Part%20One.

190. Manning Marable, "Focus on the Institutional Barriers," *Poverty and Race* (November/December 1997), Poverty and Race Research Action Council, Symposium: President Clinton's Race

Initiative, Part 1, www.prrac.org/full_text.php?text_id=352&item_id=3450&newsletter_id=35&hea der=Symposium:%20President%20Clinton's%20Race%20Initiative%20Part%20One.

191. Chester Hartman, "Notes on the President's Initiative on Race," *Poverty and Race* (November/ December 1997), Poverty and Race Research Action Council, Symposium: President Clinton's Race Initiative, Part 1, www.prrac.org/full_text.php?text_id=341&item_id=3444&newsletter_id=35&hea der=Symposium:%20President%20Clinton's%20Race%20Initiative%20Part%20One.

192. Adolph Reed, Jr., "Yackety-Yak about Race," *The Progressive* (December 1997). Reprinted in Stephen Steinberg, ed., *Race and Ethnicity in the United States* (Malden, MA: Blackwell, 2000), 62.

193. For a more sympathetic account of the Clinton initiative by a staff member, see John Goering, "An Assessment of President Clinton's Initiative on Race," *Ethnic and Racial Studies* 24:3 (May 2001), 472–84.

194. Martin Luther King, Jr., *I Have a Dream*, James Melvin Washington, ed. (New York: HarperCollins, 1992), 91.

195. If I have it right, Francis Fox Piven and Richard A. Cloward were the first to use this term, in *Poor People's Movements* (New York: Pantheon, 1977). The concept plays a central role in Doug McAdam, *Political Process and the Development of Black Insurgency, 1930–1970* (Chicago: University of Chicago Press, 1982).

196. Joe R. Feagin, "Social Justice and Sociology: Agendas for the Twenty-First Century," *American Sociological Review* 66 (Feb. 2001), 1–20.

197. Michael Burawoy, "For Public Sociology," *American Sociological Review* 70 (Feb. 2005), 4–28.

198. Lyman, "Race Relations as Social Process," 397.

PART THREE

1. Richard Rodriguez, "La Raza Cosmica," *New Perspectives Quarterly* (Winter 1991), 49.

2. Robert E. Park, *Race and Culture* (New York: Free Press, 1950), 192. Park deserves credit for introducing this idea into the sociological canon, but it was part of a much wider discourse. As early as the 1850s, Ralph Waldo Emerson wrote: "Man is the most composite of all creatures. . . . In this continent—asylum of all nations—the energy of Irish, Germans, Swedes, Poles, and Cossacks, and the European tribes—of the Africans, and of the Polynesians, will construct a new race, a new religion, a new state, a new literature, which will be as vigorous as the new Europe which came out of the smelting pot of the Dark Ages, or that which earlier emerged from . . . barbarism. La Nature aime les croisements." Quoted in Sidney Ratner, "Horace M. Kallen and Cultural Pluralism," *Modern Judaism* 4 (May 1984), 185–200.

3. Park, *Race and Culture*, 346.

4. For example, Noel Ignatiev, *How the Irish Became White* (New York: Routledge, 1995); Karen Brodkin, *How Jews Became White Folks* (New Brunswick, NJ: Rutgers University Press, 1998); Mathew Frye Jacobson, *Whiteness of a Different Color* (Cambridge, MA: Harvard University Press, 1998).

5. Park, *Race and Culture*, 204.

6. Philip Gleason, "The Melting Pot: Symbol of Fusion or Confusion?" *American Quarterly* 16 (1964), 20–46. Others who popularized the assimilationist ideal included Jacob Riis, Edward Steiner, and Mary Antin.

7. Israel Zangwill, *The Melting-Pot: Drama in Four Acts* (New York: Arno Press, 1975; orig. pub. 1909), 184.

8. This is a theme that runs through ethnic literature. See Werner Sollors, "Literature and Ethnicity," *Harvard Encyclopedia of American Ethnic Groups* (Cambridge, MA: Belknap Press, 1980), 649. Also, Werner Sollors, *Beyond Ethnicity* (New York: Oxford University Press, 1986).

9. William Thomas called this "the ethnicity paradox." See Davarian L. Baldwin, "Black

Belts and Ivory Towers: The Place of Race in U.S. Social Thought, 1892–1948," *Critical Sociology* 30:2 (2004), 407.

10. Nathan Glazer and Daniel Patrick Moynihan, *Beyond the Melting Pot* (Cambridge: M.I.T. Press, 1970; orig. ed. 1963), 290.

11. Philip Gleason, *Speaking of Diversity* (Baltimore: Johns Hopkins University Press, 1992), 71–72; emphasis in original.

12. Peter Schrag, *The Decline of the WASP* (New York: Simon & Schuster, 1971); Michael Novak, *The Rise of the Unmeltable Ethnics* (New York: Macmillan, 1971).

13. W. H. Auden, *New York Times Magazine* (March 18, 1972).

14. Park, *Race and Culture*, 150.

15. Herbert Gans, in his introduction to Neil C. Sandberg, *Ethnic Identity and Assimilation: The Polish-American Community* (New York: Praeger, 1974), vii.

16. Gunnar Myrdal, "The Case against Romantic Ethnicity," *Center Magazine* 7:4 (July-August 1974), 30.

17. Steinberg, *The Ethnic Myth: Race, Ethnicity, and Class in America* (Boston: Beacon Press, 2001; orig. pub. 1981), 51.

18. Richard Alba, "Assimilation's Quiet Tide," *The Public Interest* 119 (Spring 1995); reprinted in *Race and Ethnicity in the United States: Issues and Controversies*, Stephen Steinberg, ed. (Boston: Blackwell, 2000), 219.

19. Richard Alba and Victor Nee, *Remaking the American Mainstream* (Cambridge, MA: Harvard University Press, 1993), 91.

20. See R. W. Connell, "Why Is Classical Theory Classical?" *American Journal of Sociology* 102 (May 1997).

21. Unfortunately, this issue has rarely been engaged in the literature. One useful intervention, though with a dubious ideological subtext, is Robert Merton, "Insiders and Outsiders: A Chapter in the Sociology of Knowledge," *American Journal of Sociology* 78:1 (July 1972), 9–47.

22. In *Ethnic Studies at Chicago, 1905–45* (Urbana: University of Illinois Press, 1987), Stow Persons writes: "An outgrowth of a Baptist institution, the new University of Chicago had deep roots in Protestant Christianity" (29). Also see C. Wright Mills, "The Social Ideology of Social Pathologists," *American Journal of Sociology* 49:2 (September 1943), 165–80.

23. Mary Antin, *The Promised Land* (Boston: Houghton Mifflin, 1912), xi.

24. Horace Kallen, "Democracy Versus the Melting Pot," *The Nation* 100 (Feb. 18 and 25, 1915). See also Ratner, "Horace M. Kallen and Cultural Pluralism."

25. Hutchins Hapgood, *The Spirit of the Ghetto: Studies of the Jewish Quarter in New York* (New York: Funk & Wagnalls, c. 1909).

26. Randolph Bourne, "Trans-National America," *Atlantic Monthly* 118 (July 1916), 86–97; reprinted in *The American Intellectual Tradition*, David A. Hollinger and Charles Capper, eds. (New York: Oxford University Press, 2001), 172–81.

27. For a thorough analysis of the white ethnic revival that began in the 1970s, and its relationship to the heightened consciousness and politics of the civil rights movement and the rise of black nationalism, see Matthew Frye Jacobson, *Roots Too* (Cambridge, MA: Harvard University Press, 2006).

28. R. Fred Wacker, "Assimilation and Cultural Pluralism in American Social Thought," *Phylon* 40 (1979), 327. As the historian John Higham also observed, cultural pluralism appealed "to people who were already strongly enough positioned to imagine that permanent minority status might be advantageous.... Accordingly, cultural pluralism proved most attractive to people who were already largely assimilated. It was itself one of the products of the American melting pot." John Higham, *Send These to Me: Jews and Other Immigrants in Urban America* (New York: Atheneum, 1975), 211.

29. Ratner, "Horace M. Kallen and Cultural Pluralism."

30. Isaac B. Berkson, *Theories of Americanization: A Critical Study, With Special Reference to the Jewish Group* (New York: Teachers College, 1920).

31. Nathan Glazer, "America's Ethnic Pattern: 'Melting Pot' or 'Nation of Nations'?" *Commentary* 15 (April 1953), 408.

32. Marcus L. Hansen, "The Problem with the Third Generation Immigrant," Augustana Historical Society, Rock Island, Illinois, 1938. Reprinted with a foreword by Oscar Handlin in *Commentary* 14 (November 1952), 492–500. Eugene I. Bender and George Kagiwada, "Hansen's Law of 'Third Generation Return' and the Study of American Religio-Ethnic Groups," *Phylon* 29:4 (1968), 360. In 1974 Herbert Gans challenged whether there was an ethnic revival fueled by a third-generation return, and observed wryly that "Hansen's Law applies only to academics and intellectuals." Quoted in Sollors, *Beyond Ethnicity*, 216.

33. Milton M. Gordon, *Assimilation in American Life: The Role of Race, Religion, and National Origins* (New York: Oxford University Press, 1964). Gordon was the son of Russian Jewish immigrants, and in his autobiographical essay, he traces how the contours of his own life corresponded to his evolving intellectual project. Milton M. Gordon, "From Assimilation to Human Nature (and Back)," in *A History of Race Relations Research: First-Generation Recollections*, John H. Stanfield II, ed. (Newbury Park, CA: Sage Publications, 1993), 52–70.

34. The number of faculty in American colleges and universities expanded from 147,000 in 1940 to 247,000 in 1950, to 381,000 in 1960. The proportion of Jewish faculty rose from just 5 percent among the pre–World War II entrants to 9 percent after World War II. Everett Carll Ladd and Seymour Martin Lipset, *The Divided Academy* (New York: McGraw-Hill, 1975), 2, 88, 170; Stephen Steinberg, *The Academic Melting Pot: Catholics and Jews in American Higher Education* (New York: McGraw-Hill, 1974).

35. I pose this question from the standpoint of the sociology of knowledge. How does the ethnicity of scholars of ethnicity influence their scholarship? Nathan Glazer, who arguably was the preeminent scholar in the field, is a case in point. His first book, *American Judaism*, offered a reassuring narrative of crisis and eventual redemption, as Judaism adapted to new circumstances in America. This is a theme that was given even more general application in *Beyond the Melting Pot*, and runs through his entire oeuvre.

In John Stanfield's book of "first-generation recollections," seven of the twelve essays (seven of the ten by whites) were by Jewish scholars: Bob Blauner, Daniel Fusfeld (half-Jewish), Milton Gordon, Lewis Killian, Stanley Lieberson, Richard Robbins, and Peter Rose. Most make explicit reference to their Jewish upbringing, and the role it played in their intellectual development and their approach to the study of race and ethnicity. Stanfield, *A History of Race Relations Research*. Elsewhere Glazer has published a biographical essay that charts his trajectory from New York's East Side and the Bronx through his years at *Commentary*, as well as his immersion in radical politics at CCNY and his belated entry into academia. "From Socialism to Sociology," in *Authors of Their Own Lives: Intellectual Autobiographies*, ed. Bennett Berger (Berkeley: University of California Press, 1990), 190–209. Another contributor to that volume, Herbert Gans, writes that his "involvement with Judaism as a religion was eventually sublimated and ended by research" (447) that he conducted on Jews of Park Forest in 1949, which served as a foundation for studies that resulted in *The Levittowners* and *Urban Villagers*, and later, interventions in policy debates around race.

36. Edward Hallett Carr, *What Is History?* (New York: Knopf, 1962), 26.

37. Joel Perlmann addresses the problem of "the American Jewish periphery," which he defines as "Americans of recent Jewish origin who have only the most tenuous connections, if any, with those origins." He estimates there are nearly a million such people who hail from Jewish nuclear families and now report they are Christian. Joel Perlmann, *The American Jewish Periphery: An Overview*, Working Paper No. 473, Levy Economics Institute, Bard College, www.levy.org.

38. As Higham wrote on the last page of his book: "The lasting significance of the ethnic

revival of the late 1960's may have to do with the strengthening of nuclei rather than the guarding of boundaries." Higham, *Send These to Me*, 246.

39. Milton Gordon advanced this position. As he wrote: "It is possible for separate subsocieties to continue their existence while the cultural differences between them become progressively reduced and even in greater part eliminated." Gordon, *Assimilation in American Life*, 158.

40. A study of Jewish intermarriage reached the conclusion that "despite the hopes and assumptions, Jewish identification does not fare well in mixed marriages." Peter Y. Meddling, Gary A. Tobin, Sylvia Barack Fishman, and Mordechai Rimor, "Jewish Identity in Conversion and Mixed Marriages," in *Jews in America*, Roberta Rosenberg Farber and Chaim I. Waxman, eds. (Hanover, NH: University Press of New England, 1999), 256.

41. Calvin Goldscheider, *Studying the Jewish Future* (Seattle: University of Washington Press, 2004), 29.

42. Ibid., 12.

43. William L. Yancey, Eugene Ericksen, and Richard Juliani, "Emergent Ethnicity: A Review and Reformulation," *American Sociological Review* 31:3 (June 1976), 391–403. In *Beyond the Melting Pot*, Glazer and Moynihan make very much the same point (2nd ed., xxxiii).

44. Kathleen Neils Conzen, David A. Gerber, Ewa Morawska, George E. Pozzetta, and Rudolph J. Vecoli, "The Invention of Ethnicity: A Perspective from the U.S.A.," *Journal of American Ethnic History* 12 (Fall 1992), 5.

45. The next two sections build on an earlier paper, "The Melting Pot and the Color Line," in *Reinventing the Melting Pot*, Tamar Jacoby, ed. (New York: Basic Books, 2003), 235–48.

46. Russell A. Kazal, "Revisiting Assimilation: The Rise, Fall, and Reappraisal of a Concept in American Ethnic History," *American Historical Review*, 100:2 (April 1995), 437–71. In her 1994 article, "In Defense of the Assimilation Model," Ewa Morawska wrote: "It has been almost twenty-five years since the so-called classical model of assimilation, first formulated by Robert Park and later perfected by Milton Gordon, fell into disrepute in American ethnic studies." *Journal of American Ethnic History* 13 (1994), 76. Also, see Nathan Glazer, "Is Assimilation Dead?" *Annals of the American Association of Political and Social Science* 530 (November 1993), 122–36.

47. David A. Hollinger, *Postethnic America: Beyond Multiculturalism* (New York: Basic Books, 1995, 2000), 7–9.

48. Ibid., 8. Rey Chow also challenges the entire system of thought whereby bodies bear the signs of otherness. Indeed, she goes so far as to compare multiculturalism to a zoo where visitors are directed to view the snakes, the reptiles, the primates, et cetera. *The Protestant Ethnic and the Spirit of Capitalism* (New York: Columbia University Press, 2002), chap. 3. For a provocative analysis of the uses of domestic multiculturalism to provide cover for imperialist policies abroad, see Jodi Melamed, "The Spirit of Neoliberalism: From Racial Liberalism to Neoliberal Multiculturalism," *Social Text* 89, Vol. 24:4 (Winter 2006).

49. Min Zhou, "Are Asian Americans Becoming 'White'?" *Contexts* 3:1 (2004), 32.

50. For an acerbic analysis of the corporate fabrication and merchandizing of "Latino" ethnicity, see Arlene Dávila, *Latinos Inc.: The Marketing and Making of a People* (Berkeley: University of California Press, 2001).

51. Grace Kao and Kara Joyner, "Do Hispanic and Asian Adolescents Practice Panethnicity in Friendship Choices?" Department of Policy Analysis and Management, Cornell University, August 30 2002, http://scholar.google.com/scholar?hl=en&lr=&q=cache:BWn3jJgYPQIJ:lexis.pop.upenn.edu/news/colloquium/2002Fall/panethnic.pdf+related:f-J5G8sWnyEJ:scholar.google.com.

52. In 1990 the percentage of exogamous marriages that were interracial rather than interethnic ranged from 61 percent among Vietnamese, to 67 percent among Chinese, to 77 percent among Koreans, 80 percent among Japanese, to 88 percent among Filipinos and Indians. Sharon M. Lee

and Marilyn Fernandez, "Trends in Asian American Racial/Ethnic Intermarriage: A Comparison of 1980 and 1990 Census Data," *Sociological Perspectives* 41:2 (1998), 328. David López concluded on the basis of marriage patterns in Los Angeles in 1990, "there is no evidence that Asian Americans are shifting from national-origin to panethnic (among all Asians) marriage patterns, though pan-Asian in-marriage does certainly exist." David E. López, "Social and Linguistic Aspects of Assimilation Today," in *Handbook of International Migration: The American Experience*, Charles Hirschman, ed. (New York: Russell Sage, 1999), 220.

   53. See, for example, David Palumbo-Liu, *Asian/American: Historical Crossings of a Racial Frontier* (Stanford, CA: Stanford Univ. Press, 1999).

   54. W. Lloyd Warner and Leo Srole, *The Social Systems of American Ethnic Groups* (New Haven, CT: Yale University Press, 1945), 28.

   55. Nancy Foner has suggested that transnationalism has historical precedents, and may be only a one-generation phenomenon, with little enduring significance for later generations. *From Ellis Island to JFK: New York's Two Waves of Immigration* (New Haven, CT: Yale University Press, 2000), chap. 6. For another skeptical view of transnationalism, see Roger Waldinger and David Fitzgerald, "Transnationalism in Question," *American Journal of Sociology* 109:5 (March 2004), 1177–95.

   56. Hollinger challenges the presumption that all the "people of color" have been abused more or less equally. See his Postscript to the 2005 edition of *Postethnic America*, 230. Also, see Bob Blauner, *Still the Big News* (Philadelphia: Temple University Press, 2001), 60–63, and Iris Marion Young, *Justice and the Politics of Difference* (Princeton, NJ: Princeton University Press, 1990), chap. 2 ("Five Faces of Oppression").

   57. For example, Agence France-Presse, "Warning Raised about Exodus of Philippine Doctors and Nurses," *New York Times* (November 27, 2005); and Celia W. Dugger, "U.S. Plan to Lure Nurses May Hurt Poor Nations," *New York Times* (May 24, 2006).

   58. Hollinger, *Postethnic America*, 154.

   59. See Foner, *From Ellis Island to JFK*, esp. chaps. 3 and 8.

   60. By 1970 over 90 percent of third-generation Germans, Italians, and Poles spoke only English; the same was true of third-generation Chinese, Japanese, Koreans, and Filipinos. Richard Alba, John Logan, Amy Lutz, and Brian Stults, "Only English by the Third Generation? Loss and Preservation of the Mother Tongue among the Grandchildren of Contemporary Immigrants," *Demography* 39 (August 2002), 467–84. For a comprehensive analysis of recent trends in assimilation, see Alba and Nee, *Remaking the American Mainstream*, esp. chaps. 6 and 7.

   61. Ronald Schmidt, *Language Policy and Identity Politics in the United States* (Philadelphia: Temple University Press, 2000), 5.

   62. "U.S. Hispanics Lose Spanish over Time, Study Finds," www.banderasnews.com/0610/edat-losespanish.htm. By the same token, it has also been said that "English is the world's greatest borrower of words." Mario Pei, *What's in a Word?* (New York: Hawthorn Books, 1968), 6.

   63. López, "Social and Linguistic Aspects of Assimilation," 217. In 1998 many Latino voters in California surprised opponents of Proposition 27 banning bilingual education by voting for the measure. William Booth, "A Tongue-Lashing over Bilingual Education: An English-Immersion Proposition Vote Divides California's Latinos," *Washington Post National Weekly Edition* (March 9, 1998), 31. Poll findings seem to depend greatly on the wording of the questions. A poll by the *Los Angeles Times* found that 84 percent of Latino voters wanted to end bilingual education, but another poll by the Spanish language paper *La Opinión* found that 68 percent of Latino parents favored bilingual education.

   64. López, "Social and Linguistic Aspects of Assimilation," 217.

   65. Samuel P. Huntington, *Who Are We? The Challenges to America's Identity* (New York: Simon & Schuster, 2004), 231.

66. Geoffrey Nunberg, "Lingo Jingo: English-Only and the New Nativism," in Steinberg, ed., *Race and Ethnicity in the United States*, 299. Orig. pub.: *The American Prospect* 33 (July–August, 1997). Indeed, according to one report, by mid-century half the world's population is expected to be more or less proficient in English. Gregory Rodriquez, "English Likely Top Tongue at Home, Abroad," *New York Times* (April 7, 2002).

67. Alejandro Portes and Richard Schauffler, "Language and the Second Generation: Bilingualism Yesterday and Today," *International Migration Review* 28:4 (Winter 1994), 640–61; Alejandro Portes and Ruben G. Rumbaut, *Legacies: The Story of the Immigrant second Generation* (Berkeley: University of California Press, 2001), 119.

68. Alba et al., "Only English by the Third Generation?" 472.

69. "Health Department Presents New York City's Most Popular Baby Names for 2005," New York Department of Health and Mental Hygiene (October 11, 2006), www.nyc.gov/html/doh/html/pr2006/pr096-06.shtml.

70. Irving Howe, *World of Our Fathers* (New York: Harcourt, 1976), 253.

71. Lee and Fernandez, "Trends in Asian American Racial/Ethnic Intermarriage," 335. Also see Pyong Gap Min and Young I. Song, "Demographic Characteristics and Trends of Post-1965 Korean Immigrant Women and Men," and Gin Yong Pang, "Intraethnic, Interracial, and Interethnic Marriages among Korean American Women," in *Korean American Women: From Tradition to Modern Feminism*, Young I. Song and Ailee Moon, eds. (Westport, CT: Praeger, 1998).

72. Zhou, "Are Asian Americans Becoming 'White'?" 31.

73. Specifically, among Chinese women married to white men, 61 percent of children were labeled as white. Among Filipinos, 63 percent; Vietnamese, 64 percent; Japanese, 67 percent; Koreans, 74 percent; Asian Indians, 93 percent. In other words, there is little evidence that biracial identities are taking hold. Interestingly, the figure for Hawaiians was lowest of all: 56 percent. Mary Waters, "Multiple Ethnic Identity Choices," in *Beyond Pluralism: The Conception of Groups and Group Identities in America*, Wendy F. Katkin, Ned Landsman, and Andrea Tyree, eds. (Chicago: University of Illinois Press, 1998), 28–46. Also see Zhenchao Qian, "Options: Racial/Ethnic Identification of Children of Intermarried Couples," *Social Science Quarterly* 85:3 (September 2004), 746–65; and Y. Xie and K. Goyette, "The Racial Identification of Biracial Children with One Asian Parent: Evidence from the 1990 Census," *Social Forces* 76:2 (December 1997), 547–70.

74. For example, Mia Tuan, *Forever Foreigners or Honorary Whites?* (New Brunswick, NJ: Rutgers University Press, 1998), 37–47.

75. Zhou, "Are Asian Americans Becoming 'White'?" 30.

76. For an incisive treatment of this issue, see Frank H. Wu, *Yellow: Race in America beyond Black and White* (New York: Basic Books, 2002), chap. 3.

77. Zhenchao Qian, "Race and Social Distance: Intermarriage with Non-Latino Whites," *Race and Society* 5 (2002), 41. Generational differences are explored in Cynthia Feliciano, "Assimilation or Enduring Racial Boundaries? Generational Differences in Intermarriage among Asians and Latinos in the United States," *Race and Society* 4 (2001), 27–45. The high rate of intermarriage between Mexican Americans and non-Hispanic Whites is reported in Michael J. Rosenfeld, "Measures of Assimilation in the Marriage Market: Mexican Americans, 1970–1990," *Journal of Marriage and Family* 64 (February 2002), 152–62.

A complicating factor in assessing intermarriage among Latinos is that roughly 40 percent of mothers of Latino newborns are single. As Perlmann and Waters have observed: "How changes in cohabitation, divorce, and childbearing come to affect interethnic commingling and resultant ethnic and racial identity in the next generation are big issues for the future understanding of ethnic blending." Joel Perlmann and Mary C. Waters, "Intermarriage Then and Now: Race, Generation, and the Changing Meaning of Marriage," in *Not Just Black and White: Historical and Contemporary*

Perspectives on Immigration, Race, and Ethnicity in the United States, Nancy Foner and George M. Fredrickson, eds. (New York: Russell Sage Foundation, 2003), 275.

78. James Gaines, "From the Managing Editor," *Time*, Special Issue on "The New Face of America: How Immigrants Are Shaping the World's First Multicultural Society," 1143:21 (1993), 2. Also, "Introduction: Rethinking 'Mixed Race' Studies," in *Mixed Race Studies*, Jayne O. Ifekwunigwe, ed. (New York: Routledge, 2004), 1–3. Surveys also indicate sharp increases in the percentage of Americans who approve of interracial marriage, from 70 percent of adults in 1986 to 83 percent in 2003. Interracial dating is also on the rise. George Yancey conducted a telephone survey of English- and Spanish-speaking adults in 1999 and 2000, and found that 36 percent of whites, 56 percent of African Americans, 55 percent of Hispanic Americans, and 57 percent of Asian Americans had interdated. Alison Stein Wellner, "U.S. Attitudes toward Interracial Dating Are Liberalizing," Washington, D.C.: Population Reference Bureau (June 2005).

79. Eric Liu, *The Accidental Asian* (New York: Vintage, 1998), 56.

80. The other exception is Native Americans, a people conquered and decimated in the process of colonization of the continent, and relegated to reservations where they were subjected to a program of forced assimilation conducted by the Bureau of Indian Affairs. Of course, Native Americans have not been immune to assimilation, but for those who live on reservations, this obviously serves as an incubus for cultural preservation and development. See Stephen E. Cornell, *The Return of the Native: American Indian Political Resurgence* (New York: Oxford University Press, 1988).

81. Stephen Steinberg, "Immigration, African Americans, and Race Discourse," *New Politics* 10 (Summer 2006), www.wpunj.edu/newpol/issue39/Steinberg39.htm.

82. Douglas S. Massey, "Residential Segregation and Neighborhood Conditions in U.S. Metropolitan Areas," in *America Becoming: Racial Trends and Their Consequences*, Neil Smelser, William Julius Wilson, and Faith Mitchell, eds. (Washington, D.C.: National Academy Press, 2001), 401.

83. Qian, "Race and Social Distance," 41.

84. Stanley Lieberson, *A Matter of Taste: How Names, Fashion, and Culture Change* (New Haven, CT: Yale University Press, 2000). For a very recent intervention, see Christina A. Sue and Edward E. Telles, "Assimilation and Gender in Naming," *American Journal of Sociology*, Vol. 112:5 (March 2007): 1383–1415.

85. "'Black' Names a Resume Burden?" CBS News (September 29, 2003), www.cbsnews.com/stories/2003/09/29/national/main575685.shtml.

86. "Health Department Presents New York City's Most Popular Baby Names for 2005."

87. Stanley Lieberson and Kelly S. Mikelson, "Distinctive African American Names: An Experimental, Historical, and Linguistic Analysis of Innovation," *American Sociological Review* 60:6 (December 1995), 933.

88. "Sticks and Stones Can Break Bones, But the Wrong Name Can Make a Job Hard to Find," *New York Times* (December 12, 2002), www.irs.princeton.edu/krueger/names2.htm. The study, conducted by economist Alan Krueger, found that "applicants with white-sounding names were 50 percent more likely to be called for interviews than were those with black-sounding names." See also, "'Black' Names a Resume Burden?"

89. See William Labov's pioneering study *Language in the Inner City: Studies in Black English Vernacular* (Philadelphia: University of Pennsylvania Press, 1972).

90. Elizabeth Pleck, "Kwanzaa: An Invented Black Nationalist Tradition, 1966–1990," *Journal of American Ethnic History* 20 (Summer 2001), 3–28.

91. Louis Wirth, *The Ghetto* (Chicago: University of Chicago Press, 1928).

92. Blauner, *Still the Big News*, 98.

93. Kenneth Stampp, *The Peculiar Institution: Slavery in the Ante-bellum South* (New York: Vintage, 1956), vii. Nor was this construction one that appealed only to whites. For example, Charles

Johnson wrote: "The Negro group in America, having no unique culture of his own, lives on different planes of the American culture." Charles S. Johnson, "The Education of the Negro Child," *American Sociological Review* 1:2 (April 1936), 265. This view rested on the assumption that African culture was erased by slavery, leaving blacks with "no unique culture of their own."

94. Glazer and Moynihan, *Beyond the Melting Pot*, xix–xx. In the introduction, it is stated that Glazer wrote the chapter on "The Negroes," as well as the chapters of the Puerto Ricans, Italians, and Jews, whereas Moynihan wrote the chapter on the Irish and most of the concluding chapter (xcviii).

95. The "fine print" consisted of a long, initialed footnote. Ibid., xx.

96. Gena Dagel Caponi, ed., *Signifyin(g), Sanctifyin', & Slam Dunking: A Reader in African American Expressive Culture* (Amherst: University of Massachusetts Press, 1999).

97. Quoted in ibid., 1.

98. Quoted in ibid., 7.

99. Park, *Race and Culture*, 280.

100. See Daryl Michael Scott, *Social Policy and the Image of the Damaged Black Psyche, 1880–1996* (Chapel Hill: University of North Carolina Press, 1997), and James B. McKee, *Sociology and the Race Problem: The Failure of a Perspective* (Urbana: University of Illinois Press, 1993), chap. 8.

101. Caponi, *Signifyin(g)*, 7. Exclusive attention has been paid to popular culture, to the neglect of other sites of cultural expression. For a penetrating analysis of the cultural and political nuances of "black radio," see Micaela di Leonardo, "Neoliberalism, Nostagia, Race Politics, and the American Public Sphere: The Case of the Tom Joyner Morning Show," *Cultural Studies*, Vol. 21 (March 8, 2007). http://72.14.209.104/search?q=cache:pGjKjCu3nVIJ:www.anthropology.northwestern.edu/faculty/documents/deleonardo.pdf+%22micaela+di+leonardo%22+-+neoliberalism+-+%22race+politics%22&hl=en&ct=clnk&cd=2&gl=us

102. Charles Gallagher, "Color-blind Privilege: The Social and Political Functions of Erasing the Color Line in Post Race America," *Race, Gender and Class* 10:4 (2003), 35.

103. Bill Yousman, "Blackophilia and Blackophobia: White Youth, the Consumption of Rap Music, and White Supremacy," *Communication Theory* 4 (November 2003), 379. Later Yousman writes: "White male identification with the images of Black misogyny, homophobia, and brutal, phallocentric masculinity provided by the film, television, and recording industries, for example, does not provide material for more enlightened race and gender relations among America's youth, but rather, reinforces and reinvigorates ancient lies and misinterpretations that can only deepen the divisions that already cut and slash through America's social relations" (386). And still later: "White youth who adopt Black cultural styles may in fact be participants in a phenomenon of White fantasizing that serves only to obscure or disguise the fuller picture of the Black American experience" (387). For the classic work on white appropriation of blackness, see Eric Lott, *Love and Theft: Blackface Minstrelsy and the American Working Class* (New York: Oxford University Press, 1993).

104. Robin D. G. Kelley, *Yo' Mama's Disfunktional! Fighting the Culture Wars in Urban America* (Boston: Beacon Press, 1977), 39.

105. Yousman, "Blackophilia and Blackophobia," 387.

106. Richard Wright, *Twelve Million Black Voices* (New York: Arno Press, 1969; orig. pub. 1941), 130.

107. Orlando Patterson, "A Poverty of the Mind," *New York Times* (March 26, 2006).

108. For an even more wrongheaded diatribe against hip hop culture, see John McWhorter, *Losing the Race: Self-Sabotage in Black America* (New York: Harper Perennial, 2001).

109. W.E.B. Du Bois, *The Souls of Black Folk* (New York: Penguin, 1989), 5.

110. The "beyond race" position is exemplified by such works as Paul Gilroy's *Against Race: Imagining Political Culture beyond the Color Line* (Cambridge: MA: Harvard University Press, 2004); Antonia Darder and Rodolfo Torres's *After Race: Racism after Multiculturalism* (New York: New York

University Press, 2004); and Orlando Patterson's "Race Over," *New Republic* 222 (January 10, 2000). For a thoughtful critique of the "beyond race" position, see David Roediger, "The Retreat from Race and Class," *Monthly Review* 58:3 (July–August 2006), www.monthlyreview.org/0706roediger.htm. For an incisive analysis of the relation between race and nationality, see Nikhil Pal Singh, *Black Is a Country* (Cambridge: Harvard University Press, 2004).

111. George Yancey, *Who Is White? Latinos, Asians, and the New Black/Nonblack Divide* (Boulder, CO: Lynne Rienner, 2003). Others have raised the possibility of a black/non-black division of the American people. See Nathan Glazer, *We Are All Multiculturalists Now* (Cambridge, MA: Harvard University Press, 1997), 149; Herbert Gans, "The Possibility of a New Racial Hierarchy in the Twenty-First Century United States," in *The Cultural Territories of Race*, Michele Lamont, ed. (Chicago: University of Chicago Press, 1999), 371–90; Philip Kasinitz, "Race, Assimilation, and 'Second Generations,' Past and Present," in Foner and Fredrickson, *Not Just Black and White*, 278–98. Eduardo Bonilla-Silver has proposed a tripartite melting pot, consisting of "Whites," "Collective Black," and "Honorary Whites," the last consisting of light-skinned Latinos, Asians, and most multiracials. My crystal ball is no better than his, but I assume that the so-called Honorary Whites are rapidly being incorporated into the White category, leaving us with the old racial binary. Eduardo Bonilla-Silver, "We Are All Americans! The Latin Americanization of Racial Stratification in the USA," *Race and Society* 5 (2002), 3–17. For an incisive critique of social science representations of post-1965 black immigrants, and their tendency to recode biological notions of race as "culture," see Jemima Pierre, "Black Immigrants in the United States and the 'Cultural Narratives' of Ethnicity," *Identities: Global Studies in Culture and Power* 11 (2004), 141–70.

112. Mary Waters, *Black Identities* (New York: Russell Sage Foundation, 1999), 61.

113. Qian, "Race and Social Distance," 41. Also, Alan Aja, "Miami's Dual Melting Pot: Racial Apartheid within the Cuban Ethnic Economy," doctoral dissertation, Milano Graduate School of Management and Urban Policy, New School University, 2007.

114. Zangwill, *The Melting-Pot*, 184.

115. George Lipsitz, *The Possessive Investment in Whiteness* (Philadelphia: Temple University Press, 1998), 58. Also see Juan Flores, "'Qué Assimilated, Brother, Yo Soy Asimilao': The Structuring of Puerto Rican Identity in the United States," *Journal of Ethnic Studies* 13:3 (Fall 1985), 1–16.

116. Gary Nash, "The Great Multicultural Debate," *Contention* (1992); reprinted in Steinberg, ed., *Race and Ethnicity in the United States*, 277–93.

117. "Afro-American men and women, then, have every reason to outmarry: it will enrich the repertoire of childrearing practices among them; it will vastly expand their weak social ties and other social capital; it will help to solve the internal crisis of gender and marital relations among them; and it will complete the process of total integration as they become to other Americans not only full members of the political and moral community, but also people whom 'we' marry. When that happens, the goal of integration will have been fully achieved." Orlando Patterson, *The Ordeal of Integration* (Washington, D.C.: Civitas, 1997), 198. In 1900 Charles W. Chesnutt proposed the idea of miscegenation as the answer to the nation's race problem in a prescient essay on "The Future American." Chesnutt wrote: "If it is only by becoming white that colored people and their children are to enjoy the rights and dignities of citizenship, they will have every incentive to 'lighten the breed,' to use a current phrase, that they may claim the white man's privileges as soon as possible. . . . The races will be quite effectively amalgamated by lightening the Negroes as they would be by darkening the whites." From SallyAnn H. Ferguson, *Melus Forum* (1900), 96–107; orig. pub. *Boston Evening Transcript* (August 18, 1900), 29; (August 25, 1900), 15; (September 1, 1900), 24. The idea of miscegenation as a panacea for the race problem was resurrected by Norman Podhoretz in 1963, "My Negro Problem—and Ours," *Commentary* (February 1963). He later recanted: "I was wrong to think that miscegenation could ever result in the elimination of color 'as a fact of consciousness,' if for no

other reason than that (as Ralph Ellison bitingly remarked to me) the babies born or such marriages would still be considered black." In Paul Berman, ed., *Blacks and Jews: Alliances and Arguments* (New York: Delacourte Press, 1994), www.reportingcivilrights.org/perspectives/podhoretz.jsp. In his chapter on "Black Americans and Assimilation," in *Assimilation, American Style* (New York: Basic Books, 1997), Peter D. Salins also writes: "As more blacks and whites intermarry, there is also the possibility that the entire black-white racial dichotomy itself will be obsolete, that some day Americans—both black and white—will come to view mixed racial ancestry in exactly the same terms as mixed national and religious ancestry" (173).

118.   Stanford Lyman, "Race Relations as Social Process: Sociology's Resistance to a Civil Rights Orientation," in *Race in America: The Struggle for Equality*, Herbert Hill and James E. Jones, eds. (Madison: University of Wisconsin Press, 1993), 394.

119.   Nathan Glazer, *Affirmative Discrimination* (New York: Basic Books, 1975, 1987), 152. See also Stephen Steinberg, "Nathan Glazer and the Assassination of Affirmative Action," *New Politics* 9:3 (Summer 2003), www.wpunj.edu/~newpol/issue35/Steinberg35.htm. For an incisive analysis of the role of *Commentary* intellectuals and some Jewish agencies in mobilizing opposition to affirmative action, see Nancy McLean, *Freedom Is Not Enough* (Cambridge: Harvard University Press, 2006), chap. 6.

120.   Glazer, *Affirmative Discrimination*, 159.

121.   Oliver Cromwell Cox, *Caste, Class, & Race: A Study in Social Dynamics* (New York: Modern Reader Paperbacks, 1948), 538. Glazer, Nathan. *We Are All Multiculturalists Now* (Cambridge: Harvard University Press, 1977), 159.

122.   W.E.B. Du Bois, "On the Conservation of Races," in *Black Nationalism in America*, John H. Bracey, Jr., August Meier, and Elliott Rudwick, eds. (New York: Bobbs-Merrill, 1970), 261.

123.   A most encouraging development in recent years has been an outpouring of books that offer a critical perspective on matters of race. Collectively, they form at least the raw material out of which new paradigms evolve. Any such list is inevitably selective. The following books have all been published since 1990.

Barlow, Andrew L. *Between Fear & Hope: Globalization and Race in the United States.* Lanham, MD: Rowman & Littlefield, 2003.

Bell, Derrick A. *Faces at the Bottom of the Well: The Permanence of Racism.* New York: Basic Books, 1992.

Bonilla-Silver, Eduardo. *Racism Without Racists: Color-Blind Racism and the Persistence of Racial Inequality in the United States.* Boulder, CO: Rowman & Littlefield, 2003.

Brown, Michael K. *Race, Money, and the Welfare State.* Ithaca: Cornell University Press, 1999.

Brown, Michael K., Martin Carnoy, Elliott Currie, Troy Duster, David B. Oppenheimer, Marjorie M. Shultz, and David Wellman. *Whitewashing Race: The Myth of a Color-Blind Society.* Berkeley: University of California Press, 2003.

Bush, Melanie E. L. *Breaking the Code of Good Intentions: Everyday Forms of Whiteness.* Lanham, MD: Rowman & Littlefield, 2004.

Bush, Rod. *We Are Not What We Seem: Black Nationalism and Class Struggle in the American Century.* New York: New York University Press, 1999.

Carnoy, Martin. *Faded Dreams: The Economics and Politics of Race in America.* New York: Cambridge University Press, 1985.

Cherry, Robert. *Who Gets the Good Jobs? Combating Race and Gender Disparities.* New Brunswick, NJ: Rutgers University Press, 2000.

Collins, Sharon M. *Black Corporate Executives: The Making and Breaking of a Black Middle Class.* Philadelphia: Temple University Press, 1996.

Conley, Dalton. *Living in the Red: Race, Wealth, and Social Policy in America.* Berkeley: University of California Press, 1999.

Crenshaw, Kimberlé, Neil Gotanda, Gary Peller, and Kendall Thomas. *Critical Race Theory: The Key Writings That Formed the Movement.* New York: New Press, 1995.

di Leonardo, Micaela. *Exotics at Home: Anthropologies, Others, American Modernity.* Chicago: University of Chicago Press, 1998.

Duster, Troy. *Backdoor to Eugenics.* New York: Routledge, 1990.

Espiritu, Yen Le. *Home Bound: Filipino American Lives across Cultures, Communities, and Countries.* Berkeley: University of California Press, 2003.

Feagin, Joe. *Systemic Racism: A Theory of Oppression.* New York: Routledge, 2006.

Franklin, Raymond S. *Shadows of Race and Class.* Minneapolis: University of Minnesota Press, 1991.

Fredrickson, George M. *Black Liberation: A Comparative History of Black Ideologies in the Untied States and South Africa.* New York: Oxford University Press, 2002.

Gaines, Kevin K. *Uplifting the Race: Black Leadership, Politics, and Culture in the Twentieth Century.* Chapel Hill: University of North Carolina Press, 1996.

Gallagher, Charles, ed. *Rethinking the Color Line.* New York: McGraw-Hill, 2006.

Goldfield, Michael. *The Color of Politics: Race and the Mainsprings of American Politics.* New York: New Press, 1997.

Hacker, Andrew. *Two Nations: Black & White, Separate, Hostile, Unequal.* New York: Scribner's, 1992.

Kelley, Robin D. G. *Race Rebels: Culture, Politics, and the Black Working Class.* New York: Free Press, 1994.

Klinkner, Philip A., with Rogers M. Smith. *The Unsteady March: The Rise and Decline of Racial Equality in America.* Chicago: University of Chicago Press, 1999.

Lipsitz, George. *The Possessive Investment in Whiteness: How White People Profit from Identity Politics.* Philadelphia: Temple University Press, 1998.

Lott, Eric. *Love and Theft: Blackface Minstrelsy and the American Working Class.* New York: Oxford University Press, 1995.

Marable, Manning. *Living Black History: How Reimagining the African-American Past Can Remake America's Racial Future.* New York: Basic Civitas Books, 2006.

Marable, Manning, Immanuel Ness, and Joseph Wilson. *Race and Labor Matters in the New U.S. Economy.* Lantham, MD: Rowman & Littlefield, 2006.

McKee, James B. *Sociology and the Race Problem: A Failure of Perspective.* Urbana: University of Illinois Press, 1993.

McLean, Nancy. *Freedom Is Not Enough: The Opening of the American Workplace.* Cambridge: Harvard University Press, 2006.

Mills, Charles W. *The Racial Contract.* Ithaca, NY: Cornell University Press, 1997.

Mullings, Leith. *On Our Own Terms: Race, Class, and Gender in the Lives of African American Women.* New York: Routledge, 1997.

Ness, Immanuel. *Immigrants, Unions, and the New U.S. Labor Market.* Philadelphia: Temple University Press, 2005.

Neubeck, Kenneth J., and Noel A. Cazanave. *Welfare Racism: Playing the Race Card against America's Poor.* New York: Routledge, 2001.

Oliver, Melvin L., and Thomas M. Shapiro. *Black Wealth/White Wealth: A New Perspective of Racial Inequality.* New York: Routledge, 1995.

Reed, Adolph, Jr. *Stirrings in the Jug: Black Politics in the Post-Segregation Era.* Minneapolis: University of Minnesota Press, 1990.

Reed, Adolph, Jr., *Without Justice for All: The New Liberalism and the Retreat from Racial Inequality.* Boulder, CO: Westview Press, 1999.

Robinson, Dean E. *Black Nationalism in American Politics and Thought.* New York: Cambridge University Press, 2001.

Roediger, David R. *Colored White: Transcending the Racial Past.* Berkeley: University of California Press, 2002.

Shelby, Tommie. *We Who Are Dark: The Philosophical Foundations of Black Solidarity.* Cambridge, MA: Harvard University Press, 2005.

Singh, Nikhil Pal. *Black Is a Country: Race and the Unfinished Struggle for Democracy.* Cambridge: Harvard University Press, 2004.

Squires, Gregory D., and Charis E. Kubrin. *Privileged Places: Race, Residence, and the Structure of Opportunity.* Boulder, CO: Lynne Rienner, 2006.

Wellman, David T. *Portraits of White Racism.* 2nd ed. New York: Cambridge University Press, 1993.

Williams, Terry M., and William Kornblum. *The Uptown Kids: Struggle and Hope in the Projects.* New York: Putnam, 1994.

Winant, Howard. *The World Is a Ghetto: Race and Democracy Since World War II.* New York: Basic Books, 2001.

Wu, Frank H. *Yellow: Race in America beyond Black and White.* New York: Basic Books, 2002.

124. Godfrey Hodgson, *America in Our Time: From World War II to Nixon* (New York: Vintage, 1976), 188.

INDEX

affirmative action, 68, 90, 100, 106, 110, 143, 144
African Americans: African American dialect,
135–36; culture of, 67, 101–2, 136–40,
175n103, 176n111; as exception to melting
pot, 31–32, 133–42, 145, 175n111; and the
ghetto, 136, 138; vs. immigrants, 31–32,
91–92, 111–14, 125, 128, 133–42, 145, 159n12;
interdating among, 174n78; Kwanzaa,
136; labor competition with immigrants,
134, 174n81; lynching of, 41, 42, 43, 54;
migration to Northern cities, 1, 41, 47, 78,
79, 134; and miscegenation, 143, 176n117;
names of children, 135, 174n88; relations
with Jews, 60; slavery, 11, 24–25, 44, 45–46,
69–70, 71, 74, 85, 92, 102, 134, 138, 140,
141, 174n94. *See also* black colleges; black
families; black middle class; black radical
tradition
Afro-Latinos, 141; dual melting pot, 140–41,
176n113; intermarriage, 141
Aja, Alan: "Miami's Dual Melting Pot: Racial
Apartheid within the Cuban Ethnic
Economy," 176n113
Alba, Richard, 117, 169n19, 172n60; *Remaking
the American Mainstream,* 172n60

Allen, Robert: *Black Awakening in Capitalist
America,* 164n142
Allport, Gordon: *The Nature of Prejudice,* 103
Amenia Conference of 1916, 79–80
American Communist Party, 78–79, 91; and
NAACP, 14
American Journal of Sociology, 33–34, 35, 38, 46,
53, 58, 76
American Sociological Association, 53–54,
58–59, 67, 109, 155n33, 157n62
American Sociological Association, 1963
meeting of: Leventman at, 14, 18, 38;
presidential address of Everett Hughes/
"Race Relations and the Sociological
Imagination," 10–12, 13, 14, 15–18,
88; Record's paper "The Politics of
Desegregation," 14; sessions on
"Race and Ethnic Relations" at, 14; topics
at, 14, 89
American Sociological Review, 18, 31
*Annals of the American Academy of Political
and Social Science:* special issue on "The
Negro's Progress in Fifty Years," 44
Antin, Mary, 168n6; *The Promised Land,* 118
antithetical scholarship, 146–47, 177n123

Aptheker, Herbert: criticism of Myrdal's
American Dilemma, 2; and Du Bois, 14
Arendt, Hanna, 8
Asian Americans: ethnic identity, 125, 126–27,
132, 171nn51,52; interdating among, 174n78;
intermarriage among, 132, 135; language
loss among, 130; names of children among,
131, 135
Asian immigrants, 124, 128–29, 135
assimilation, 33, 134–36, 142–43; Park on, 31–33,
43, 50, 51, 52, 53, 111–14, 116, 134–35, 142,
160n47, 171n46; race, 43, 73, 79, 168n6.
See also intermarriage; language loss;
melting pot
Association of Black Sociologists, 97
Autobiography of Malcolm X, The, 89

Baker, Lee D.: From Savage to Negro, 164n126
Baker, Newton: on slavery, 85
Baldwin, Davarian, 155n30; on black scholars,
61
Baldwin, James, 89
Barlow, Andrew L.: Between Fear & Hope:
Globalization in the United States, 177n123
Baron, Harold M.: The Negro Worker in the
Chicago Labor Market, 164n142
beliefs, racial. See racism
Bell, Derrick, 98; Faces at the Bottom of the Well:
The Permanence of Racism, 177n123
Bemis, Edward, 37–39, 75
Bennett, Larry: "The New Face of Urban
Renewal: The Near North Redevelopment
Initiative and the Cabrini-Green
Neighborhood," 167n174
Berkson, Isaac: Theories of Americanization,
120, 121
bilingual education, 127, 130, 143, 172n63
Birmingham, Alabama, 90; civil rights protests
in, 6, 7, 12
black colleges: black sociologists at, 3, 15, 58–59,
154, 160n48; Fisk University, 58, 60, 62,
154n17; Howard University, 30, 58, 63, 67,
68, 80, 154n17
black culture, 67, 101–2, 136–40, 175n103, 176n111
black families: Frazier on, 66–67
black middle class, 34, 44–45, 96, 97, 110, 134
black radical tradition, 12–13, 63–65, 68–72,
75–76, 109

Blauner, Robert, 95, 164n126, 170n35; on
the black ghetto, 136; on colonized
minorities, 128; and Marxism, 90, 91,
95; and Park, 165n148; Racial Oppression
in America, 16, 19, 91–92, 165n148;
Still the Big News: Racial Oppression in
America, 165n148, 172n56; "Toward the
Decolonization of Social Research,"
161n58; at University of California,
Berkeley, 91, 95, 165nn149,155; at
University of Chicago, 91
Blumer, Herbert, 155n33; on Park, 20; at
University of Chicago, 91
Boas, Franz, 70
Boggs, James: Racism and the Class Struggle,
164n142
Bonilla-Silver, Eduardo: Racism Without Racists,
177n123; "We Are All Americans! The Latin
Americanization of Racial Stratification in
the USA," 175n111, 177n123; on tripartite
melting pot, 176n111
Bourdieu, Pierre, 102
Bourne, Randolph, 119
Bracey, John, 51, 160n30
Brodkin, Karen: How Jews Became White Folks,
168n4
Brown, Michael K., Race, Money, and the
Welfare State and Whitewashing Race: The
Myth of a Color-Blind Society, 177n123
Brown v. Board of Education, 1, 87
Bulmer, Martin, 157nn62,76, 159n23
Bunche, Ralph, 80, 81, 163n116
Burawoy, Michael, 109–10
Burgess, Ernest W., 66; Introduction to the
Science of Sociology, 19–20, 49–50, 65,
155n31, 159n12; relationship with Park, 19–
20, 42; at University of Chicago, 19–20
Bush, Melanie E. L.: Breaking the Code of Good
Intentions: Everyday Forms of Whiteness,
177n123
Bush, Rod: We Are Not What We Seem, 163n108,
177n123

capitalism, 64, 69–71, 74, 77
Caponi, Gena Dagel: Signifyin(g), Sanctifyin',
and Slam Dunking, 137–38
Caribbean immigrants, 124, 125, 128, 131, 141. See
also dual melting pot

Carmichael, Stokely: *Black Power*, 89–90
Carnegie Corp., 1, 4, 84–87, 92, 157n62
Carnoy, Martin: *Faded Dreams: The Economics
and Politics of Race in America* and
*Whitewashing Race: The Myth of a Color-
Blind Society*, 177n123
Carr, Edward: *What Is History?*, 3, 121
caste, 13, 144, 157n79
Cazanave, Noel A., 157n69; *Welfare Racism:
Playing the Race Card against America's
Poor*, 178n123
Cherry, Robert: *Who Gets The Good Jobs?
Combating Race and Gender Disparities*,
177n123
Chesnutt, Charles W.: "The Future American,"
176n117
Chicago: ethnic communities in, 111–12; Hyde
Park Improvement Protective Club, 42,
158n3; migration of Southern blacks to, 41–
42, 47; race riot of 1919, 42–43, 47–49, 61–
62, 67, 75, 93, 159n23; racial discrimination
in, 102–3; racial segregation in, 6, 41–42,
47–48, 62, 102
children of immigrants, 114–15, 119, 121, 124–25,
129, 130–31, 132
Chinese Americans: intermarriage among, 132,
171n52, 173n73; language loss among, 131,
172n60
Chinese immigrants, 112, 113, 125, 128–29
Chow, Rey, 171n48
Civil Rights Act of 1875, 142
Civil Rights Act of 1964, 7–8, 84, 101
Civil Rights Revolution, 5–19, 141–42, 147,
169n27; and black radical tradition, 12–13,
19; and economic inequality, 80–81; and
immigration policy, 124, 134; as insurgency,
109, 168n195; March on Washington, 6–7,
10, 15, 18; and political science, 8; and
sociology, 4, 8–19, 27, 38, 73, 84, 87–89,
109. *See also* King, Martin Luther, Jr.
Clark, Kenneth: *An American Dilemma Revisited*,
1; on class and race, 97; relationship with
Myrdal, 1, 153n2; testimony before Kerner
commission, 93–94
class: black middle class, 34, 44–45, 96, 97,
110, 134; class origin of sociologists,
10–12; and immigrant population, 129;
in Marxism, 76–81, 91; Park on race and,

96; the poor, 68, 80, 90, 96, 99, 100,
102–3, 106, 107, 140; race vs. class debate,
76–81, 91, 94, 96–97, 99–100, 107, 157n79,
163nn107,108,116,126; and sociology, 11–12,
73, 76–81; Wilson on, 96–102
Clinton, Bill, 77; race initiative of, 104–8;
welfare policy, 106; and Wilson's *Truly
Disadvantaged*, 99, 100, 166n170
Cloward, Richard A.: *Poor People's Movements*,
168n195
Cold War, 7, 9
Cole, Alyson: *The Cult of True Victimhood*, 96
Collins, Sharon M.: *Black Corporate Executives:
The Making and Breaking of a Black Middle
Class*, 177n123
colonialism, 54, 92; in Congo, 21–25, 55, 82;
and Park's race relations cycle, 51, 52–53,
55–56, 82
Commentary, 120, 170nn32,35, 176n117
Communist International: Sixth World
Congress, 78
compensatory programs for blacks, 89
Congo Free State: Belgian colonialism in, 21–25,
30, 82, 156n56
Congo Reform Association, 21–25, 30, 31, 32,
63, 82
Conley, Dalton: *Living in the Red: Race, Wealth,
and Social Policy in America*, 177n123
Connell, R. W.: on sociology and imperialism,
55–56; "Why is Classical Theory Classical,"
55–56, 162n95
Conrad, Joseph: *Heart of Darkness*, 22
Conzen, Kathleen Neils, 123–24
Cornell, Stephen E.: *The Return of the Native*,
174n80
Coser, Lewis: on Park, 155nn31,33, 158n92,
160160n30
Cox, Oliver C., 3, 12, 68–69, 71, 85, 146,
164n126; on caste, 13, 144; *Caste, Class,
& Race*, 12, 13–14, 69, 70–71; criticism
of Myrdal's *American Dilemma*, 2, 3; on
Frazier, 66; and Marxism, 12, 69–71, 74;
on Myrdal, 144; on Park, 70–71; on racial
prejudice, 12, 69–70, 74; relationship with
Park, 61; on slavery, 69–70, 71
Crenshaw, Kimberlé: *Critical Race Theory: The
Key Writings that Formed the Movement*,
178n123

Cuban Americans: intermarriage among, 133; language loss among, 130–31

cultural pluralism, 115, 122; Berkson on, 120, 121; Glazer on, 144; Gordon on, 121; Higham on, 169n28; and Jews, 118–20, 121; Kallen on, 118–20, 121; and multiculturalism, 124

Currie, Elliott: *Whitewashing Race: The Myth of a Color-Blind Society*, 177n123

Darder, Antonia: *After Race: Racism after Multiculturalism*, 175n110

Dávila, Arlene: *Latinos Inc.*, 171n50

Davis, Angela, 89

Debs, Eugene V., 77

Deegan, Mary Jo: *Jane Addams and the Men of the Chicago School*, 158n92

Degler, Carl: "The Negro in America: Where Myrdal Went Wrong," 88–89

Democratic Party, 9, 94, 99

Dewey, John, 42

di Leonardo, Micaela: *Exotics at Home: Anthropologies, Others, American Modernity*, 164n142, 178n123; "Neoliberalism, Nostalgia, Race Politics, and the American Public Sphere: The Case of the Tom Joyner Morning Show," 175n101

Dominican Americans: language loss among, 131

Drake, St. Clair, 31

D'Souza, Dinesh: on black culture, 100–101, 102; critics of, 101, 103–4; *The End of Racism*, 28, 100–104; on institutionalized racism, 101–2; on racial discrimination, 100–101, 102–3; vs. Washington, 28, 101; vs. Wilson, 101–4

dual melting pot, 140–41, 176n113. *See also* assimilation; intermarriage; melting pot

Du Bois, W.E.B., 13, 54, 67, 146, 164n126; attitudes toward, 11; at *The Crisis*, 76; and Debs, 77; on double-consciousness, 141; on historiography, 76; on human brotherhood, 145; on lynchings, 42; on Negroes as "ordinary human beings," 46, 73; "On the Conservation of Races," 145; *The Philadelphia Negro*, 32–33, 76, 155n30; and *Phylon*, 13; on protest, 14, 79; on race-conscious solutions, 107; *The Souls of Black Folk*, 25, 32–33; on Washington, 25

Durkheim, Emile, 106

Duster, Troy, 165n155; *Backdoor to Eugenics* and *Whitewashing Race: The Myth of a Color-Blind Society*, 177n123

Edwards, G. Franklin: on Frazier, 63

Edwards, Harry: *The Revolt of the Black Athlete*, 165n143

Ellison, Ralph, 89, 176n117

Ely, Richard, 36–37, 38, 75

Embree, Edwin, 60

Ericksen, Eugene: "Emergent Ethnicity," 123

Espiritu, Yen Le: *Home Bound: Filipino American Lives across Cultures, Communities, and Countries*, 178n123

ethnicity, 111–47; cultural pluralism, 115, 118–20, 120, 121, 122, 124, 144, 169n28; ethnic communities, 111–12, 114, 127–28, 136, 168n9; ethnic studies programs, 121; ethno-racial pentagon, 125; and gender revolution, 117; intermarriage across ethnic lines, 117, 122–23, 125, 132–33, 135, 141, 143, 171m40, 171n52, 173nn73,77; and naming of children, 131; Park on, 50, 111–14, 116, 142, 159n12, 160n47, 171n46; vs. race, 31–32, 46, 91–92, 111–14, 124–25, 127, 128, 133–42, 159n12, 160n47; of sociologists, 118–20, 169n21, 170nn35,37; and sociology, 4, 91–92, 111–14; white ethnic revival, 119–20, 169n27. *See also* European immigrants

Ethnic Myth, The, 116

European immigrants: vs. blacks, 31–32, 46, 91–92, 111–14, 125, 128, 134; children of, 114–15, 119, 121, 129; Euro-Americans, 124–26; grandchildren of, 116, 120, 129; and loss of language, 129–30, 172n60; and nationality quotas, 112, 124; vs. non-European immigrants, 124–33; Park on, 111–14; prejudice against, 111–14; thesis of third-generation return, 120

evolutionary social change, 10, 43, 47, 155n30; and race relations cycle, 20, 44, 49–53, 55–56. *See also* melting pot, the

exogamy: ethnic, 117, 122–23, 125, 132–33, 135, 141, 143, 171n40, 171n52, 173nn73,77; racial, 133, 135, 143, 171n52, 173n73, 174n78

Faulkner, William, 8

Feagin, Joe, 109; *Systemic Racism: A Theory of Oppression*, 178n123
Feliciano, Cynthia, 173n77
Fernandez, Marilyn, 171n52
Filipino Americans: intermarriage among, 132, 171n52, 173n73; language loss among, 131, 172n60
Filipino immigrants, 125
financing of universities and scholarship, 36–38, 75, 95–96; foundations, 1, 4, 37, 59, 59–60, 61–62, 66, 81, 84–87, 92, 95, 96, 99, 110, 157n62; grants, 59–60, 66, 85–86, 92, 95, 98, 100, 110, 165n155
Fisk University, 58, 60, 62, 154n17
Fitzgerald, David: "Transnationalism in Question," 172n55
Fitzhugh, George: *Sociology for the South*, 50
Flores, Juan, "Qué Assimilated, Brother, Yo Soy Assimilao: The Structuring of Puerto Rican Identity in the United States," 176n115
Foner, Nancy, 182n95, 183n77, 185n111; on transnationalism, 172n55
foundations, 81, 95, 96, 110; Carnegie Corp., 1, 4, 84–87, 92, 157n62; Peabody Fund, 59; Rockefeller Foundation, 66; Rosenwald Fund, 59–60, 61–62; Russell Sage Foundation, 37, 99
Franklin, John Hope, 104; Franklin Report, 105–8; on scholars, 56
Franklin, Raymond: *The Political Economy of Racism*, 165n142; *Shadows of Race and Class*, 178n123
Frazier, E. Franklin: on foundations, 59; and Harlem riot of 1935, 67–68; at Howard University, 58–59, 63, 67, 68; *The Negro in the United States*, 67; *The Pathology of Race Prejudice*, 64–66, 162n78; Platt on, 59, 63, 64–65, 67; relationship with Park, 61, 63, 66–67, 155n33; at Tuskegee, 63; at University of Chicago, 66–67
Frederickson, George M.: *Black Liberation: A Comparative History of Black Ideologies in the United States and South Africa*, 178n123
Furner, Mary: *Advocacy & Objectivity*, 36, 37

Gaines, Kevin: *Uplifting the Race*, 156n58, 178n123
Gallagher, Charles: on hip hop culture among whites, 139; *Rethinking the Color Line*, 178n123
gangsta rap, 67, 139, 140
Gans, Herbert, 116, 170n32; *The Levittowners*, 170n35; "The Possibility of a New Racial Hierarchy in the Twenty-First Century United States," 175n111; *Urban Villagers*, 170n35
Geschwender, James A.: *The Black Revolt*, 164n142
Gilman, Charlotte Perkins: "A Suggestion on the Negro Problem," 53, 160n32
Gilpin, Patrick J., 155n30, 159n23
Gilroy, Paul: *Against Race: Imagining Political Culture beyond the Color Line*, 175n110
Glazer, Nathan: and affirmative action, 120, 144; *Affirmative Discrimination*, 144; *American Judaism*, 170n35; "America's Ethnic Pattern: 'Melting Pot' or 'Nation of Nations'?," 120, 144; *Beyond the Melting Pot*, 115–16, 117, 118, 120, 122, 137, 138, 170n35, 171n43; on black culture, 137, 138; on cultural pluralism, 144; *We Are All Multiculturalists Now*, 143–44, 176n111, 177n119, 178n121; on Wilson, 166n165
Gleason, Philip, 115
Goering, John, on Clinton's Race Initiative, 168n193
Goffman, Erving: *Stigma*, 46
Goldfield, Michael: *The Color of Politics: Race and the Mainsprings of American Politics*, 178n123
Goldscheider, Calvin: on exogamy among Jews, 123
Gordon, Milton, 170n35; *Assimilation in American Life*, 120–21, 170n33, 171n39; on cultural pluralism, 121, 171n39; on ethnic assimilation, 171n46
Gotanda, Neil: *Critical Race Theory: The Key Writings that Formed the Movement*, 178n123
grandchildren of immigrants, 116, 120, 129, 130, 131, 132, 170n32, 172n60
Greeley, Andrew: *Why Can't They Be Like Us? America's White Ethnic Groups*, 119

Hacker, Andrew: *Two Nations: Black & White, Separate, Hostile, Unequal*, 178n123
Hamilton, Charles: *Black Power*, 89–90

Handlin, Oscar, 120
Hansberry, Lorraine, 89
Hansen, Marcus: thesis of third-generation
    return, 120
Hapgood, Hutchins, 119
Harper, William R., 37–38
Harris, Abram, Jr., 79–80
Hart-Cellar Act of 1965, 124, 134
Hartman, Chester, 107
Harvard University: black PhDs in sociology
    from, 14; Park at, 21; Woodson at, 75
Hier, Sean, "Structures of Orthodoxy and the
    Sociological Exclusion of Oliver C. Cox,"
    69
Higham, John: on cultural pluralism, 169n28;
    on ethnic revival of 1960's, 122, 170n38
hip hop culture, 67, 138–39, 140
Hispanic Americans. See Latinos
Hodgson, Godfrey: on SNCC, 147
Hollinger, David: on assimilation of immigrants,
    129; on the ethno-racial pentagon, 125, 126;
    Postethnic America, 125, 145, 172n56
Howard University, 30, 58, 63, 67, 68, 80, 154n17
Howe, Irving, 116; on Jewish immigrants, 131–32
Hughes, Everett, 109; on Burgess, 20; on Park,
    20, 155n30; presidential address at 1963
    meeting of the American Sociological
    Association, 10–12, 13, 15–18, 38, 88;
    relationship with Park, 16, 20, 82, 155n30,
    159n14; review of Cox's Caste, Class, &
    Race, 13–14; at University of Chicago,
    16, 91
Hughes, Henry: A Treatise on Sociology, 50
Huntington, Samuel: on Mexican immigrants,
    130, 131; Who Are We?, 130

Ignatiev, Noel: How the Irish Became White,
    168n4
immigrants, 50, 145; vs. African Americans,
    31–32, 91–92, 125, 128, 133–42, 145, 159n12;
    children of, 114–15, 119, 121, 124–25, 129,
    130–31, 132; and ethnic communities, 111–
    12, 114, 127–28, 136, 168n9; grandchildren
    of, 116, 120, 129, 130, 131, 132, 170n32,
    172n60. See also European immigrants
imperialism: and Congo Free State, 21–24; and
    Park's race relations cycle, 51, 52–53, 55–57,
    61; and Social Darwinism, 54–57

Indians, Asian: intermarriage among, 132,
    171n52, 173n73
institutionalized racism, 3, 107; vs. Clinton's
    race initiative, 110; vs. individual racism,
    89–90, 101–2, 105
intermarriage: across ethnic lines, 117, 122–23,
    125, 132–33, 135, 141, 143, 171n40, 174n78;
    across racial lines, 133, 135, 143, 171n52,
    173n73, 174n78; for Afro-Latinos, 141,
    176n113; for Asians, 132, 135, 171n52,
    173nn72–77; attitudes toward, 174n78; for
    Latinos as a whole, 132–33, 141, 173nn77,78.
    See also assimilation; dual melting pot;
    melting pot
Italian immigrants, 123, 126, 171n43

Jackson, Walter, 86, 87, 153n2
Jacobson, Matthew Frye: Roots Too, 169n27;
    Whiteness of a Different Color, 168n4
James, C.L.R.: attitudes toward, 12; "The
    Revolutionary Answer to the Negro
    Problem in the U.S.A.," 12–13
Janowitz, Morris, 20, 29, 155n31
Japanese Americans: Exclusion Act of 1924,
    160n47; intermarriage among, 132, 171n52,
    173n73; internment of, 128; language loss
    among, 131, 172n60; and Park, 160n47
Jewish Americans: exogamy among, 122–23,
    171n40; relations with blacks, 60; as
    scholars of ethnicity, 118–21, 170nn34,35
Jewish immigrants, 118–20, 121, 126, 131–32,
    170n37
Johnson, Charles S.: and Chicago race riot of
    1919, 47–49, 61–62, 75, 159n23; criticisms
    of, 49, 161n62; "The Economic Basis of
    Race Relations," 96–97; The Education of
    the Negro Child, 174n91; Growing up in the
    Black Belt, 62; on lack of Negro culture,
    174n93; The Negro in Chicago, 47–49, 62;
    relationship with Park, 43, 47, 49, 61–62,
    75, 96–97, 159nn14,23; Shadow of the
    Plantation, 62
Jones, Butler, 160n48; on Johnson, 62; on Park,
    60–61; on surrogate control, 61, 161n62
Joyner, Kara: "Do Hispanics and Asian
    Adolescents Practice Panethnicity in
    Friendship Choices?," 171n51
Juliani, Richard: "Emergent Ethnicity," 123

Kallen, Horace: on cultural pluralism, 118–20, 121; "Democracy Versus the Melting Pot: With Special Reference to the Jewish Group," 118–20

Kao, Grace: "Do Hispanics and Asian Adolescents Practice Panethnicity in Friendship Choices?," 171n51

Kasinitz, Philip: "Race, Assimilation, and 'Second Generations', Past and Present," 175n111

Kelley, Robin D. G., 162n98; on gangsta rap, 139; *Hammer and Hoe: Alabama Communists during the Great Depression,* 163n112; *Race Rebels: Culture, Politics, and the Black Working Class,* 178n123; *Yo' Mama's Disfunktional! Fighting the Culture Wars in Urban America,* 175n104

Keppel, Frederick, 85, 86

Kerner Commission report, 92–94, 105–6, 165n150

Killian, Lewis, 163n121

Kim, Claire, 105

King, Martin Luther, Jr.: in Albany, Georgia, 6; assassination of, 92; in Birmingham, Alabama, 6; in Freedom Walk in Detroit, 6; "Letter from the Birmingham Jail," 108–10; March on Washington, 6–7, 10, 15, 18; on poverty, 80; on racial oppression, 16; *Stride toward Freedom,* 89

Klein, Joe: on Wilson, 103

Klineberg, Otto, 58

Klinker, Philip A.: *The Unsteady March: The Rise and Decline of Racial Equality in America,* 178n123

Kopkind, Andrew, 92–93; "White on Black: The Riot Commission and the Rhetoric of Reform," 165n150

Korean Americans: intermarriage among, 132, 171n52, 173n73; language loss among, 131, 172n60

Kornblum, William: *Uptown Kids: Struggle and Hope in the Projects,* 178n123

Kubrin, Charis E.: *Privileged Places; Race, Residence, and the Structure of Opportunity,* 178n123

Kuhn, Thomas, 91; on paradigm change, 17–18, 57–58, 72, 88, 95–96

Ku Klux Klan, 41, 44

Kwanzaa, 136

labor unions, 35, 36, 37; craft unions, 48; exclusion of blacks from, 46, 48, 68, 88

Ladd, Everett Carl, 170n34

Ladner, Joyce A.: *The Death of White Sociology,* 94, 96, 165n143

LaGuardia, Fiorello, 67–68

language loss, 129–31, 135, 172n60

Latin American immigrants, 124, 128, 129, 135

Latinos: and bilingual education, 172n63; ethnic identity among, 125, 126–27, 171n50, 175n111; interdating among, 174n78; intermarriage among, 132–33, 135, 141, 173n77; language loss among, 130–31; names of children among, 131, 135

Lee, Sharon M., 171n52

Legget, John: *Class, Race and Labor,* 164n142

Leopold II and Congo Free State, 21–24, 30

Lester, Julius, 89

Leventman, Seymour, 14, 18

Lewis, David Levering, 163n108

Liebow, Eliot, 165n155

Lipset, Seymour Martin, 170n34

Lipsitz, George, 142; *The Possessive Investment in Whiteness: How White People Profit from Identity Politics,* 178n123

Lipsky, Michael: *Commission Politics,* 165n143

Liu, Eric: *The Accidental Asian,* 133

Logan, John, 172n60

López, David, 130, 171n52

Los Angeles, 130, 171n52

Lott, Eric: *Love and Theft: Blackface Minstrelsy and the American Working Class,* 175n103, 178n123

Lusane, Clarence: on Clinton's race initiative, 105, 107

Lyman, Stanford, 5; *The Black American in Sociological Thought,* 164n142; on Chicago school of sociology, 50; on Park, 162n75; "Race Relations as Social Process; Sociology's Resistance to a Civil Rights Orientation," 9–10; on sociology, 9–10, 50, 110, 143

lynchings, 41, 42, 43, 54

Maddern, Darlene Alvarez, 157n69

Mahoney, Ron, 78–79

Mailer, Norman, 8
Malcolm X, 89
Manifest Destiny, 56
Marable, Manning: on Clinton's race initiative,
    107; *Living Black History: How Reimagining
    the African-American Past Can Remake
    America's Racial Future*, 178n123; *Race and
    Labor Matters in the New U.S. Economy*,
    178n123
marriage across ethnic lines, 117, 122–23, 125,
    132–33
Marx, Gary: *Protest and Prejudice*, 165n143;
    "Two Cheers for the National Riot
    (Kerner) Commission Report," 165n150
Marx, Karl, 106, 146; on craft unions, 48; on
    slavery, 74
Marxism: and Blauner, 90, 91; class in, 76–81,
    91; and Cox, 69–71; as epistemology
    of oppression, 72, 162n98; historical
    materialism, 39, 69–71; Myrdal's attitudes
    toward, 2; and racial oppression, 16, 69–78,
    91, 109, 162n98; rejection of, 2, 3, 12, 38–39,
    53, 69, 70, 71–72, 75, 76, 95, 164n126.
    See also American Communist Party;
    Communist International
Massey, Douglas S., 135, 174n82
Masuoka, Jitsuichi, 159n14
Matthews, Donald R., 153n3
Matthews, Fred, 47; *Quest for an American
    Sociology: Robert E. Park and the Chicago
    School*, 26, 31, 158n91, 159n12
McAdam, Doug: *Political Process and the
    Development of Black Insurgency*, 168n195
McAuley, Christopher: on Cox, 68
McCarthyism, 8
McCone Commission, 93
McIver, Robert: *The More Perfect Union*, 83
McKee, James: *Sociology and the Race Problem*,
    18, 81–83, 163n126, 175n100, 178n123
McLaughlin, Neil, 97
McLean, Nancy: *Freedom Is Not Enough:
    The Opening of the American Workplace*,
    177n119, 178n123
Meddling, Peter Y., 171n40
Meier, August, 51, 160n30; *From Plantation to
    Ghetto*, 164n142
Melamed, Jodi: "The Spirit of Neoliberalism:
    From Racial Liberalism to Neoliberal

Multiculturalism," 171n48
melting pot, the: African Americans as
    exception to, 31–32, 133–42, 145, 175n111;
    and the ethno-racial pentagon, 125, 126;
    Higham on, 169n28; Native Americans as
    exception to, 174n80; and non-European
    immigrants, 124–33, 134–35; Park on, 111,
    112–13, 116, 118, 133, 168n2; rejection of,
    114–24, 142; Zangwill's *The Melting-Pot*,
    114. *See also* assimilation; dual melting pot;
    intermarriage
Merton, Robert: "Insiders and Outsiders: A
    Chapter in the Sociology of Knowledge,"
    169n21
Messenger, The, 64, 67
Metzger, Walter: *Academic Freedom in the Age of
    the University*, 36
Mexican Americans/Chicanos, 112, 113, 116, 128;
    intermarriage among, 133, 173n77; language
    loss among, 130, 131
Mexican-American War, 56, 130
Mexican immigrants, 130
Miller, Herbert, 159n12
Miller, Kelley, 63
Mills, Charles W.: on epistemology of
    ignorance, 11, 72; *The Racial Contract*, 11,
    41, 52–53, 73, 178n123
Mills, C. Wright, 39, 95; on sociological
    imagination, 15
miscegenation, 143, 176n117
Morawska, Ewa: "In Defense of the
    Assimilation Model," 171n46
Morris, Aldon, 80
Moss, James: "In Defense of Black Studies," 15
Moton, Robert R., 63
Moynihan, Daniel Patrick: *Beyond the Melting
    Pot*, 115–16, 117, 118, 122, 137, 171n43; on
    Wilson, 98
Mullings, Leith: *On Our Own Terms: Race,
    Class, and Gender in the Lives of African
    American Women*, 178n123
multiculturalism, 124–33, 143–44, 145, 171n48
Myrdal, Gunnar: *An American Dilemma*,
    1–4, 84–89, 92; *An American Dilemma
    Revisited*, 1; attitudes toward American
    sociologists, 4, 14; attitudes toward
    Marxism, 2; Cox on, 144; critics of, 2–3,
    87–89; on the ethnic movement, 116;

influence of, 3, 105; monetary compensation, 85, 164n132; and Park, 87; relationship with Carnegie Corp., 1, 4, 84–87, 92, 95, 164n132; relationship with Clark, 1, 153n2; views on racial differences, 86; vs. Wilson, 97–98

NAACP, 12, 63; Amenia Conference of 1916, 79–80; and Communist Party, 14; *The Crisis*, 76
Nash, Gary: "The Hidden History of Mestizo America," 143
National Advisory Commission on Civil Disorders. *See* Kerner Commission
National Urban League: *Opportunity*, 62
Native Americans, 51, 56, 92, 112, 113, 116, 125, 127, 174n80
Nee, Victor: *Remaking the American Mainstream*, 169n19, 172n60
Ness, Immanuel: *Immigrants, Unions, and the New U.S. Labor Market*, 178n123; *Race and Labor Matters in the New U.S. Economy*, 178n123
Neubeck, Kenneth J.: *Welfare Racism: Playing the Race Card against America's Poor*, 178n123
New Deal, 86, 107
Newton, Huey: *To Die for People*, 89
New York City: civil rights demonstrations in, 6; employment discrimination in, 68; ethnic communities in, 115–16; Harlem riot of 1935, 67–68, 85, 93; Harlem riot of 1943, 93; names of black children in, 135
New York Times Magazine: Degler's "The Negro in America: Where Myrdal Went Wrong," 88–89
Niagara Movement, 12
Niebuhr, Reinhold, 8
Nixon, Richard, 94
Northern cities: black migration to, 1, 41, 47, 78, 79, 134
Novak, Michael: *The Rise of the Unmeltable Ethnics*, 116, 119
Nunberg, Geoffrey, 130

Oliver, Melvin L.: *Black Wealth/White Wealth*, 178n123
Olson, David J.: *Commission Politics*, 165n143

One America in the 21st Century: Forging a New Future, 105
Oppenheimer, David B.: *Whitewashing Race: The Myth of a Color-Blind Society*, 177n123
Otis, Johnny, 138
Owen, Chandler, 64

Park, Robert Ezra, 19–34, 95; and abstractions, 55, 160n47, 165n148; and Bemis, 38; biological inferiority of blacks rejected by, 28, 50, 70, 72, 86, 102; on black temperament, 138; character traits of, 20–21; and Chicago race riot of 1919, 43, 47, 49, 75; as Chicago Urban League director, 43, 47, 62; on class and race, 96; on class differentiation among blacks, 44–45; and Congo Reform Association, 21–25, 30, 31, 32, 63, 82; on detachment, 42; on education, 46–47, 50, 60; on ethnic and racial minorities, 111–14, 159n12; on ethnic assimilation, 50, 111–14, 116, 142, 160n47, 171n46; on European immigrants, 31–32; at Fisk University, 60, 62; in Germany, 21; at Harvard, 21; influence of, 16, 19–20, 30–31, 47, 59–62, 66, 70–71, 82, 95, 96–97, 114, 155nn30,31,33, 165n148; and Japanese Americans on West Coast, 160n47; on the melting pot, 111, 112–13, 116, 118, 133, 168n2; and Myrdal, 87; as newspaper reporter, 21; on progress, 24; on race relations cycle, 20, 44, 49–53, 81–84, 112–13, 157n79, 160nn30,47; on racial accommodation, 27, 43, 50, 51, 52, 53; on racial assimilation, 31–33, 43, 51, 52, 53; on racial conflict, 50, 51, 53, 56; on racial contact, 50, 51, 53; on racial progress, 24–25, 26, 27–29, 43, 44–46, 50–51, 52, 55–56, 56, 72, 160n47; on racial temperament, 65, 162n75; relationship with Burgess, 19–20, 42; relationship with Cox, 61; relationship with Frazier, 61, 63, 66–67, 155n33; relationship with Hughes, 16, 20, 82, 155n33, 159n14; relationship with Johnson, 43, 47, 49, 61–62, 75, 96–97, 159nn14,23; relationship with Small, 29, 38, 44; relationship with Thomas, 27–28, 29–30, 31, 44, 50, 55, 157n62, 159n12; relationship with Washington, 23, 24–29, 30–31, 32–33, 34, 44, 46–47, 52, 60–61, 63,

156n53, 161n62; relationship with Wright,
19; sociology as moral enterprise rejected
by, 42; at University of Chicago, 16, 18, 19,
25, 27, 29–34, 38, 43, 47, 49, 59, 60–61, 72,
101, 111–14, 118, 155n30; vs. Wilson, 44–45
Park, Robert Ezra, works of: "An Autobiographical Note," 20–21, 24, 158n92;
"The Blood-Money of the Congo," 23, 31,
32, 55; "Cruelty in the Congo Country,"
25, 31–32, 55; "Human Migration and
the Marginal Man," 159n12; *Introduction
to the Science of Sociology,* 19–20, 49–51,
65, 155n31, 159n12; "A King in Business,"
22–23, 31, 32, 55; *The Man Farthest Down,*
26; "Masse und Publikum," 21; *My Larger
Education,* 26; *The Nature of Race Relations,*
96; "Negro Home Life and Standards of
Living," 44–47, 73, 159nn13,14; *Race and
Culture,* 20, 50, 82, 155n30, 159n14, 168n2;
"Racial Assimilation in Secondary Groups,
With Particular Reference to the Negro,"
31–33; *The Story of the Negro,* 23, 25, 26,
47, 156n53; "The Terrible Story of the
Congo," 23
Parks, Rosa, 5
Parsons, Talcott, 18
Patterson, Orlando: "A Poverty of the
Mind," 140; on hip hop culture, 140; on
miscegenation, 143, 176n117; *The Ordeal of
Integration,* 176n117; "Race Over," 175n110
Pei, Mario: *What's in a Word?,* 172n62
Peller, Gary: *Critical Race Theory: The Key
Writings that Formed the Movement,*
178n123
Perlman, Joel, 170n37, 173n77
Persons, Stow: *Ethnic Studies at Chicago,* 42,
159n12; on the long view, 43; on Park and
Thomas, 158n12; on Park's emphasis on
detachment, 42; on University of Chicago,
169n22
Pettigrew, Thomas, 163n124
Phylon, 13, 16
Pierre, Jemima: "Black Immigrants in the
United States and the 'Cultural Narratives'
of Ethnicity," 176n111
Pittsburgh Courier, 60
Piven, Frances Fox: on Clinton's race initiative,
107; *Poor People's Movements,* 168n195

Platt, Anthony: *E. Franklin Frazier Reconsidered,*
63, 154n17; on Frazier, 59, 63, 64–65, 66, 67
Pleck, Elizabeth, 136
Plessy, Homer, 143
Podhoretz, Normal: "My Negro Problem—and
Ours," 176n117
policy recommendations: in Franklin report,
105–6, 107; in Kerner Commission report,
93–94; in The Negro in Chicago, 48; in
report on Harlem riot of 1935, 68
political action: rejected in sociology, 31, 32–33,
34–35, 38–39
political science: *American Political Science
Review,* 8; and Civil Rights Revolution, 8
Polsgrove, Carol: *Divided Minds: Intellectuals
and the Civil Rights Movement,* 8–9
poverty, 68, 80, 90, 96, 99, 100, 102–3, 106,
107, 140
Progressive Era, 35–36, 39, 41
Proposition 27 (California), 172n63
Puerto Ricans: and assimilation, 142;
intermarriage among, 133, 141

Qian, Zhenchao, 173nn73,77, 174n83, 176n113

"race relations": as euphemism, 43–44, 55–56;
vs. "racial oppression," 16–17, 39, 43–44,
46–47, 53, 58, 73–74, 108, 154n23
race relations cycle: accommodation, 50, 51,
52, 53; assimilation, 50, 51, 53; conflict,
50, 51, 53; contact, 50, 51, 53, 56; and
evolutionary social change, 20, 49–53,
55–56; and imperialism, 51, 52–53, 55–57,
61; Park on, 20, 44, 49–53, 81–84, 112–13,
157n79, 160nn30,47. See also scholarship of
confrontation
race relations industry, 82–83, 163n121
racial accommodation: Park on, 27, 43, 50, 51,
52, 53; Washington on, 27, 52
racial districting, 106
racial equality, 8, 50, 65, 75, 83, 86, 110, 157n79
racial hierarchy, 11, 28–29, 50, 55–57, 66–67,
72, 73, 83
racial intermarriage, 133, 135, 143, 171n52, 173n73,
174n78
racial pacification, 43, 108–9
racial progress: Gilman on, 53, 160n32; and
the inverted metric, 45–46, 48; Park on,

24–25, 26, 27–29, 43, 44–46, 50–51, 52,
55–56, 56, 72, 160n47; and slavery, 24–25;
Washington on, 24–25, 26, 27–29, 156n58
racism: Allport's definition of prejudice, 103;
attitudes vs. conditions, 57, 82–83; as
biological/scientific, 9, 28, 50, 53–55, 57,
66, 70, 72, 74, 86, 102; Cox on racial
prejudice, 12, 69–70, 74; among employers,
102–3, 134, 135, 174n88; as institutionalized,
89–90, 101–2, 105–6, 108, 110; Jim Crow
system, 5, 7, 12, 16, 26, 28, 33, 35–36, 41, 75,
79, 80, 81, 82, 85, 86, 87, 140, 141; Marxism
and racial oppression, 16, 69–78, 91, 109;
in the North, 33, 86, 134; prejudiced beliefs
and attitudes, 2, 17, 57, 70, 71–72, 74,
82–83, 88–89, 90, 100–103, 105, 163n124;
and race relations industry, 82–83, 163n121;
race vs. class debate, 76–81, 91, 94, 96–97,
99–100, 107, 157n79, 163nn107,108,116,126;
residential segregation, 135; slavery, 11, 24–
25, 44, 45–46, 69–70, 71, 74, 85, 92, 102,
134, 138, 140, 141, 174n94; as social/cultural,
9, 54–55, 57–58, 66–67, 72, 74, 101, 102;
structural foundations of, 2, 12, 15, 17, 69–
71, 74–75, 83, 89–90, 105–6, 110, 144
Randolph, A. Philip, 64
Rauschenbush, Winifred: *Robert E. Park:
Biography of a Sociologist,* 29, 30
Reconstruction, 8, 31, 35, 41, 94, 142
Record, C. Wilson: "The Politics of
Desegregation," 14; *Race and Radicalism,*
14, 164n142
Reddick, Lawrence Dunbar, 9, 11
Redfield, Robert, 155n33, 159n14
Reed, Adolph, Jr., 99, 167nn172, 174, 181; on
Clinton's race initiative, 105; *Stirrings in
the Jug: Black Politics in the Post-Segregation
Era* and *Without Justice for All: The New
Liberalism and Our Retreat from Racial
Equality,* 178n123; "Yakety-Yak about
Race," 108
Reisman, David, 8
residential segregation, 41–42, 47–48, 62, 102,
135, 136, 138, 140
Resnik, Solomon: *The Political Economy of
Racism,* 165n142
Rex, John, 163n126
Reynolds, Gretchen, 99–100

Riis, Jacob, 168n6
Ringer, Benjamin, 1–2
Robbins, Richard, 170n35
Robinson, Cedric: on Du Bois, 76
Robinson, Dean E.: *Black Nationalism in
American Politics and Thought,* 178n123
Rockefeller, John D., 30, 38
Rodriquez, Gregory, 172n66
Rodriquez, Richard: "La Raza Cosmica," 111
Roediger, David R.: *Colored White: Transcending
the Racial Past,* 178n123; "The Retreat from
Race and Class," 175n110
Roosevelt, Franklin D., 77
Rose, Peter, 166n168, 170n35
Rosenfeld, Michael J., 173n77
Rosenwald, Julius, 59–60, 61–62
Ross, Dorothy, 37
Ross, Edward, 75
Rudwick, Elliott, 51, 160n30; *From Plantation to
Ghetto,* 164n142
rules of epistemology of ignorance:
ahistoricism, 47, 48, 57; detachment, 42,
47; vs. epistemology of wishful thinking,
117; evasion, 42–43, 48; the inverted metric,
45–46, 48; the moral calculus of race, 46;
the racial optic, 66–67; reductionism, 57;
sophism, 43–44; transcendentalism, 43;
vilify racists, not social system, 71
rules of epistemology of wishful thinking:
defining assimilation out of existence,
117–18; defining ethnicity down, 122–23;
the ethnic academy, 118–21; knowing where
to fish, 121–22; redefining assimilation as
ethnogenesis, 123–24
Rumsfeld, Donald, 24
Rustin, Bayard, 6–7

Sage, Russell, 37; Russell Sage Foundation, 37,
99
Said, Edward, 109; on antithetical scholarship,
146
Salins, Peter D.: *Assimilation, American Style,*
176n117
Sartre, Jean-Paul, 1
Schmidt, Ronald: on language of immigrants,
129
scholarship of confrontation, 89–94, 109,
164n142

school desegregation, 1, 87, 106

Schmidt, Romald, 129

Schrag, Peter: *The Decline of the WASP,* 116

Schwendinger, Herman and Julia: *The Sociologists of the Chair,* 53–55, 72, 162n97

Scott, Daryl Michael: *Social Policy and the Image of the Damaged Black Psyche,* 175n100

Sears, Roebuck & Co., 59, 60

segregation, 43, 44, 93, 140–41; Jim Crow system, 5, 7, 12, 16, 26, 28, 33, 35–36, 41, 75, 79, 80, 81, 82, 85, 86, 87, 140, 141; and race relations industry, 82–83; residential segregation, 41–42, 47–48, 62, 135, 136, 138, 140

Shapiro, Thomas: *Black Wealth/White Wealth,* 178n123

Shelby, Tommie: *We Who Are Dark: The Philosophical Foundations of Black Solidarity,* 178n123

Shultz, Marjorie M.: *Whitewashing Race: The Myth of a Color-Blind Society,* 177n123

Simmel, Georg, 21, 155n30

Simons, Sarah: on racial progress, 46; "Social Assimilation," 33–34

Singh, Nikhil Pal: *Race Is a Country: Race and the Unfinished Struggle for Democracy,* 175n110, 179n123

Small, Albion, 52, 109; rejection of reform by, 38, 43; relationship with Bemis, 38; relationship with Park, 29, 38, 44; "Scholarship and Social Agitation," 35

Smith, Rogers M.: *The Unsteady March: The Rise and Decline of Racial Equality in America,* 179n123

SNCC (Student Non-Violent Coordinating Committee), 147

Sobel, Lester A., 153n2

Social Darwinism, 9, 50, 53–55, 56–57

socialism, 63, 64, 77, 158n91. *See also* American Communist Party; Marxism

sociology: black sociologists, 3, 14–15, 57–72, 154, 160n48; and Civil Rights Revolution, 4, 8–19, 27, 38, 73, 84, 87–89, 109; and class, 11–12, 73, 76–81; concept of caste in, 13, 157n79; doctrine of objectivity in, 9, 34–39, 69, 70, 76, 146; as elitist, 10–12; the ethnic academy, 118–12; euphemisms in, 43–44; exclusion of women, 39,

158n92; intellectual stasis in, 18–19, 20, 34, 84; Lyman on, 9–10, 50, 110, 143; and moderate social change, 11–12, 81–84; and morality of racism, 9, 11, 33, 42, 50; and racial status quo, 9, 11–12, 17, 27, 42, 66, 70, 86, 110; rejection of Marxism in, 2, 3, 12, 38–39, 53, 69, 70, 71–72, 75, 76, 95, 164n126; rejection of political action/advocacy in, 34–39, 43, 83–84, 86, 158n91, 162n97; relationship to imperialism, 51, 52–57; role of obfuscating abstractions in, 14, 47, 48, 49, 55, 79, 160n47, 165n48; and values, 9, 11, 16, 33, 34–39, 42, 46, 50, 83–84, 109–10, 158n6. *See also* rules of epistemology of ignorance; rules of epistemology of wishful thinking; sociology of knowledge

sociology of knowledge: ethnicity of sociologists, 118–20, 169n21, 170nn35,37; foundations, 1, 4, 37, 59, 59–60, 61–62, 66, 81, 84–87, 92, 95, 96, 99, 110, 157n62; grants, 59–60, 66, 85–86, 92, 95, 98, 100, 110, 165n155; iconic figures, 95, 97–99, 101–2; and imperialism, 54–56; power elite, 95–96, 97–99, 110; and sociology's canon, 3, 20, 64–65, 70–71, 72, 75–76, 97–99, 101–2, 109

Sollors, Werner: *Beyond Ethnicity,* 168n8; "Literature and Ethnicity," 168n8

Solomon, Mark: *The Cry Was Unity,* 78–79

Solow, Robert, 98

Southern, David W., 164n132

Southern blacks: migration to Northern cities, 1, 41, 47, 78, 79, 134; vs. Northern blacks, 46

Spanish-American War, 56

Spencer, Herbert, 50, 53, 54–55

Squires, Gregory D.: *Privileged Places: Race, Residence, and the Structure of Opportunity,* 178n123

Srole, Leo, 114, 127

Stampp, Kenneth: *The Peculiar Institution,* 137

Stanfield, John, 27, 170n35; on Park, 157n79; *Philanthropy and Jim Crow in American Social Science,* 84–85

Steiner, Edward, 168n6

structural foundations of racism, 2, 12, 15, 17, 69–71, 74–75, 83, 144; institutionalized racism, 3, 89–90, 101–2, 105–6, 107, 108, 110

Student Non-Violent Coordinating Committee (SNCC), 147

Sue, Christina A.: "Assimilation and Gender in Naming," 174n84

Supreme Court of the United States, 6; *Brown v. Board of Education,* 1

Tabb, William: *The Political Economy of the Black Ghetto,* 164n142

Telles, Edward E.: "Assimilation and Gender in Naming," 174n84

Thomas, Kendall: *Critical Race Theory: The Key Writings that Formed the Movement,* 179n123

Thomas, William I., 9, 160n47; "Education and Cultural Traits," 33; on the ethnicity paradox, 168n9; and *Old World Traits Transplanted,* 159n12; relationship with Park, 27–28, 29–30, 31, 44, 50, 55, 157n62, 159n12; at University of Chicago, 27, 29, 33, 157nn62,76

Thrasher, Max Bennett, 156n50

Time Magazine, 98; cover in 1993, 133

Tompkins, E. Berkeley: *Anti-Imperialism in the United States,* 56

Torres, Rodolfo: *After Race: Racism after Multiculturalism,* 175n110

transnationalism, 128, 172n55

Turner, Ralph, 155n30; on Park, 50

Tuskegee Institute: conference on "The Education of Primitive Man," 27–28, 33, 50, 55; Frazier at, 63; and Rosenwald Fund, 59. *See also* Washington, Booker T.

University of California, Berkeley: Blauner at, 91, 95, 165n155; Institute of Race and Community Studies/Institute for the Study of Social Change, 165n155; Third World Strike of 1969, 165n155

University of Chicago: Bemis at, 37–39; black PhDs in sociology from, 14; Blauner at, 91; Burgess at, 19–20; Chicago school of race relations, 19, 27, 28, 30, 33–34, 41–42, 50, 55, 56, 57–58, 59–61, 65, 66–67, 69, 72, 73, 91–92, 101, 109, 114, 118, 146, 155n30, 161n62; exclusion of women, 158n92; Frazier at, 66–67; Park at, 16, 18, 19, 25, 27, 29–34, 38, 43, 47, 49, 59, 60–61,

72, 101, 111–14, 118, 155n30; Persons on, 169n22; and race riot of 1919, 42–43; and Rosenwald Fund, 59–60; Simons at, 33–34; Small at, 29, 35, 38; Thomas at, 27, 29, 33, 157nn62,76; Wilson at, 34

University of the Toilers of the East, 78–79

University of Wisconsin: black PhDs in sociology from, 14; Ely at, 36–37

values: racial equality, 8, 50, 65, 75, 83, 86, 110, 157n79; and sociology, 9, 11, 16, 33, 34–39, 42, 46, 50, 83–84, 109–10, 158n6

Vietnamese Americans: intermarriage among, 132, 171n52, 173n73

Voting Rights Act of 1965, 7–8

Wacker, R. Fred: "Assimilation and Pluralism in American Social Thought," 119

Waldinger, Roger: "Transnationalism in Question," 172n55

Wallace, George, 94

Ward, Lester, 33; views on race, 53–54, 160n36

Warner, W. Lloyd, 114, 127

Warren, Robert Penn, 8

Washington, Booker T.: vs. D'Souza, 28, 101; *My Larger Education,* 26; *The Man Farthest Down,* 26; public image of, 26–27; on racial progress, 24–25, 26, 27–29, 156n58; relationship with Park, 23, 24–29, 30–31, 32–33, 34, 44, 46–47, 52, 60–61, 63, 156n53, 161n62; relationship with Thrasher, 156n50; speech at the 1895 Atlanta Exposition, 34; *The Story of the Negro,* 23, 25, 26, 47, 156n53; *Up From Slavery,* 24–25, 26, 28–29, 45–46, 59, 156n50; views on education, 27–29, 32, 34, 46–47, 60, 63; views on political action, 32, 34; views on racial accommodation, 27, 52; views on racial hierarchy, 28–29; views on racial progress, 44, 45–46; vs. Wilson, 34

Waskow, Arthur: *From Race Riot to Sit-In,* 159n24

Waters, Mary, 132, 141, 173nn73,77

Watkins, Mel, 89

Watts riot of 1965, 88, 93

Weber, Max, 106; "Science as a Vocation," 34–35

Wellman, David, 166n155; *Portraits of White Racism,* 165n143, 179n123; "Toward the

Decolonization of Social Research,"
  161n58; *Whitewashing Race: The Myth of a
  Color-Blind Society,* 177n123
West, Michael Rudolph: on Washington,
  154n23, 156n58
whiteness studies, 113, 168n4
Wideman, John Edgar, 138
Wilkins, Roy, 79
Williams, Terry M.: *The Uptown Kids: Struggle
  and Hope in the Projects,* 179n123
Willis, Paul, 102
Wilson, Joseph: *Race and Labor Matters in the
  New U.S. Economy,* 179n123
Wilson, William Julius: on affirmative action,
  100; on black culture, 102; on black middle
  class, 96; on class differentiation among
  blacks, 44–45, 157n79; and Clinton,
  99, 100, 166n170; critics of, 97, 98; *The
  Declining Significance of Race,* 34, 95,
  96–100, 101–2, 118, 166nn165,168; vs.
  D'Souza, 101–4; financial support of, 95;
  influence of, 95, 96, 97–100, 101–2; vs.
  Myrdal, 97–98; vs. Park, 44–45; on racial
  discrimination, 102–3; Seidman Award
  in Political Economy received by, 98; *The
  Truly Disadvantaged,* 99, 100, 166n170;
  at University of Chicago, 34; views on
  education, 34; views on political action, 34;
  vs. Washington, 34; *When Work Disappears,*
  95, 102–4
Wilson, Woodrow, 41, 42
Winant, Howard, 16; *The World Is a Ghetto:
  Race and Democracy since World War II,*
  178n123

Windelband, Wilhelm, 21
Winston, Michael R., 154n17
Wirth, Louis, 136, 155n33, 159n14
Woodson, Carter G.: *The Miseducation of the
  Negro,* 75
Woodward, C. Vann, 8
working class: and blacks, 46, 48, 68, 76–81;
  and Marxism, 76–81
Wright, Richard, 89; on black culture, 139–40;
  relationship with Park, 19
Wu, Frank H., *Yellow: Race in America beyond
  Black and White,* 173n76, 178n123

Yancey, George: *Who Is White? Latinos, Asians,
  and the New Black/Nonblack Divide,*
  173n78, 175n111; interracial dating, 174n78
Yancey, William, 174n78; "Emergent Ethnicity,"
  123
Young, Iris Marion: *Justice and the Politics of
  Difference,* 172n56
Young, James O.: *Black Writers of the 1930s,*
  163n107
Yousman, Bill: "Blackophilia and Blackophobia:
  White Youth, the Consumption of Rap
  Music, and White Supremacy," 139,
  175n103

Zangwill, Israel: *The Melting-Pot,* 114, 119, 135,
  142
Zhou, Min, 125
Zinn, Howard: *You Can't Be Neutral on a
  Moving Train,* 84
Znaniecki, Florian, 160n47

3144